CULTURE WARS

THE THREAT TO YOUR FAMILY AND YOUR FREEDOM

MARIE ALENA CASTLE

SEE SHARP PRESS ◆ TUCSON, ARIZONA

For information contact:

See Sharp Press
P.O. Box 1731
Tucson, AZ 85702

www.seesharppress.com

Castle, Marie Alena.
    Culture wars : the threat to your family and your freedom / Marie Alena Castle ;
introduction by Tim Gorski – Tucson, Ariz. : See Sharp Press, 2013.
    Includes bibliographical references and index.
    235 p. ; 23 cm.
    ISBN 978-1-937276-47-8 1937276473

Contents: Introduction -- Preface -- 1. Interpreting the Constitution -- 2. The
Theology of Sex -- 3. Dumb as a Rock: Theology and Nature's Sexual Diversity --
4. Women and Religion: An Abusive Relationship -- 5. Theology Based Healthcare --
6. No Right to Know: Science, Education and Free Expression -- 7. Religion and Taxes:
Freeloading at its Finest -- 8. The Nation's Most Favored Welfare Recipient -- 9. Public
Religion: Insults and Injuries -- 10. To the Barricades.

1. Social values - Political aspects. 2. Culture conflict – Religious aspects. 3. Social
conflict – Religious aspects. 4. Church and state – United States.

CONTENTS

Dedicated to the memory of

Sue Rockne

religious liberal, political activist, friend and mentor,

and formidable lobbyist for reproductive rights

and separation of religion from government.

Her file folder on authoritarian religion's

assaults on our liberties was labeled,

"Tax the Bastards!"

She died too soon.

There are not enough like her.

We need so many.

INTRODUCTION

If you are a believer—if you are committed to a theology—you should read this book. Yes, it is written by an atheist. But, no, it is not just about finding fault with theological doctrines, though it does that. This book is not so much against believers as against believers imposing their religious beliefs on others. Most believers do not want that. In fact, most believers will be surprised and deeply distressed at how well-meaning ideas are sometimes result in dreadful public policies with horrifying effects. *Culture Wars* explains how this is happening, right now, in our nation.

If you are an unbeliever, you have much to learn from this book, as well. Yes, it will explore the substance and absurdity of many theological doctrines, though not in such detail or at such length as in many other books. But unlike other books criticizing religion and its doctrines, the purpose here is different. This book is unique in not only showing how silly and wrong many religious beliefs are, but in showing how and why they affect the laws and legal institutions we live under. *Culture Wars* shows how these entanglements corrupt our government and hurt all of us.

If you simply do not care about religion or do not have strong opinions about it, then you really, really need to read this book. We stand, here in the early 21st century, at the doorway of a world filled with new technologies and innovations that promise to improve human life and diminish suffering and misery. Stem cell research, to name just one example, could greatly reduce or eliminate many chronic degenerative diseases. And religious authoritarians are trying to stop it dead in its tracks. Even if you don't care much about other people's religious convictions, you can rest assured that the most zealous and unreasonable religious believers are doing their best to deform and destroy our future and yours.

Of course, everyone knows that here in the United States we enjoy religious liberty. Our Constitution—the First Amendment, specifically, backed by the 14th Amendment—means that we're supposed to have complete separation of state and church at all levels of government. Thomas Jefferson called it a "Wall of Separation" between the government and religion. This "wall" guarantees (or should guarantee) that no one is forced, via law and our legal institutions, to obey religious dictates. Marie Alena Castle shows in this book that current reality is far from this ideal. In fact, she shows that what "everyone knows" about this subject is in some cases devastatingly wrong, that we are, in fact, continually subjected to legal strictures and public policies that violate our religious liberties and state/church separation.

The United States was founded on the self-evident principle that everyone possesses intrinsic, inalienable and equal rights. Thomas Jefferson ridiculed the idea that some people are "born with saddles on their backs" while others are naturally "booted and spurred, ready to ride them legitimately." Yet Jefferson himself owned slaves. It took a bloody civil war to end the appalling institution of slavery, and we still suffer from its legacy. What will it take, and how long will it take, for us to finally make concrete the First Amendment's guarantee of state-church separation and religious liberty? There is already a war underway, the outcome of which is uncertain, that will answer this question. This book outlines some aspects of this "culture war" that politically powerful religious groups and leaders are waging against our liberties. At stake are not just important principles of American freedom, due process, and equal treatment under the law, but, in some circumstances, our lives.

There are those who dismiss complaints about violations of state-church separation as frivolous, especially when such protests come from atheists. So what if a creche is displayed in a government building? they say. So what if The Ten Commandments hang above a judge in a courtroom? So what if our money has "In God We Trust" on it? So what if everyone must recite "under God" in the nation's official loyalty oath? But the question is not whether these things are worse than chattel slavery. It is whether these things are at odds with and undermine our nation's founding principles. They are and they do. All of these things are violations of our religious liberties.

But, as this book explains, there are much worse consequences of state-church entanglement. Religious groups and leaders actively promote government intrusion into the most private and personal aspects of our lives. How and whom we love; our reproductive rights; how we choose to form families and have children; protection of children from neglect and abuse; and even the choices we make when we face serious health problems or are dying. Religious authoritarians want massive government intrusion in all of these basic aspects of life. Objections to these intrusions are not frivolous.

Religious leaders offer a multitude of reasons why their religious doctrines should be the law of the land. "We are a Christian Nation!" is usually the first "explanation." Never mind that one could just as easily argue that Iran is a Muslim nation and should therefore be under shariah law. This is so obvious that many on the religious right promote their authoritarian claims as "scientific" rather than religious. The most blatant example of this is the labeling of creationism as "Intelligent Design." Many religious groups go far beyond such deceptive labeling and endlessly repeat demonstrably false claims, such as that birth control pills and abortion cause cancer, that gays are pedophiles, and that "legitimate rape" (as Missouri Congressman Todd Akin put it) cannot cause pregnancy. They then cite these specious claims as justification for meddlesome, intrusive laws.

Worse, religious leaders claim that defenders of state-church separation are anti-religious bigots or even persecutors of religious believers. For example, the public policy that requires medical insurance to include contraceptive coverage is being challenged as "going against the religious convictions" of Catholic employers (who provide insurance to their employees). This is like saying that employers religiously opposed to the germ theory of disease (it is "just a theory" after all) should be able to exclude antibiotics from insurance coverage. In fact, what such claims reveal is that the religious zealots making them are not persecuted in any sense of the word (in an 80% Christian nation!), but rather seek special privileges for religions and religious believers.

You will enjoy reading *Culture Wars*. Even if you are already a reasonably well informed advocate of religious liberty and state-church separation, there are things here that will make you sit bolt upright and say, "What?! I didn't know that!" And the author presents the facts in an engaging and entertaining way. Her warmth and depth of experience come through well, especially when she relates personal experiences and events. This is not an exhaustive treatment of a subject that deserves—but has never gotten— much attention. That book is yet to be written. But this is an excellent introduction, with many references and citations, to a subject that has for far too long been neglected. And, as the author points out, there is now an urgency to recognizing and addressing these problems before they become much worse.

— Dr. Tim Gorski, Pastor, North Texas Church of Freethought

PREFACE

*"The legitimate powers of government extend to such acts only as are
injurious to others. But it does me no injury for my neighbor
to say there are twenty gods, or no god. It neither
picks my pocket nor breaks my leg."*

—Thomas Jefferson, *Notes on Virginia*, 1782

What Jefferson says in the opening quotation would be true enough if religious beliefs were only a matter of personal opinion, like belief in tarot cards or astrology. But they have never been. Rather, they are usually intrusive. Religions, far too often, attempt to institutionalize their theologies, even though the laws and social customs dictated by those theologies may be injurious to others.

This is a report from the trenches. I am not a personally unaffected outside observer pondering the social-political dilemmas that center on religious beliefs. I have stood face to face with religious theocrats and seen the coldness in their eyes, and I've experienced the hardness of their hearts. I have been to the funerals of their victims and watched beautiful human potential shredded in the service of their barbaric beliefs. I have fought mightily to keep that sadistic worldview out of our laws. I am not done yet. Humanity deserves better.

Some think we have freedom of (and from) religion in America because of our Constitution—the first in the world to separate government from religion. They are wrong.

Much has been made of the supposed success of state-church separation exemplified by John F. Kennedy's 1960 campaign speech to the Greater Houston Ministerial Association about the importance of secular issues, such as poverty, hunger, education and health care, and the irrelevance of religious belief in dealing with them:

I believe in an America where the separation of church and state is absolute—where no Catholic prelate would tell the President (should he be Catholic) how to act, and no Protestant minister would tell his parishioners for whom to vote—where no church or church school is granted any public funds or political preference—and where no man is denied public office merely because his religion differs from the President who might appoint him or the people who might elect him.

I believe in an America that is officially neither Catholic, Protestant nor Jewish—where no public official either requests or accepts instructions on public policy from the Pope, the National Council of Churches or any other ecclesiastical source—where no religious body seeks to impose its will directly or indirectly upon the general populace or the public acts of its officials—and where religious liberty is so indivisible that an act against one church is treated as an act against all.

For while this year it may be a Catholic against whom the finger of suspicion is pointed, in other years it has been, and may someday be again, a Jew—or a Quaker—or a Unitarian—or a Baptist. It was Virginia's harassment of Baptist preachers, for example, that led to Jefferson's statute of religious freedom. Today I may be the victim—but tomorrow it may be you—until the whole fabric of our harmonious society is ripped apart at a time of great national peril.

. . . I ask you tonight . . . to judge me on the basis of 14 years in Congress—on my declared stands against an Ambassador to the Vatican, against unconstitutional aid to parochial schools, and against any boycott of the public schools (which I attended myself). . . . Whatever issue may come before me as President, if I should be elected—on birth control, divorce, censorship, gambling or any other subject—I will make my decision in accordance with . . . what my conscience tells me to be in the national interest, and without regard to outside religious pressure or dictates. And no power or threat of punishment could cause me to decide otherwise . . .

Yet, at the time Kennedy spoke, there was no real separation of religion and government. Religious institutions had it all. Their views on social morality were already part of our legal system; the law forced everyone to follow their moral dictates. Despite this, the Catholic Church unabashedly claimed support for freedom of conscience, as expressed in a 1938 book, *The Faith of Millions*, by the Rev. John A. O'Brien, Ph.D. Regarding Protestant fears of papal control—fears responsible for defeating the Catholic governor of New York, Al Smith for President in 1928—O'Brien wrote:

[I]n the century and a half of our national existence there has never been a single instance of a Catholic proving false to his civic duties because of any pull exerted upon him by his religious faith. No matter how much men may speculate about a theoretical conflict of civil and spiritual loyalties on the part of Catholics, the stark fact remains that no Catholic incumbent has ever yet discovered any obligation arising from his Catholic faith at variance with that which presses inexorably upon his conscience to discharge to the full the duties of his civil office.

It was easy enough for O'Brien to make that claim in 1938, because the laws then supported the dominant religious beliefs, however much they violated the freedom of conscience of those who believed differently. None of the religion-based laws had then, and do not have now, any credible secular justification. Most were state laws, sometimes inconsistently enforced, making them appear to be only a reflection of local cultural habits and prejudices—as just the way things were done. Their violations of the First Amendment's "no establishment of religion" clause generally went unnoticed. Violations included:

- Racial discrimination and Jim Crow laws
- Blue laws restricting what businesses could sell and when
- Severe restriction of access to contraceptives and sterilization
- Prohibition of abortion
- Prohibition of reality-based sex education
- Censorship of books and all other media
- Prohibition of homosexuality
- Laws against atheists holding public office
- Denial or restriction of child custody for nonreligious parents
- Restriction of grounds for divorce
- Prohibition of cohabitation
- Prayer and Bible reading in public schools.
- Prohibition of suicide, even to shorten unbearable suffering
- Preferential tax exemptions for religion.
- "Morals squads" enforcing laws against gambling, drinking, erotic dancing, and non-marital consensual sex.
- Religious language replacing secular statements on our national motto, money, and pledge of allegiance.

Much of this began changing in the 1960s with widespread and sometimes violent challenges to "the way things were always done." Television coverage of the Vietnam War raised doubts and questions never before asked about political authority. The development of the pill gave women a level of control over their reproductive functions—and therefore their lives—that was never before possible, thus encouraging a rebellion against religious authority. A general sense of disgust with nonsensical repressive laws sparked a whole host of freedom movements among historically mistreated groups.

The first inklings of change toward separating religion from government had already appeared following the 1947 Supreme Court ruling in *Everson v. Board of Education*. This landmark decision was the first to make the religion clauses of the First Amendment binding on the states by applying the Due Process clause of the Fourteenth Amendment. Prior to *Everson*, many states had been granting special privileges to religious denominations. In *Everson*, the plaintiff contested New Jersey's reimbursement to parents for the transportation costs of sending their children to private schools, 96% of which were Catholic parochial schools. In his ruling, Justice Hugo Black wrote:

> The "establishment of religion" clause of the First Amendment means at least this: Neither a state nor the Federal Government can set up a church. Neither can pass laws which aid one religion, aid all religions, or prefer one religion over another. Neither can force nor influence a person to go to or to remain away from church against his will or force him to profess a belief or disbelief in any religion. No person can be punished for entertaining or professing religious beliefs or disbeliefs, for church attendance or non-attendance. No tax in any amount, large or small, can be levied to support any religious activities or institutions, whatever they may be called, or whatever form they may adopt to teach or practice religion. Neither a state nor the Federal government can, openly or secretly, participate in the affairs of any religious organizations or groups and vice versa. In the words of Jefferson, the clause against establishment of religion by law was intended to erect a "wall of separation" between church and state.

The *McCollum v. Board of Education* ruling followed in 1948. It ended the "released time" practice in Illinois of allowing religious organizations to use the public schools, during school hours, to conduct religious instruction classes. This practice required the unconstitutional involvement of the school system in administering, organizing, and supporting the classes.

However, the turn toward secularism embodied in these and later rulings, and, starting in the 1960s, increased resistance to repressive, religion-based laws, and awakened the authoritarian religions to the danger such rebellion posed to them. If the laws went, so would their status as the moral arbiters of society. They set up political, social action, and public relations campaigns. To make matters worse, they attracted political allies who, although disinterested in the religious agenda, paid it lip service to manipulate authoritarian religious believers into supporting their goals of lessening government control over corporations, banks, and the environment, and in favor of ever more regressive taxation and greater wealth and income inequality. As this religious/economic movement developed, with little organized opposition, it became more extreme, adopting a political take-no-prisoners attitude which made reasoned debate almost impossible.

And the dysfunction continues and worsens, with no relief in sight, causing one to suspect that in the future these times may be regarded, in comparison, as the good old days. We are in the midst of a long-running culture war. Government support of women's rights, gay rights, and anything that helps disadvantaged people is defined as evil, making government itself evil, except when enforcing moral dictates. So, the logical outcome of the religious right movement would be reversion to theocracy—with no separation between religion and government, a certain end to many of the liberties we cherish, and a grossly unfair, devil-take-the-hindmost economic system.

Could this happen in our democracy? Not if enough voters care about protecting our freedoms. But it appears that not enough do. In the 2010 mid-term elections, with the federal government extremely dysfunctional, only 41% of the electorate voted. That means 59% either did not know or did not care about the issues, so they stayed home. A majority of those who voted elected candidates who supported an authoritarian religion-based society where compromise for the common good is impossible.

Once a dogmatic religious belief is seen as a critical component of a society's moral values, it is almost impossible to dislodge it. True believers do not compromise what they believe is their god's will. They can and do kill and die for their beliefs—a fact attested to by history and current events. That's a disconcerting thought for those who value democratic freedoms, but one that should encourage action to avoid this awful outcome.

As the culture war escalated, almost everything Kennedy said he would not allow soon came into being through religious pressure and accommodative Supreme Court rulings. Presidents began seeking advice from the likes of Billy Graham, Ted Haggard, and the Catholic hierarchy. Religious schools and activities received taxpayer support (though indirectly, to circumvent state-church separation issues), and religious institutions began to impose their beliefs through electoral politics. Ronald Reagan, as Governor of California in 1967, said his administration would be based on the teachings of Jesus. He then had Billy Graham address the state legislature twice and asked him to discuss the second coming of Christ with his cabinet. When Graham held one of his religious crusades in Anaheim, Reagan attended it and said, "I'm sure there will be those who question my participation here tonight. People have become so concerned with church-state separation that we have interpreted freedom of religion into freedom from religion."[1]

As President, Reagan maintained his one-sided view of state-church separation by appointing the first U.S. ambassador to the Vatican. (The Vatican became a "state" in 1929 thanks to Mussolini and his Lateran Pact. At the signing of the Pact, Pope Pius XII called Mussolini "a gift of Providence, a man free of the prejudices of the liberal school.")

Reagan's lack of understanding of the First Amendment and church-state separation could be stunning. For example, consider this statement: "We establish no religion in this country. We command no worship. We mandate no belief, nor will we ever. Church and state are and must remain separate." Sounds good, doesn't it? Not quite. That supposedly pro-separation statement was made on October 21, 1984, at Temple Hillel in Valley Stream, New York. Reagan was referring to a Connecticut Supreme Court ruling that denied religious employees the right to impose their beliefs on an employer and all the employees. The religious employees had demanded a strict workplace-wide adherence to their Sabbath religious practices at much inconvenience to everyone else. Reagan (as he said in his speech) was actually urging the U.S. Supreme Court to overturn the Connecticut decision and allow the religious imposition. "This is what I mean by freedom of religion," he said, "and that's what we feel the Constitution intends." The U.S. Supreme Court thought differently and upheld the Connecticut Supreme Court's ruling. The ruling (and wouldn't it be nice if there were more like this applied to every topic in this book?) said:

The Connecticut statute, by providing Sabbath observers with an absolute and unqualified right not to work on their chosen Sabbath, violates the Establishment Clause. To meet constitutional requirements under that Clause, a statute must not only have a secular purpose and not foster entanglement of government with religion, its primary effect must not advance or inhibit religion. *Lemon v. Kurtzman*, 403 U.S. 602. The Connecticut statute imposes on employers and employees an absolute duty to conform their business practices to the particular religious practices of an employee by enforcing observance of the Sabbath that the latter unilaterally designate. The State thus commands that Sabbath religious concerns automatically control over all secular interests at the workplace; the statute takes no account of the convenience or interests of the employer or those of other employees who do not observe a Sabbath. In granting unyielding weighting in favor of Sabbath observers over all other interests, the statute has a primary effect that impermissibly advances a particular religious practice.[2]

In opposition to this viewpoint, and reflecting the skewed view of state-church separation Reagan favored, the Catholic hierarchy and Jerry Falwell's newly formed Moral Majority had already begun attempting to return society to the 1950s, triggered by the 1973 *Roe v. Wade* decision on abortion. As a result of the efforts of the Catholic Church, allied with Protestant fundamentalists and the Mormon hierarchy, we have been locked in what the media call a culture war for decades. Productive, civil political discussion is all but gone. The Republican party, once a respectable and worthy political institution, has become mired in religious litmus tests for its candidates, and uses religious wedge issues (gay marriage, abortion rights, etc.) to induce religiously conservative blue-collar voters to vote against their own economic interests.

John F. Kennedy's concern that religious hostilities might some day cause "the whole fabric of our harmonious society (to be) ripped apart" foreshadowed the divisive culture war that has destroyed rational political and social discourse since the 1960s century. This war is actually a religious war, instigated and maintained by Catholic, Mormon, and Protestant religious leaders, that pits authoritarian religion against both nonbelievers and liberal religionists. Their weapons today are propaganda, political organizing, and legal strategies—rather than the wholesale bloodshed of past centuries. Their goal is to reinstate the social control they had at the time Kennedy was assuming they did not have it.

Kennedy was mistaken then, and we as a nation are mistaken now if we think we are not a religious country. Despite our secular Constitution, we are still very much a Christian nation. Although the First Amendment created a wall of separation between religion and government, that wall has always been so porous as to be almost useless. In a nation that values freedom, no one should be controlled by the religious beliefs of others. Yet we are so immersed in theocratic laws that we no longer see them for what they are or understand the injuries they cause.

These laws have social and personal costs. Although many people escape some of them, no one escapes them all. Even those who favor some of these laws are likely to resent others. All of them are unconstitutional, because they do nothing but support unverifiable sectarian dogma. They are an establishment of religion in its most egregious form. Far worse than forcing government god-talk on us, they force us to live—and even die—by religious doctrines we don't accept and may abhor.

In November 2011, as reported in the *New York Times*,[3] the culture war took an astonishing turn when the United States Conference of Catholic Bishops (USCCB) suddenly shifted its tactics. Instead of continuing to oppose abortion rights, gay rights, stem cell research and other "values" issues on the grounds of morality, the bishops began to claim the Church was a victim. Their "Religious Liberty Drive" is trying to redefine the culture war as a government assault on the Catholic Church's religious freedom. Archbishop (now a cardinal) Timothy M. Dolan of New York said, "We see in our culture a drive to neuter religion," and a move "to push religion back into the sacristy." Dolan was promoting a politicized religion that overrides the civil rights and civil liberties of everyone who thinks or believes differently. This is divisive and arrogant. And yes, religion should be politically neutered and pushed back into the sacristy, where it belongs.

What set Dolan off was the federal government's decision to stop funding social programs operated by the Catholic Church on the government's behalf if the Church insisted on imposing its doctrinal beliefs on its non-Catholic employees and recipients of it services. These impositions included denial of contraceptives or morning after pills to women trying to avoid pregnancy due to rape, incest, the possibility of grave health problems, or death. The Church would not allow abortion even under the most dire circumstances—including possible (in some cases certain) death from being denied it. The Church wouldn't even allow referrals in such cases. Similarly, it would not allow adoption (or foster care) by same-sex couples.

This is sheer brutality but, in the view of the Catholic bishops, they have "religious freedom" to brutalize people in this way, and to stop them is to discriminate against *them* because of their beliefs. They claim the government is taking away their liberty, but what kind of liberty is it that denies the liberty of others? This is a form of "religious liberty" no one should support: the "liberty" to control others. If churches want to exercise their "religious liberty" by denying services to those who do not conform to their doctrines, they should reject government funding and provide the services on their own dime.

The Catholic bishops are a powerful lobby, although they appear to have more influence with legislators than with their own church members. They distribute a voters guide called "Forming Consciences for Faithful Citizenship" in every election. However, according to a recent poll, only 16% of Catholics knew of the document, and only 3% read it.[4] On birth control the pope actually speaks for only 2% of Catholics. The 98% majority use or have used contraceptives.[5] Apparently, not many Catholics are interested in having the Church tell them what to do. They seem quite able to make their own decisions.

But this hardly matters if the Catholic/fundamentalist/Mormon political juggernaut succeeds in getting state and federal judges and Supreme Court justices appointed who are willing to interpret the religion clauses of the First Amendment in such a way as to increase the social and political power of religion. One more conservative Supreme Court justice could tip the balance, Cardinal Dolan could get his "religious freedom" to override our civil rights and civil liberties. Our Constitution protects us only to the extent the Supreme Court allows it to.

Belief in gods, whether one or twenty, really does pick our pockets and break our legs—and not just metaphorically—when sectarian doctrines become entrenched in our laws. These doctrines are abusive and mean-spirited, disdaining the most basic elements of common decency in the service of unverifiable beliefs and ecclesiastical power.

This has to stop. I am by nature a "cause" person, always drawn to the call to mount the barricades when civil rights and liberties are under siege. I am also an atheist—the kind whose principles require opposing religions that violate human rights and human-centered values. Therefore, I don't bother with generalized "religion-bashing," only with aspects of religion that inflict harm on innocent people. I find I share this concern with many moderate religionists. Like all atheists, I have no belief in an afterlife or a supernatural deity. What I do have is a deep yearning to see this life, the only one we have, as the best it can be for all of us. Yet that better life remains out of reach for many reasons. Some are related directly to the subject of this book: archaic laws, policies, and practices that do nothing but ensure the continuance of suffering while providing government validation for the self-indulgent, mystical yearnings of authoritarian religious institutions.

I find no good secular reasons for oppressive laws that target women, racial and sexual minorities, harmless sexual relationships, children, the hopelessly ill, working people, and even the tax paying population in general. What I do find is that we are all, in one way or another, being mugged by mythology without realizing it. It is not just "Your money or your life." It is "Your money *and* your life!"

Our Constitution mandates separation of religion from government. Oppressive religion-based laws are not "separation"; they are an entanglement that serves only to validate and enforce particular beliefs, and impose the resulting hardships, restrictions, injustices, abuses, financial costs, and—at best—tiresome inconveniences, on the whole of society. These laws, for no good secular reason, take our money, criminalize harmless sexual interactions, compromise our personal relationships, override our freedom to control our reproductive functions, adversely affect our health, dumb down our educational system, interfere with scientific research, and diminish our quality of life.

Advocates for religion-based laws sometimes acknowledge their harmful effects, but dismiss the effects as necessary to promote the common good. They always cite abstractions ("moral values," "the common good," etc.) and ignore the real suffering these laws inflict on real people. These laws have no rational purpose, Assuming that the slippery abstraction "the common good" exists, it's best served by taking theology out of our laws and leaving religious beliefs to individuals. Let those who want to run their own lives on religious principles do so, but don't let them run the lives of others.

There is probably more support for this "keep it private" view than one might think. I attended a day-long symposium on religion in public life on April 28, 1998, in Minneapolis. It was sponsored by PBS and hosted by the well-known Lutheran theologian Martin Marty. I was one of two atheists among the 100 religious and civic leaders invited to attend. The focus was on countering the rise of the religious right. During Marty's keynote address, he noted our atheist presence and said, "It is the role of unbelievers to force religions to be benign." He urged us to be more open in challenging the assaults of the religious right.

The purpose of *Culture Wars* is to do just that by showing the extent to which we are living under the rules of a form of Christianity more suited to the Middle Ages than the 21st century. We are awash in antiquated laws that cost us money and adversely affect how well we live—and die.

This book identifies those laws—at least the worst and most common ones. Although *Culture Wars* is divided into chapters on specific topics, there is considerable overlap, which is difficult to avoid—the topics are interconnected. In some way, every topic affects every other topic due to the pervasiveness and structural (though not rational) coherence of the theological worldview. This book explains that worldview and its archaic theological basis, and illustrates the harm it causes. It exposes the fraudulent "secular" arguments for the laws that validate that worldview and force it on others. *Culture Wars* is a call to mount the barricades once again to challenge unconstitutional laws, repeal them, and make our lives a little more fulfilling, a little less stressful, and a lot more free.

---

1. Bothwell, Cecil, *The Prince of War: Billy Graham's Crusade for a Wholly Christian Empire*, Brave Ulysses Book, 2007, p. 157.

2. See http://open.salon.com/blog/douglas_berger/2012/04/03/putting_reagans_church_state_quote_in_context._shows_a_hypocrisy.

3. Laurie Goodstein, "Bishops Open 'Religious Liberty' Drive," *The New York Times*, Nov. 11, 2011, http://www.nytimes.com/2011/11/15/us/bishops-renew-fight-on-abortion-and-gay-marriage.html.

4. Ibid.

5. Catholics for Choice, www.CatholicsForChoice.org

ACKNOWLEDGMENTS

Writing this book was not easy, since there is so much going on politically that is directly relevant to the topic, and things change daily. Not even the past holds still, what with recent U.S. Supreme Court rulings undermining achievements in state-church separation.

A lot of people helped by giving generously of their expertise. It is an honor to have this opportunity to give them a big THANK YOU. Their assistance in making this book as accurate, informative and useful as possible was invaluable. They contributed much to the down-to-earth, grass-roots orientation of this book—they've helped show how archaic, theology-based laws harm all of us. No ivory tower stuff here! I've tried not to leave anyone out, and if I did, I apologize. And, of course, if any part of this book is deficient, it is entirely my doing, not theirs.

Let me start by briefly recognizing those whose indirect and unintended help I certainly did find invaluable, but who are not fit to be in the same room with decent human beings. They are the authoritarian religious misanthropes who have injected their bizarre theology and inhumane doctrinal demands into our laws, and who have sucked much of the joy out of life for their victims. Just quoting the pompous theology and Bible-thumping claims coming from the Vatican and Protestant fundamentalist extremists gives credibility to my assertions. So I hereby acknowledge their willingness (actually arrogance) in being so forthcoming with their self-incriminating pronouncements.

Now let's get to the good guys—and they even include politicians! First I need to recognize three irreplaceable people who looked forward to reading my book, who cheered me on and up, but were taken by death while I was writing it.

One was my dear Quaker friend and long-time political colleague, D Perry Kidder, a sensitive, lyrical writer of short stories and memoirs. We occasionally attended each other's Quaker/atheist events and she had agreed to edit my book, but that was not to be.

Another was John B. (Jack) Massen, also a longtime friend, who was an atheist colleague. Jack's moral vision and ethical principles were inspiring to those of us seeking a peaceful world free of religious divisiveness.

Finally, there was my son, Bill Nagengast, the third of my five children. He died in a motorcycle accident on I-35 in Oklahoma on his way home from visiting his daughter and her family in California. Bill had such a generous spirit, always full of the joy of living. I saw him for the last time a few weeks earlier when he came over with his chainsaw to trim my tree branches. He worked away so enthusiastically that I told him he didn't have to do such a good job. He said, with his usual cheerful exuberance, "But that's the only kind of a job I know how to do!"

There is one more friend, still living, who deserves a special recognition—Jeri Rasmussen, now lost to the memory death of Alzheimers. We were colleagues in fending off the assaults of the anti-abortion zealots when she was managing an abortion clinic in the face of constant death threats. A liberal religionist, she loved being a guest on our atheist public access TV show where she could give her unvarnished opinion of misogynistic theocrats.

There have been too many sad losses of the kind of people we need so badly and have so few of. Still among us, and may they stay that way for a long time, are many other good people who kept me going and shined, polished, and dusted this book's prose to make it presentable.

George Erickson, in northern Minnesota, edited my book with professional skill. A published author himself, he has written several arctic adventure books with a scientific slant based on his own explorations. One of the books, *True North: Exploring the Great Wilderness by Bush Plane*, was a bestseller in Canada.

The introduction for this book was written by Tim Gorski, M.D., in Texas. A secular pastor of his North Texas Church of Freethought, Dr. Gorski's writing reflects the masterful "sermons" he gives. He also made sure my statements on reproductive medical issues were accurate.

Niles Ross, in Iowa, was a bottomless source of first hand information about hospital policies and practices, who made the sections on health care at the administrative level so informative.

Randall Tigue, a constitutional lawyer in Minnesota and board member of Atheists For Human Rights as well as State Director for American Atheists, helped tremendously in keeping my discussion of legal issues understandable and accurate. (Not easy, given the sometimes murky nature of legal prose.)

William Sierichs Jr., in Louisiana, a journalist and researcher in religious history, provided interesting historical information about religious institutional behavior that is generally unknown but illuminates the contentious censorial mindset that still impacts society today.

Roy Sablosky, in California, provided excellent material about charitable tax deductions. He turned a much-needed light on the world of preferential tax treatment for religious as well as secular nonprofits.

Kirk Buchanan, in California, was especially encouraging. As a former Catholic priest—now an atheist—he was able to assure me that my assessment of Catholic theology was entirely appropriate.

Arvonne Fraser, author of *She's No Lady: Politics, Family, and International Feminism*. and a well known civic leader in Minnesota and in national and international human rights circles, provided much inspiration for me as I worked on this book through her grassroots-to-global activism

I owe a very special thanks to my publisher, Chaz Bufe of See Sharp Press. He is responsible for my going where I had never gone before—or wanted to—when he invited me to write this book. As with so much of my life, it was another "fools rush in" experience. I never imagined how complex serious book publishing can be. Fortunately, Chaz sprung requirements on me only as needed, so I never knew what I would be getting into, only what I was getting into at the moment. Looking back, that ignorance was indeed bliss—more or less. Chaz did a commendable job of keeping me out of pitfalls I had not been aware of in his final editing of the book. He said part of his job was to watch out for his authors, and he did it with great patience and skill.

Then there are the people who provided me with their experiences so I could show the real-world impact of religion-based laws. They deserve my sincere admiration and thanks, especially Cecil Bothwell, Dick Hewetson, Jacqueline (Jackie) Marquis, Erica Rogers, and Rita and Doug Swan of CHILD Inc.

Many people provided information and support, and/or skillfully reviewed parts of this book. They include: John Annen, Sanford Berman, Caroline Brunner, Paul Craven, Margaret Downey, Jane Everhart, Rick Gellman, Bruce Hurtley, Scott Jackson (my grandson), Susan Jackson (my daughter), Paul Keller, Sarah Hurwicz Kogut, Ron Kroll, Tom Lawson, Brad Mattson, Marianne Maves (my daughter), Guy and Victoria McCoy, Scott Muir, Andy Mulcahy, Julia Nagengast (my daughter), Mike Nagengast (my son), Nancy Ruhland, Sybil Smith, Oliver Steinberg, and William van Druten, M.D.

I want to especially thank the organizations that fight for our right to be free of religious coercion, andwhose ongoing efforts show the vast extent of the problem. There are many, large and small, so I can list only a few: American Atheists, American Civil Liberties Union, American Humanist Association, Americans for Religious Liberty, Americans United for Separation of Church & State, CHILD Inc., Final Exit Network, and Freedom From Religion Foundation. Other organizations especially worthy of thanks are those that take on their own fellow religionists in the hope of civilizing them, such as Catholics for Choice (www.catholicsforchoice. org). May their tribe increase.

Lastly, my sincere appreciation goes to those Minnesota politicians who do their best to keep our laws religion free. All of them belie the stereotype of the "crooked politician." All are honest and decent, with a sincere desire to promote the common good. Some have left office for personal reasons; others lost election to religious-right fanatics running deceitful campaigns. I can mention only those no longer in office because such mention can no longer jeopardize their political careers. Among the most notable have been congressman and Minneapolis mayor Don Fraser; state senator and congressman Bill Luther; state senator Jane Ranum; state representative Phil Carruthers; state representative Andy Dawkins and his wife, state senator Ellen Anderson; and state senator Don Betzold.

Other politicians who deserve my (and everyone's) respect cannot be named here because they are currently in office and therefore vulnerable to religious-right targeting. They work behind the scenes as best they can to modify or eliminate unfair preferential treatment of religious institutions and end religious intrusions into our personal lives. They are slandered nearly constantly just for being politicians by people who make gratuitous assumptions, but they are heroes. If they read this book, they will know who they are and that I thank them.

—Marie Alena Castle, Minneapolis, March 2013

1

INTERPRETING THE CONSTITUTION

"I believe I have rights because I exist, in spite of my government, not because of my government. Judge Bork believes that rights flow from the majority, through the Constitution to individuals, a notion I reject."

—Senator Joseph Biden, hearings on nomination of
Robert Bork to the U.S. Supreme Court, 1987

The First Amendment's religion clause begins: "Congress shall make no law . . ." But Congress does make those laws, and we pay for them with our money, our health, our freedom . . . and sometimes our lives.

The social and political chaos generated by our culture war would not exist if laws that serve only theological beliefs were declared unconstitutional, as violations of the Establishment Clause of the First Amendment. Unfortunately, and disturbingly, we have at least one Supreme Court Justice, Antonin Scalia, who openly rejects the concept of state-church separation, while the Court as a whole, judging by its rulings under Chief Justice John Roberts, appears to be leaning increasingly toward supporting religious beliefs rather than maintaining government neutrality.

Jeffrey Toobin, in his 2012 book, *The Oath: The Obama White House and the Supreme Court,* writes that Roberts has expressed contempt for what he calls the "fluid and wide-ranging jurisprudence" of the Court that brought about so much civil rights progress under Chief Justices Earl Warren and Warren Burger during the 1960s, '70s and '80s. This progress included improvements in protection for minorities, state-church separation, the ability of citizens to challenge governmental as well as business practices, and the establishment of women's right to abortion. When William Rehnquist became Chief Justice in 1986, all of these rights and liberties (called "excesses" by Justice Roberts) came under attack. Now, as Toobin documents, it has become "Roberts' mission to lead the counterrevolution" to finish the job.[1]

There is great danger in this. We have long assumed that our freedoms are protected by the Constitution, but this is not true. The Constitution does absolutely nothing to protect us until and unless a Supreme Court ruling spells out that protection—or, in some cases, denies it, as in the notorious 1857 *Dred Scott* decision that affirmed the status of slaves as property.

In reality, we are governed not by the Constitution but by constitutional law, which is based on the Supreme Court's interpretation of the Constitution. However, there can be no interpretation unless a law is challenged, as is required by the Constitution itself. Article III, Sec. 2 limits federal judicial power to controversies arising under the laws and Constitution of the United States. Unless someone brings a legal challenge to a particular law or practice, there is no controversy over which the Court has any legal authority. Without (a) Supreme Court ruling(s), freedoms can exist in some states while being denied in others. Although state-church violations have been rampant throughout our history (and are still rampant today), no significant challenges came before the Court until the 1940s. The reasons are understandable. It takes considerable personal courage and financial resources to challenge such abuses.

Before the founding of the American Civil Liberties Union (ACLU) in 1920, individuals who wanted to litigate a state-church violation would have had to bear the considerable legal costs themselves, so no one did. The ACLU changed that by supplying plaintiffs with the attorneys and funds needed for cases it deemed important. Since then, other state-church separationist groups have supplied funding, as has the federal government. In 1976, Congress passed the Civil Right's Attorneys Fee Award Act. It provides that any governmental unit that enacts an unconstitutional law must pay the attorneys' fees and costs for a party that successfully challenges that law.[2]

But even with legal fees covered, plaintiffs have often faced daunting perils. Challenges frequently result in death threats, social ostracism, and job or business losses due to the hostility of those who want religious beliefs and practices enshrined in law. Plaintiffs often have to file a challenge anonymously, go into hiding, or move far away to ensure their safety.

In addition to these problems, there is always the possibility of a ruling that *furthers* state-church entanglement rather than removing it, thus setting a legal precedent that makes the success of subsequent challenges on the same issue almost impossible. Here is an example of how legal challenges are sometimes withheld—and therefore justice denied—when the Supreme Court is unreliable regarding the First Amendment: On June 7, 2001, the ACLU of Ohio announced that it would not appeal the ruling of the full 6th Circuit Court that Ohio's motto, "With God All Things Are Possible" was constitutional. The ruling overturned a previous three-judge panel ruling that the motto infringed on the First Amendment of the Constitution. The reason the ACLU decided not to take the case to the Supreme Court was that the current conservative bloc on the court had hacked away at the wall of separation of church and state in previous rulings. According to an article in the *Columbus Dispatch* at that time, Raymond Vasvari, legal director for the ACLU of Ohio, said: "It's no secret that there's a conservative bloc on the Supreme Court that takes a skeptical view of church and state separation. For now, this will be the last word."

In 2007, in *Hein v. Freedom From Religion Foundation* (FFRF),[3] the Supreme Court ruled that taxpayers do not have standing to challenge the constitutionality of expenditures by the executive branch of government. FFRF had argued that the use of money appropriated by Congress to support faith-based social programs was unconstitutional. The Court ruled, however, that the funds involved had actually been appropriated for use by the executive branch for unspecified purposes and the President was therefore free to use those funds as he wished. This, of course, means that public money can be spent on religious activities as long as it is laundered through an appropriation designated for *carte blanche* use by the President.

Taxpayer money laundering seems to be the up-and-coming preferred strategy in circumventing the First Amendment—as well as state constitutions, which tend to be more specific and therefore stronger in prohibiting taxpayer support for religious activities and institutions—especially schools. In 2011, in the *Arizona Christian School Tuition Organization v. Winn*[4] case, the Supreme Court ruled that taxpayers do not have standing in federal court to challenge state tax credits for contributions to school-tuition organizations that then provide scholarships to students at private schools, including religious schools. (In 2010, in Arizona, this amounted to $60 million, 92% of which went to religious schools.[5]) The effect of this is that, instead of giving money directly and unconstitutionally to religious schools, the state can "launder" it through an organization that takes a parental donation and turns it over to the school of the parent's choice. The parent is then reimbursed by the state in the form of a dollar-for-dollar tax credit in the amount of the tuition donation.

The Roberts Court based its ruling on the plaintiff not having claimed a personal financial injury. This effectively negated the 1968 Warren Court's ruling in *Flast v Cohen* that taxpayers could sue to stop government expenditures that violated the Establishment Clause. Chief Justice Warren had argued that, without this right, the courts would have no avenue (that is, no controversy brought to them) leading to examination of constitutional violations.[6]

So now one needs to show a personal financial injury. But is it not injurious to be forced indirectly to support religious schools? Tuition tax credits come from taxes paid by citizens, citizens who did not expect their taxes to end up in a money laundering scheme designed to circumvent the First Amendment. One would think that challenging such a constitutional runaround would be an essential prerogative—even a duty—of a citizen in a constitutional democracy. But the U.S. Supreme Court thinks otherwise. So now we must show that a state-church violation does tangible harm to us personally. Destroying the civil liberties the Constitution was created to protect is apparently not harmful enough.

Even when there is personal injury, religious institutional prerogatives often outweigh the rights of victims. For example, in 2012 the Supreme Court ruled in favor of a religious school in *Hosanna-Tabor Evangelical Lutheran Church and School v. Equal Employment Opportunity Commission*. The case concerned the church's claim that it had an unrestricted right to discriminate on the basis of race, sex, disability and other characteristics regardless of secular laws prohibiting such action; therefore, its firing of a teacher because of a medical condition should be allowed. Several civil liberties and religious organizations asked the Court to rule for the plaintiff, saying that the right of religions to discriminate in their personnel practices should not apply in situations not related directly to the institution's religious mission. They argued that religion-specific justifications for discrimination should not be extended into—as an *amicus* brief filed by Americans United for Separation of Church & State said—"a shield for all forms of discrimination and retaliation, regardless of motivation."[7] The Roberts Court, judging by its ruling, evidently thought such discrimination was perfectly acceptable—as long as it resulted from religious belief.

Because the Supreme Court's interpretations can be, and inevitably are, influenced by the ideological mindset of the justices, constitutional law can just as easily destroy our freedoms as protect them. The current makeup of the Court is such that there is reason to fear a destructive phase is at hand, and that the Court will uphold at least some, if not all, of our theology-based laws if they are challenged. But those of us who love freedom and the civil rights and liberties promised by our Constitution must accept the danger. There may be some hills worth dying on, and so—although care must be taken—challenges must be made. Religious beliefs must be removed from government and privatized if we are to remain a nation dedicated to liberty and justice for all.

The Problem with Challenging Religion-Based Laws

Challenges to theology-based laws are seldom, if ever, presented as challenges to violations of the First Amendment's establishment of religion clause. Instead, plaintiffs often employ secular right-to-privacy or equal-treatment arguments. Such arguments are often convoluted in comparison with establishment clause arguments, but are common due to the Court's unreliability on First Amendment issues.

It is important to note how subjective the Court's interpretations can be. For example, Robert Bork, well known as President Ronald Reagan's unsuccessful nominee for appointment to the U.S. Supreme Court in 1987, was defeated because of strong opposition to his belief that the Constitution conferred no right to privacy in matters relating to women's reproductive decisions, that the civil rights decisions of the Warren and Burger courts were made in error, and that the Federal government had no right to impose standards of voting fairness on the states.[8] An October 24, 1987 article in the *New York Times* about the Senate debate on the confirmation, contained the following. It shows the philosophical differences that underlie so many Court decisions and the impact they can have on our rights:

> Later, in closing the debate, the Judiciary Committee chairman [Senator Joe Biden] said: "This has been a great debate, a debate about fundamental principle, about how one interprets the Constitution." Senator Biden repeated the statement with which he opened Judge Bork's confirmation hearings last month, and which he has made a theme for the entire proceeding. "I believe I have rights because I exist, in spite of my government, not because of my government," he said. "Judge Bork believes that rights flow from the majority, through the Constitution to individuals, a notion I reject."[9]

Currently on the U.S. Supreme Court, Justice Antonin Scalia echoes Bork's views of the limited scope of the Constitution and the apparently unlimited power of whatever constitutes the majority of voters. His exact words are instructive as to the value of the Constitution in protecting our civil rights and civil liberties. This is what he said during a Q&A interview published by The Daily Journal Corporation:

> **Q.** In 1868, when the 39th Congress was debating and ultimately proposing the 14th Amendment, I don't think anybody would have thought that equal protection applied to sex discrimination, or certainly not to sexual orientation. So does that mean that we've gone off in error by applying the 14th Amendment to both?
>
> **A.** Yes, yes. Sorry, to tell you that. . . . But, you know, if indeed the current society has come to different views, that's fine. You do not need the Constitution to reflect the wishes of the current society. Certainly the Constitution does not require discrimination on the basis of sex. The only issue is whether it prohibits it. It doesn't. Nobody ever thought that that's what it meant. Nobody ever voted for that. If the current society wants to outlaw discrimination by sex, hey we have things called legislatures, and they enact things called laws. You don't need a Constitution to keep things up-to-date. all you need is a legislature and a ballot box. You don't like the death penalty anymore, that's fine. You want a right to abortion? There's nothing in the Constitution about that. But that doesn't mean you cannot prohibit it. Persuade your fellow citizens it's a good idea and pass a law. That's what democracy is all about. It's not about nine superannuated judges who have been there too long, imposing these demands on society.[10]

Chief Justice John Roberts expressed a similar sentiment in July, 2012, in explaining the sometimes ideologically inconsistent way he voted: "It is not our job to protect the people from the consequences of their political choices,"[11] he said. Really? Doesn't the Constitution exist precisely to protect a minority from the harmful consequences of the majority's political choices when its civil rights and civil liberties are at stake? And isn't it the job of the Supreme Court to see that the Constitution does just that? Not according to Justice Roberts.

It's true that you don't need a Constitution if you think the majority should rule at all times. But we do have a Constitution, whose very purpose is to protect the rights of the minority against the tyranny of the majority. It's also true that when Thomas Jefferson wrote, "All men are created equal," he meant, literally, only men, not women, and only white men, not blacks, and only white men who owned property. Women were, at that time, considered men's property (and in some respects, still are). Slavery was also enshrined in the law. So were many other religion-based laws and policies (some still in operation—the motivation for this book). But, countering that, the Constitution and the Bill of Rights provided for a government that would adjust to changing times.

All references to religion in the Constitution were exclusionary—religion and government were not to be involved with each other. How would Bork and Scalia establish justice consistently if that were left to majority rule? How could the blessings of liberty be secured (and for whom?) if we had liberty in some states but not in other states, whenever the whims of a state's current majority decreed it? How could we be equal citizens under the law or have the basic right to privacy in our personal lives if that were based on the shifting sands of majoritarian rule? What would it mean to be "the land of the free" if our freedom depended, election by election, on the whims of whatever group had at least 50% plus 1 of the votes?

The rights Bork and Scalia cannot find in the Constitution, and that Roberts considers "excesses," have tended to be rights that run counter to archaic religious beliefs embedded in our laws, such as those related to sexuality and reproduction. The very fact that these laws are based on religious beliefs shows they do not belong in our laws at all. They are an establishment of religion in the most harmful way possible. Of course, the current religious right activists who agree with Bork and Scalia don't accept the concept of state-church separation any more than they accept the concept of liberty and justice for all. They believe that might makes right— that they should have the "freedom" to impose their religious beliefs on others, and their chosen method is the law.

If theology-based laws were challenged forthrightly on First Amendment grounds as an establishment of religion, the courts would be faced with a clear issue: Is this law based on a religious belief and, if so, does it still have a *valid* secular purpose that justifies supporting it? (*Valid* is important. After all, one can—and society once did—find a secular economic purpose for slavery; but let's hope our civilization has advanced enough to find that unacceptable.) The religious basis of a law and its (supposed) valid secular purpose either exist or they do not.

The following chapters in this book will attempt to resolve this question for at least the most destructive theology-based laws. An establishment of religion is not just about government god-talk, pledges of allegiance, and slogans on money. It is also about the far more harmful establishment of religious doctrine through laws that affect our life, liberty and pursuit of happiness.

Again, why is the establishment clause used so little in challenging laws that essentially force everyone to bow to the dictates of religious beliefs?

The answer is fairly straightforward. The clause was adopted as a response to the centuries of religious wars and persecution in Europe. This nation's founders, a mix of Christians and Deists, were determined to keep America free of such bloody strife. They assumed that the religion clauses of the First Amendment would be effective in disentangling government from religion.

However, as a consequence, they also effectively disentangled religion from public discourse lest public hostilities break out. As a further consequence, it has become politically and socially incorrect to criticize religious beliefs publicly, with harmful religious behavior euphemized as "socially conservative" behavior, as though religion had nothing to do with it. Thus, the obvious religious nature of many laws is seldom if ever used to argue that they are unconstitutional. When anyone points out this elephant in the room, he or she is accused of "religion bashing," no matter how objective their arguments—and so secularists tend to avoid such arguments.

This is a mistake. If democracy and free speech mean anything, they should mean that we have the right to engage religious institutions freely and openly in debates about the beliefs they want to impose on all of us--just as we debate political parties' socio-economic positions. We should debate their theological arguments, not just their specious "secular" arguments. If they fear exposing their antiquated and unverifiable dogma to public scrutiny, that is all the more reason to scrutinize it.

1. Toobin, Jeffrey, *The Oath: The Obama White House and the Supreme Court*, Doubleday, New York, NY, 2012, p.39. Toobin, a staff writer for *The New Yorker*, is author of *The Nine*, a best-selling book that is also about the U.S. Supreme Court.

2. This information was supplied by Randall Tigue, a constitutional law attorney who had all his fees paid by the State of Idaho under this Act when he successfully challenged the state's actions regarding a Day of Prayer event in 2005.

3. *Hein, Jay, et al. (Dir., White House Office of Faith-Based and Community Initiatives) v. Freedom From Religion Foundation, Inc., et al*, June 25, 2007, 551 U.S. 587

4. *Arizona Christian School Tuition Organization v. Winn*, No. 09-987, April 4, 2011. See www.martindale.com/litigation-law/article_Faegre-Benson-LLP.

5. *Voice of Reason*, Spring 2011, No. 2.

6. Toobin, op cit, p. 82.

7. See http://www.au.org/media/press-releases/archives/2011/08/2011-08-09-hosanna-tabor.pdf. (Information regarding outcome of case supplied by attorney Randall Tigue.)

8. See numerous sources quoted and referenced at htto://en.wikipedia.org/wiki/Robert_Bork_Supreme_Court_nominee

9. See www.nytimes.com/1987/10/24/politics/24REAG.html

10. *The Daily Journal Corporation* interview, titled "The Originalist," part of "Legally Speaking," a series of in-depth interviews with prominent lawyers, judges and academics, co-produced by California Lawyer and UC Hastings College of the Law, as reported by http://www.callawyer.com/common/print.cfm

11. Quoted by Michael Kinsley, "Love it or hate it, Citizens United was the right decision," *Minneapolis Star Tribune* editorial page, July 12, 2012.

2

The Theology of Sex

"I learned two things growing up in Texas. 1: God loves you, and you're going to burn in hell forever. 2: Sex is the dirtiest and most dangerous thing you can possibly do, so save it for someone you love."

—Molly Ivins

This chapter covers sex and the medieval views of it supported by the Catholic Church's papal-infallibility-based theology and the Protestant fundamentalists' inerrant-Bible-based beliefs. I am not going to give these views much respect, because there is nothing about them that deserves it.

According to numerous surveys, most Catholics don't care much for their Church's archaic views on sex, and the liberal Protestant religions have given up such views entirely. However, because of the political influence exerted by religious institutions, medieval religious views are affecting our laws and our lives in harmful ways.

Fortunately, many current theologians are developing more contemporary, human-centered positions. These people are not a problem. They may, in fact, be part of an eventual solution—if they can help get rid of the absurd and authoritarian beliefs described below.

Because so many of the religion-based laws discussed in this book reflect an obsession with sex, an introduction to the supporting theology is needed. Regardless of the appeal this theology may have for its proponents, repressive, religious "moral" beliefs have no value whatsoever in a secular society. In fact, such beliefs have less than no value: archaic theology-based laws—especially those related to sex—do immeasurable harm.

Ironically, that harm falls often upon its facilitators—those supposedly celibate priests who demand that everyone avoid religiously non-approved sex. These are men who entered seminaries around age 13, innocent and eager to become servants of God. But they are human, and that includes having innate yearnings that can be severely at odds with a vow of celibacy. They fight against their natural urges, and I believe most of them succeed to an extent and find satisfaction in their vocation, but others do not. Some act upon their yearnings in destructive, tragically newsworthy ways, and others, probably much more commonly, live wistful, lonely lives.

One Catholic priest, John A. O'Brien, writes the following in his book, *The Faith of Millions*, in a chapter on the joy and fulfillment marriage brings to men. (He doesn't say much about what it brings to women, other than economic support.)

> Among the worst miseries of life is that of unrelieved loneliness. To go to one's dwelling at evening, only to find it empty of any person interested in your struggles, rejoicing in your achievements, softening the sting of defeat with the balm of sympathy and understanding, is to live in a darkened chamber whither the sunshine of human comradeship and love scarcely penetrates. As other forms of life, when deprived of the sun's rays, wither and die, so human life, robbed of the sunshine of love and sympathy, loses its zest, its enthusiasm and its vigor. Love is the radiance which brightens the world of human life with the sunshine of happiness.[1]

It's easy to sense here the unrelieved loneliness of a dedicated priest who entered the ministry too soon to know what he would be sacrificing. Where do such men go if the loneliness becomes unbearable? To prostitutes? To vulnerable altar boys? There is no "sunshine of love and sympathy" there, only the "sloppy fusion of genitalia" (as I once heard it rather graphically described). This is very sad.

But back to theology. If we're going to discuss the theological underpinnings of our laws, the underpinnings of the theology itself need explanation. As a start, get a copy of the 60-page Pastoral Letter of the United States Conference of Catholic Bishops titled "Marriage: Love and Life in the Divine Plan," then pause to wonder what planet its authors are from.[2] In this pastoral letter, the real world is nowhere to be seen. It delivers only mystical musings that glorify an existence based in the imagination and ruled by directives no one with any real life experience would recognize as even sane. In this imaginary world, sex is only for procreation by one man and one woman—and limited to the missionary position!—united until death in a monogamous marriage. Sex in any other context, for any other purpose, is immoral, evil and depraved. All problems arising from adhering to this limited view of sex can be resolved by prayer and reliance on the grace of God through receiving the sacraments.

The Pastoral Letter's entire premise is based on accepting—as an historical, literal, reality—the biblical creation story of Adam and Eve. As the Letter says, "Conflicts, quarrels, and misunderstandings can be found in all marriages. They reflect the impact of Original Sin, which (quoting the United States Catholic Catechism for Adults) 'disrupted the original communion of man and woman.'"[3]

That's fine for those who can believe it, but the Catholic bishops, along with their Protestant fundamentalist counterparts, campaign endlessly for laws based on this mythical world view. The following chapters will discuss those laws. This one will focus on the underlying theology that the advocates for those laws evidently prefer you didn't know about, since they carefully ignore their own theology in their public arguments.

Sex as the Transmitter of Sin and Death

Of all bodily processes, sex seems to always have been especially unsettling to the religious mind—at least in the Abrahamic religions. (Belief systems based on nature worship or multiple gods are less inhibited; Hinduism's ancient sex instruction book, the Kama Sutra, even provides graphic examples.) Some cultures, for non-religious reasons, have tended to worry that sexual activity could make one physically vulnerable. For example, the ancient pagan Greek belief was that sex was "dangerous, hard to control, harmful to health, and draining," and that it should be engaged in infrequently, preferably only for begetting children. As for women, the Greeks didn't see any harm in sexual activity for them because they were "not affected by the loss of energy through the loss of semen."[4] They apparently considered perils of pregnancy and childbirth irrelevant.

In contrast to pagan and polytheistic views of sex, from its earliest days the Christian view has insisted that sex is harmful—in a sinful rather than physical sense. This view has manifested itself in an astonishing number of attempts to control and limit sex, in the process turning sex into the focal point of morality—so much so that many Christians seem to regard sexual behavior as the only aspect of morality. And all this about a natural function that, of itself, has no moral implications. Only the irresponsible (or coercive) use of sex has moral aspects, as when such use is careless of consequences, exploitive, deliberately or thoughtlessly hurtful, or just plain stupid. Given the power of the sex drive, unwise sexual encounters are extremely common. After all, who hasn't been there?

In Christian theology, this is all our fault. All the troubles humans endure have been caused by "the fall" in the Garden of Eden. Eve was deceived by the serpent and seduced Adam into eating the forbidden fruit—said to be a metaphor for sex. That mythical unwise sexual encounter was the Original Sin that doomed humanity to pain, suffering, disease and death.

Or maybe not. As myths go, this one has interesting competition. The creation story in the Bible was not the only one making the rounds when the Bible was created. The Bible we have today has only a few of the many gospels, epistles, legends, historical fictions, and spiritual commentaries that were circulating at the time.

Of the creation stories, the best one, the intriguing tale of Adam's first wife,[5] was left out. It's absolutely fascinating. It tells of how the Most High God first created Lileth to be Adam's wife. Both Adam and Lileth were created equal, out of dirt. Because of that equal creation, Lileth insisted on having full equality with her husband. That being denied her, she left him. Adam complained to God so God made him another wife, Eve. This time, God used one of Adam's ribs, so Eve could not claim to be his equal. How desperate the fear of equality or the need for control must have been that the storytellers felt compelled to reverse the natural process by having Eve "born" of man. The Bible's version of the story has Adam almost gloating when he says (in Genesis 2:23): "This one, at last, is bone of my bones and flesh of my flesh; This one shall be called 'woman' for out of her man this one has been taken."

Ancient writings are full of fables that make man the original "child-bearer" in some magical way, thus denying woman that status. Also, in the non-biblical but endlessly intriguing creation story, the serpent's role changes the sex picture significantly:

> Among the animals, the serpent was notable. Of all of them he had the most excellent qualities. Like man, he stood upright and in height was equal to the camel. His superior mental gifts caused him to become an infidel. It likewise explains his envy of man, especially of his conjugal relations. Envy made him meditate ways and means of bringing about the death of Adam. Knowing that Adam, in his zeal to keep Eve from eating of the Tree of Knowledge, had told her to not even touch it, he formed a plan.

(You have to admire the writing—humans have always been such great storytellers.) Here we learn that eating the forbidden fruit was not a euphemism for having sex. Adam and Lileth and Eve had been going at it all along, which seems to have bothered the serpent. The serpent's plan was to talk Eve into just touching the tree so that when nothing happened she could be persuaded to eat the fruit, then get Adam to eat it. The plan worked beautifully. . . . By the way, the fruit was a fig, not an apple. That's why Adam and Eve covered themselves with fig leaves to hide their newly discovered "shame." The fig tree was the only one that allowed its leaves to be taken, due to its role in the downfall of humanity. (Read the story. Very compelling. Persuasive even, as these things go. It would make a great movie.)

Although the cause of Original Sin differs in the biblical and non-biblical versions (disobeying an order versus having sex), and both are equally ridiculous, the Bible's compilers went with the one that blames sex. Why? you ask. Well, it created a handy explanation for how Original Sin could be passed on through succeeding generations, by attaching itself to the soul of each fertilized egg through sex at conception.[6] The sex-as-forbidden-fruit narrative also provided an explanation for the strength of the sex drive, which makes controlling it so difficult—Original Sin gave the sex drive that power![7] (Actually, it was evolution through natural selection that did it. The stronger one's sex drive, the higher one's reproductive rate, resulting in a preponderance of individuals in the gene pool with strong sex drives.) There are a couple of problems with these theological inventions:

First, souls are supposedly created individually by God at the moment of conception, so the only way they can acquire Original Sin is for God to put it there deliberately. Sex alone couldn't do that because it only creates the body. This instillation of sin looks like a punishment for engaging in sex, although God had ordered humans, in Genesis 1:28, to "be fruitful and multiply." Theology has an amazing ability to put humans between a rock and a hard place.

Second, the soul cannot enter the fertilized egg at the moment of conception because it needs a reasonably operational body to function. This is evident from the Catholic Church's instruction for the baptism of infants that was in force for 700 years, until 1917, in its *Codex Juris Canonici*. Canon Law 748 said severely defective babies ("monstrosities") must be baptized conditionally just in case they are "ensouled persons." Current canon law leaves this instruction out, although "ensouled" status is still a necessary consideration. What, after all, is a priest to do when he is called to baptize conjoined twins, one of which consists of only part of a body?

Years ago, when freak shows were still common, I saw a fully formed woman being exhibited who had most of another body growing out of her side—torso, arms, one leg, no head. I suppose that would qualify as a "monstrosity" in canon law. Were there two souls there or one? How much of an attached body must exist for it to be considered a separate, baptizable person? Would two heads with one body do it? How about two bodies with one head? If a soul is present, where would it reside? Anywhere in the body? In every cell? Only in the brain? If only in the brain, there is no possibility of "ensoulment" at the moment of conception. If anywhere or everywhere in the body, wouldn't any partially formed conjoined twin be eligible for baptism? Not long ago, the media reported on a girl in India who was born with two sets of arms and legs--obviously a twinning that did not go well. Would the conjoined set of limbs qualify for baptism?

This is an example of the problems the advocates of archaic theology face, given their locked-in belief in Original Sin as historical fact. This theological rigidity also exposes a more basic problem. If the Original Sin story is taken as a metaphor (the only way it can make sense), the end result—the Bible's crucifixion and redemption story—must also be taken as a metaphor (also the only way it can make sense). But there goes the historicity—the very foundation upon which Christianity is based. The stories stand together as either all (easily disprovable) history or all (interestingly creative) metaphor. We'll leave it to the theologians to work that one out.

The Original Sin story really is just a religious fable, very likely created to explain why life is hard, bad things happen, childbearing is difficult and, less admirably, to justify male ownership and subjugation of women. Creative writers have always speculated about how things observed in nature came to be. Aesop's Fables, Rudyard Kipling's Just So Stories, and many other works, are replete with such entertaining tales. The Garden of Eden story is of the same genre as "How the Leopard Got its Spots." For believers who accept it as fact, it serves nicely, but cruelly, as the ultimate guilt trip, one that compels them to seek the solace and salvation promised by religion. Consider this Catholic priest's answer to a questioner's objection to the severity of the punishment for Original Sin:

> I do deny that God has treated the human race unjustly. It has deserved far more suffering than it has received, and has not deserved the great blessings God has deigned to bestow on it.[8]

How comforting.

The reliance on Original Sin to explain life's hardships creates a theological version of "Alice in Wonderland" where one disappears down a metaphysical rabbit hole and things get curiouser and curiouser. The absurdity starts with a talking snake . . . goes to a man made of clay and a woman made of his rib . . . has them tricked into eating a forbidden fruit that gives them the knowledge of good and evil (which they didn't have before, so why were they wrong in eating it?) . . . goes on to justify patriarchal, misogynistic views of women and decrees that any sex act done in any but the missionary position is immoral . . . winds down with doctrinal fiats pounding on fertility technology . . . and hits rock bottom with the current insane assertion that there are microscopic, single-celled persons who must be saved at all costs, and must be afforded the same rights as sentient human beings—with dozens of laws being proposed and enacted to ensure just that.

Thanks to theology's endless theater of the absurd, human society has been dragged down the rabbit hole since its beginnings. Here are a few examples of what it's like in that theological Wonderland.

The Varieties of Theological Sex Absurdities

This is a summary of the more noteworthy theological absurdities that have caused hundreds—no, thousands—of years of misery and frustration. We'll deal with Catholic beliefs, because that church's views tend to dominate our culture. The Catholic Church's strength and influence derive from its being the only institution that has existed continuously for nearly 2,000 years, and from its global, monolithic, hierarchical structure that enforces doctrinal discipline. No other religious institution comes close to the Catholic Church's theological depth and breadth, however much that distances it from reality.

More importantly, it has always insisted that the law enforce its views on moral issues. Every election year brings dogma-driven voters' guides along with threats of excommunication for Catholic politicians who refuse to support the official Catholic position on laws related to sex, marriage and reproduction. Fundamentalist Protestants agree with the Catholic Church on "moral" (i.e., sexual) issues generally (with some exceptions regarding divorce and contraception), while basing their position on Bible verses alone. Together, these authoritarians are a formidable threat to our secular democracy and freedom of conscience.

Basically, the Christian theology of sex covers about two millennia of obsessing over one idea—that sex is a necessary evil to be used only for procreation, always open to the transmission of life, and not to be thought about lustfully or acted upon in any circumstances other than within a monogamous marriage between one man and one woman united for life in the sacrament of matrimony. Here is an excerpt from a Catholic pamphlet titled "How to Conquer the Most Common Sin of Impurity."[9] It follows a list of four actions (all innocuous thoughts, mostly sex related) that lead to the dreaded mortal sin described, inexplicably, as "self-abuse":

> These principles apply equally to married and single persons, and equally to men and to women. They flow directly from the established premise that sex actions and sex pleasure must never be deliberately separated from the sublime primary purpose for which God designed them, a purpose that even in marriage must never be destroyed or frustrated.

The problem here is with the claim that there is an "established premise" supporting these tightly constrained, irrational, religion-based conclusions regarding sex and marriage. The pamphlet states:

> It is from these basic concepts and principles that we draw a knowledge of the natural law forbidding any deliberate indulgence in sex pleasure outside of marriage, whether alone or with others, and any deliberate frustration or destruction of the purpose of sex in marriage.

Aha! So it is from unverifiable religion-based assumptions that we derive the "natural law" that all sex is sinful except when tightly constrained as specified. Once again, we have to wonder what planet such ideas come from. The self-evident fact is that "natural law" is only a description of how nature works. We get that from observation and testing. It's not something that was enacted into "law." It just describes what is. Where sex is concerned, from what we can observe and test, "natural law" does not conform to religious "basic concepts and principles."

But religious belief (dressed up as "natural law") is there, and so down the rabbit hole we go, where the following acts are considered so evil that they deserve eternal hellfire—or at least a few theology-based laws and public policies to complicate the lives of those who don't buy any of this. Let's look at a few specific sexual practices.

Masturbation. We have here the ultimate safe sex—effective, harmless, free, and readily available. In the great scheme of things, it is no more significant than scratching an itch. Yet sex-phobic religions have elevated it to a matter of cosmic importance. For example:

[O]ne addicted to solitary acts of impurity is corrupt and depraved . . . The only way to protect the higher interests of all human beings, both individually and socially, is to cling to or return to Christian standards. Sex has duties as well as privileges. It is an opportunity for self-sacrifice, and the serving of God as well as the best interests of the human race. The procreation of children is the explanation and justification of sex indulgences. That is lawful only in the married state. Outside marriage, therefore, all indulgences in sex pleasure deliberately sought is a perversion, immoral, and sinful before God.[10]

To put this foolishness in context, keep in mind that it is brought to you by the same people who see leftover frozen embryos in fertility clinics as "snowflake children" to be adopted by a willing uterus, and who seek a "personhood amendment" to the Constitution that declares fertilized eggs to be persons with all the attendant rights to life, liberty and the pursuit of happiness. . . . Well, at least until birth. They never show much (if any) concern for the life, liberty and pursuit of happiness of actual individuals—those already born.

The idea that sex might be enjoyed without any adverse consequences is apparently too horrible for some religious folks to contemplate. Two examples:

In 1995, the religious right pressured President Bill Clinton to remove Dr. Joycelyn Elders as U.S. Surgeon General because of the huge controversy that erupted when she suggested that the subject of masturbation could usefully be included in high school sex education classes. She was accused of wanting it taught (although it hardly requires teaching). As Dr. Elders said, "God taught us how," and the only thing students need to learn is that "masturbation never got anybody pregnant, does not make anybody go crazy, and what we're about is preventing HIV in our bright young people."[11]

Notice theology's shifting sands here, as Dr. Elders, a religious liberal, redefines the reproductive-purpose-only theology of the religiously conservative to move it closer to reality. And she's right. If one believes in God, it makes sense to say, "God taught us how," because humans come equipped knowing how to enjoy sex in many ways. If the transmission of life were the only purpose of sex, one would expect that to be the only way it could be enjoyed. Obviously it's not. Religious speculation about lessons from God aside, it is far more likely that solo sex is a harmless consequence of the variety-loving evolutionary process. No doubt it is actually beneficial when other types of sexual outlets are unavailable or unwise.

Then, in 2010, Christine O'Donnell, a Tea Party candidate for the US Senate in Delaware, won the Republican primary. She became notorious because of her statements that she was not a witch (no, I'm not kidding) and that masturbation should be outlawed because she considered it adultery, which is based on lust, which the Bible opposes. Could one ask for a better illustration of the underlying theocratic assumptions about sex, and the willingness of believers to enshrine those assumptions in restrictive laws and social policies?

Interestingly, theologians have paid little attention to female masturbation, beyond a generalized opposition to sex free of reproductive consequences. Almost all attention is on the male experience. Perhaps it's due to concern about men "wasting their seed," even though the supply never seems to run out. Several planets could be populated with a few ejaculations. Women have no "seed" they are physically able to "waste," other than by avoiding sex during an ovulatory period . . . but wait! Isn't that what they do when they follow the Vatican-approved rhythm method of birth control!?

Contraception. This is a problem only because theocrats have no workable understanding of sex or are willfully ignorant. In this regard, ranking in first place in all-time, world-class, dumb-as-a-rock stupidity is the Vatican. The Protestant fundamentalists, whose position is a bit more nuanced, are mostly horrified by teens enjoying sex; the Vatican is horrified by *anyone* enjoying it—except in the most carefully controlled and approved libido-deadening situations.

The papal view of evolution as having a God-given purpose reinforces this ignorance. Since sex so often leads to procreation, the Vatican assumes that procreation is its purpose. Well, not quite. Nothing evolves for a purpose. Evolution is a mindless process that has no purpose, only consequences, some of which we interpret as bad, some as good, depending on their effects on us. The consequences of consensual sex include physical pleasure, the transmission of microbial life (disease), and the transmission of human life. So what purpose do we humans assign to these consequences? Simple observation shows the primary purpose of sex is almost always pleasure. The transmission of disease and life are side effects, with disease being unwelcome and life often welcomed, but sometimes not.

The archaic Catholic theological view of contraception simply ignores this very obvious reality, and so is replete with contradictions and jaw-dropping absurdities. The following is from the Pastoral Letter cited above.[12] Does any of it look like a reflection of reality? Quoting from an earlier pastoral letter, the bishops say:

> By using contraception, married couples may think that they are avoiding problems or easing tensions, that they are exerting control over their lives. At the same time, they may think they are doing nothing harmful to their marriages. In reality, the deliberate separation of the procreative and unitive meanings of marriage has the potential to damage or destroy the marriage. Also, it results in many other negative consequences, both personal and social.

> Conjugal love is diminished whenever the union of a husband and wife is reduced to a means of self-gratification. The procreative capacity of male and female is dehumanized, reduced to a kind of internal biological technology that one masters and controls just like any other technology.

> . . . The procreative capacity of man and woman should not be treated as just another means of technology, as also happens with in vitro fertilization (IVF) or cloning. When that happens, human life itself is degraded because it becomes, more and more, something produced or manufactured in various ways, ways that will only multiply as science advances. Children begin to be seen less as gifts received in a personal communion of mutual self-giving, and increasingly as a lifestyle choice, a commodity to which all consumers are entitled. There is a true issue of the dignity of human life at stake here.

It would have been helpful if the bishops had provided examples of the supposed damage, the supposed destruction and negative consequences, the supposed diminished conjugal love, and the supposed treatment of children as a commodity. I know of none of this, neither in my own personal experience, nor that of my relatives and friends, nor in stories from others—not even in literary fiction. On the other hand, don't all of us know many examples of the harm done by lack of contraception? Don't we all know of it from our personal experiences and associations, as well as from observing the effects of poverty and overpopulation?

Contraception is closely related to masturbation in the medieval theological view. The church actually defines it as mutual masturbation ("reciprocal vice"). Here's the infallible doctrine, taken verbatim from one of my old Catholic books, officially authorized with the imprimatur of John Gregory Murray, archbishop of St. Paul, with a Preface by the highly renowned Msgr. Fulton J. Sheen, famous for having his own prime time TV show in the '60s. It answers the question, "Where is birth control forbidden in Scripture?"

It is rather grimly hinted at in the case of Onan as recorded in Genesis 38:10, for Onan was struck dead by God. [Onan was supposed to impregnate his brother's widow, as was the custom, but he did not want to do that, so when he had sex with her, he "spilled his seed on the ground."] And Scripture describes his contraceptive practice as a detestable thing. However, it would not matter in the least if there were no concrete reference to birth control in Scripture. Scripture gives the general principles of morality, and lays down clearly the obligations of marriage. Birth control by contraception is immoral of its very nature, being but reciprocal vice; and violates the Christian obligation of marriage. No sane person would deny the immorality of one's becoming a cocaine fiend. Yet that is not mentioned in Scripture. The natural moral law existed before a line of Scripture was written, and still exists, being in no way abolished by Scripture.[13]

OK, let's see how this works. Contraception is immoral because it is mutual masturbation, which is immoral, just as using cocaine is immoral. This argument falls apart every step of the way, because harmful effects are simply assumed, not demonstrated, based on an assumed immorality based on unverifiable religious beliefs. (And never mind that masturbation is by definition a solo act.) Only the misuse of cocaine (which is not immoral, just stupid) can be demonstrated to cause harm to one's health and ability to function. The author preaches that great spiritual and temporal harm is caused by masturbation and contraception, but of course gives no concrete examples of such harm. What we get are endless repetitions of "rabbit hole" thinking, such as the following, which is useful only in showing definitively the craziness that results when theology attempts to deal with sex:

> Man's intelligence must rule blind passion by self-control, not abdicate in favor of the irresponsible beast. Like the conductor of an orchestra, the mind of man must coordinate perfectly all the impulses of that marvelous instrument called the body of man. Introduce into this temple of art an unclean brute beast, and what becomes of reason? Contraceptive birth control weakens the flesh, poisons the blood, tangles the nerves with disorderly destructive and spasmodic violence, and renders those guilty of it less and less fit to be parents at all.[14]

Now let's take a more realistic look at this vacuous claptrap. The best and most comprehensive book I have ever come across on the theology of sex is *Eunuchs for the Kingdom of Heaven: Women, Sexuality and the Cath-*

olic Church, by Uta Ranke-Heinemann. She is a Catholic theologian, but one who has taken it upon herself to investigate and discredit the Catholic Church's theological absurdities and give them the boot they deserve. Here she observes the Vatican's "fruits of theological imbecility" as it has struggled to maintain doctrinal consistency since the advent of the pill forced it up and out of the rabbit hole, giving Pope Pius XII a unique problem.

> Since his predecessor, Pius XI, had condemned any kind of sterilization for the purpose of preventing conception, the pill had to be banned as well. No surprise there; we cannot expect a pope to deviate from the opinions of his predecessor. Papal infallibility serves as a brake on independent thinking. But Pius XI was unable to provide Pius XII with a special justification for rejecting the pill, because there was no pill in 1930.

> Here Pius XII had to be creative. . . . The pope means that nature's intention, procreation, may under no circumstances be thwarted, even when nature cannot bear the procreation, and the woman will die on account of the pregnancy. The pope, then, is defending a morality that marches over corpses.[15]

Well said, but there is more. Sterilization runs against the Catholic Church's prohibition against mutilating the body for non-therapeutic reasons, because the Church holds that the body the temple of the Holy Spirit and belongs to God. The 1994 Catechism of the Catholic Church, #2297, states, "Except when performed for strictly therapeutic medical reasons, directly intended amputations, mutilations, and sterilizations are against the moral law." When done to avoid pregnancy or to have a more "uninhibited and guilt-free sex life,"[16] as the Secretary General of the Bishops' Conference of Bogota, Colombia, said in 2010, it is immoral. If so, why didn't the Church see anything immoral about it during the Baroque Period (1600–1750) when it approved the castration of young male singers to preserve their soprano voices for church choirs? This was deemed necessary because high voices were needed and women were not allowed to participate in church services. That's not exactly a "strictly therapeutic medical reason." The effects on these boys (called the *castrati*—"the castrated ones") as they grew older included personality disorders and an inability to lead a normal sex life. Most of them had poorly developed sex organs and the growth of their limbs was distorted. Apparently, it was better to mutilate those temples of the Holy Spirit and destroy those boys' lives than to allow women to sing in church choirs.[17]

The Missionary Position. This is something theology no longer dwells on much (at least not directly), but it deserves some attention to highlight the appalling lack of intellectual competence at work these past two thousand years. Here is Ranke-Heinemann again, quoting St. Thomas Aquinas (1225?–74), called "the Angelic Doctor," the Church's preeminent theologian whose writings are widely quoted by church authorities and form the basis for much of Catholic doctrine.

> Deviation from the missionary position, [Thomas Aquinas] believes, is one of a series of unnatural vices that were classified, in a system going back to Augustine, as worse than intercourse with one's own mother. This ban on other sexual positions does not quite fit into Thomas's schema, because the other unnatural vices he catalogues have the common feature of excluding generation. In exceptional cases he does allow other positions, when couples cannot have sex any other way for medical reasons. . . . Thomas holds that the other most seriously sinful—because they are unnatural—vices, worse than incest, rape and adultery, are masturbation, bestiality, homosexuality, anal and oral intercourse, and coitus interruptus (Summa Theologiae II/II q. 154 a. II). Thomas appears to put deviation from the missionary position on the list of the most serious sins because he thought that, like the other acts on this list, which prevented conception, this one, if nothing else, made conception more difficult.[18]

What is difficult here is to see anything that makes sense. However, the Catholic Church does seem to have at least qualified the sinfulness of non-missionary-position sex since then. This is hearsay, but according to what I've been told about the advice given by at least one Catholic priest, all sex positions are now OK "as long as you end up in the right place." Perhaps we can consider that as some kind of progress. But maybe not. There still remains the theological position on the missionary position regarding its effect on people whose disabilities make that unworkable. Canon law does not consider a marriage valid if the couple is sexually incapacitated, although procreation is possible for them in some circumstances. Once again, Ranke-Heinemann separates the real world from what is going on down in that rabbit hole:

> [F]or some paraplegics . . . Catholic marriage law is as unbearable now as it ever was. . . . The Church dictates the precise form of the conjugal act to everybody and does this in a way that demotes a paraplegic and his partner to the level of infants, because according to Catholic sexual morality intimacies are allowed only in marriage and only in connection with the

standardized intercourse conceded by the Church. This sort of interference in everyone's right to marriage is intolerable and shows once more that the celibates running the Church would be better advised not to get mixed up in such matters.[19]

Then there's the matter of condoms. There's no need to go into the well known theological hostility toward them as contraceptives. But when the AIDS virus entered the human population, the hostility reached a level of depravity almost unimaginable. Quoting Ranke-Heinemann:

> With the International Congress of moral theologians held in Rome in November 1988, the papal campaign against contraception reached new heights. If the pope weren't the pope, his position might put him at odds with the state penal code. According to John Paul II and his spokesman, Carlo Caffarra, head of the Pontifical Institute for Marriage and Family Matters, a hemophiliac with AIDS may not have intercourse with his wife, ever, not even after her menopause, because God has forbidden condoms. And if the hemophiliac husband can't manage to abstain, it's better for him to infect his wife than to use a condom. Catholic sexual morality has turned into a morality of horror.[20]

But can the woman refuse to have sex under such conditions? Possibly, if it is certain—not just highly probable—that her life is in danger.[21] However, public outrage over this twisted view of morality may be having some effect. In 2009, when Pope Benedict XVI, on a visit to Africa, said condoms could not be used to combat AIDS because they might make the epidemic worse, outrage followed. And so, in 2010, the pope cautiously made it public that condoms may be considered a lesser evil to prevent the spread of AIDS in homosexual relationships.[22] Janet Smith, a Vatican advisor who teaches ethics at Sacred Heart Major Seminary in Detroit, spun the about-face this way:

> The Holy Father is simply observing that for some homosexual prostitutes, the use of a condom may indicate an awakening of a moral sense, an awakening that sexual pleasure is not the highest value.

Or is it that, since there can be no transmission of life in homosexual sex, and the participants are probably bound for hell anyway, why not at least try to keep AIDS from spreading? Regardless, the door is now open to possibly protecting the wives of AIDS-infected men—at least those who are past menopause. It's a start.

But refusing to have sex just to prevent pregnancy is also forbidden, and always has been. Spouses are obliged to fulfill their "marital duty" to each other to prevent the other person from "stumbling into fornication." OK, so we can see that a husband can demand his marital rights and his wife could comply, willingly or not, because she just has to lie there. Regardless of any harmful consequences to the wife, at least she has saved her husband from "stumbling into fornication."[23] On the other hand, if the wife demands her marital rights, she is out of luck if her husband can't "get it up." Her demands are useless and if she stumbles into fornication because of that it will be her own sinful fault, not her husband's. Medieval theology clearly considers the woman's desires and circumstances as of no importance. (Of course, now that men have Viagra . . .)

Better Dead than Raped. On the other hand, refusing to have sex is not only allowed but demanded when a woman is attacked by a rapist. It's about protecting one's chastity. The Catholic Church hauls out the saints to glorify this sad choice. It has something of a tradition of conferring sainthood on women who resist a rapist at the cost of their lives.

The first step to sainthood is beatification, which earns the recipient the title of "blessed." The most recent example of this recognition of holiness came in 1987 when Pope John Paul II beatified two Italian women who had allowed themselves to be killed rather than submit to rape. One of the women was murdered in 1957 at the age of 26. The other was murdered in 1935 at the age of 16.

In 1950, another Italian girl, Maria Goretti, was elevated from the ranks of blessed to full sainthood. She had died in 1902 at age 12 at the hands of a rapist, Alexander, an 18-year-old neighbor. Pope Pius XII canonized her as a model of sexual purity, declaring her the patroness of youth, young women, purity, and victims of rape.

Maria's tragic story was the preeminent morality tale for young girls when I was going to Catholic school, as Maria's canonization approached. It's still being promoted; she's still being held up as a role model for chastity. As the catholic.org web site says, "She is called a martyr because she fought against Alexander's attempts at sexual assault." I well remember the nuns telling us the inspiring story of that assault: how Maria had been stabbed to death while resisting rape, how she cried out that she would not submit because to do so would be a mortal sin, how Alexander was sent to prison, where in due time he piously repented and spent his last years praying for forgiveness to the saint he had such an important role in creating.

Of course, every woman who is killed resisting rape does not get honored by the Catholic Church. To be canonized, the facts of the woman's life—and death—must show that:

1. She was an intensely devout and dutiful servant of the Church throughout her life;

2. She had made it clear in words and deeds that she would rather die than commit a sin;

3. Her death was a direct result of her refusal to submit to rape. In other words, she knew she could save herself by submitting, but chose death rather than offend God by sinning.

What is a rational person to make of this? What can we say of a theology that advances the belief that a woman, when she is threatened by a rapist, must not even consider submitting when the knife is at her throat? What kind of moral teaching is this that says a woman who submits to rape, rather than be killed, commits a sin of any kind? How many women have died at the hands of rapists because their Catholic indoctrination so confused them when they were under attack that they could not save themselves?

This raises another question: Why is submitting to rape when one's life is in danger a sin? Is it that sexually repressed Catholic theologians assume that any time a woman engages in sex, regardless of circumstances, she enjoys it? Is it that their theology compels them to regard any sexual activity outside of monogamous marriage for the purpose or procreation as sinful? One has to wonder at the workings of the celibate priestly mind, that these men would think a terrified woman, desperately trying to save her life, would enjoy such an encounter.

But perhaps there is another rationale underlying the Church's better-dead-than-raped theology. It is patriarchal religious beliefs, after all, that have promoted the idea that women have no value in their own right, but only as they serve men's purposes, as men's property. Female virginity is mandated by patriarchal religions as a way of ensuring male sexual control over women—of keeping women "unspoiled" until they become a man's property through marriage. If Catholic theologians have so little respect for a woman's humanity, if they consider her men's property, why wouldn't they encourage her to die rather than have that property "spoiled"?

Fertility Technology. Here we are dealing with couples who want to have children, not avoid having them. One would think the Church would be supportive. But no, the Church considers it just another descent into immorality. Why? Because fertility testing requires a man to ejaculate into a cup, usually while looking at a pornographic magazine to help the process along. This is how fertility clinics, necessarily, get the sperm needed for artificial insemination. But the theological pinheads see only lustful thoughts and sex that is not open to the transmission of life, with no wife involved and the man not even in the missionary position. All they see is "self-abuse," masturbation.

A woman teacher in a Catholic school in Indiana was actually fired for using fertility treatments in an effort to get pregnant with her husband. Normal people would think that admirable, but the woman's parish priest called her a "grave, immoral sinner."[24]

However, all is not lost, for a way has been found to provide sperm for fertility testing while still having sexual intercourse in the theologically correct way. All you need is a leaky condom.[25]

Then there's in vitro fertilization (for which no leaky loopholes have been found) that might allow a couple to have a child. The sperm get mixed in a petri dish with the woman's eggs, so embryos can develop and be implanted in the woman's uterus. Several embryos have to be created to ensure that at least one takes hold. The rest are destroyed or frozen for possible later use. This brings us up against the theology of abortion, where a fertilized egg is proclaimed to be a person. Yes!—a microscopic single-celled person the size of the period at the end of this sentence. This is human imagination run amok—a clear case of insanity. But that's their story, and the "pro-life" fanatics are sticking to it.

The religious mind is nothing if not inventive. Because abortion is sometimes necessary to save a woman's life, the theologians have been forced to find a way to avoid public outrage if deaths due to pregnancy get out of hand. One of the causes of such deaths is ectopic pregnancy (where a fertilized egg attaches itself to something outside the uterus, sometimes the woman's intestines, but usually within one of the two fallopian tubes). An embryo cannot get very big in there, and must be removed quickly (within say, the first seven or eight weeks) or it will cause the woman's death. And, of course, the embryo will die, too. this is a case of an abnormal pregnancy in an abnormal place—but that's nature's "intelligent design" for you.

Yet the Catholic Church decrees that no abortion can be performed. Ever. Even in the case of ectopic pregnancy. What to do? This is where the theology of secondary effects comes in. To deliberately remove the fetus would be considered murder. But to remove a fallopian tube that is causing trouble by entrapping the fetus is OK. If the fetus dies, that is considered an unintended secondary effect. Sounds like a way out? Not quite. If the fetus is removed from the tube the woman's ability to bear children is preserved. If the tube (which just happens to contain a fetus) is removed, her childbearing ability is severely compromised if not ended. But that doesn't matter to those who put dogma before people.

Finally, there's yet another problem, and it's a theological biggie. If Original Sin is transmitted through sexual intercourse, but there is no intercourse—only sperm ejaculated into a petri dish and mixed with some eggs retrieved from a woman's ovaries—how will Original Sin be transmitted? Maybe the Church hopes to avoid that conundrum by getting laws passed that outlaw this form of fertility technology, but the problem remains. Lots of babies are out there that have been created this way without intercourse. Lots of fertilized eggs and embryos created the same way are stored in clinic freezers. Do any of them have souls? If not, how can they be considered real persons? If so, did God implant the soul but not the Original Sin because sexual intercourse wasn't involved? Would such persons be immaculate conceptions, incapable of sinning?

The theologians have their work cut out for them. For those of us not living down that rabbit hole, our work is cut out for us too, and it consists of keeping such theological absurdities from determining our laws.

Reality vs. Theology

It's time to come out of the rabbit hole. The insane views outlined above are purely religious views that have no place in our diverse, secular culture. Some directly affect only those who believe the doctrines, but may entail indirect social costs that affect the larger community. Some are the basis of many of the sex-related laws we still live under, while others formed the basis of laws that have been repealed or declared unconstitutional Regardless, the underlying theology clouds our entire legal and social policy approach to sex-related issues.

Laws criminalizing birth control services were ruled unconstitutional only as recently as 1965 when the US Supreme Court declared them a violation of the right to marital privacy in *Griswold v. Connecticut*. Laws criminalizing anal and oral sex were declared unconstitutional in 2002 in *Lawrence v. Texas*. Although the Lawrence ruling was based on the right to privacy, Justice Kennedy noted that centuries of religion-based hatred of homosexuality underlay the anti-sodomy laws, and Justice O'Connor concurred, calling the laws "a bare desire to harm a politically unpopular group."[26]

Given how embedded our theology-based laws are, one might ask whether it would have been better in the long run if both *Griswold* and *Lawrence* had been argued as violations of the First Amendment's Establishment Clause. The right to privacy is an implied right, which leaves it open to being compromised by subsequent interpretations—something that has indeed been happening, most notably in the ongoing attempts to overturn *Roe v. Wade*. Arguments based on the Establishment Clause might have produced clearer rulings. Laws against contraception and homosexuality either have a religious basis or they do not. They either serve a valid secular purpose or they do not.[27] The same either-or argument applies to all the restrictive theology-based laws we live under. To mean anything at all, the Establishment Clause must be concerned with something more than whether religious mottoes and patriotic pledges are constitutional. It must extend to laws that do real harm to real people.

As things stand, the *Griswold* and *Lawrence* right-to-privacy rulings become progressively more compromised as religious-right legislators redefine almost all contraceptives as abortifacients,[2] restrict sex education, and spout dire and entirely false warnings about homosexual relationships' effect on society. There is a major ongoing legislative effort to further restrict abortion rights, defund Planned Parenthood, outlaw same-sex marriage, and restrict access to contraception. What is the secular justification for any of this?

---

1. John A. O'Brien, Ph.D., *The Faith of Millions*, Part IV, The Church and Marriage, Chapter 25, "Why No Divorce?" p. 296, "The Light of Love." Our Sunday Visitor Press, Huntington, IN, 1938.

2. USCCB, Marriage: Love and Life in the Divine Plan, a Pastoral Letter of the United States Conference of Catholic Bishops, Nov. 17, 2009. To order a copy, visit www. usccbpublishing.org and click on "New Titles."

3. USCCB, Introduction: The Blessing and Gift of Marriage, p. 2

4. Ranke-Heinemann, Uta, *Eunuchs for the Kingdom of Heaven*, trans. by Peter Heinegg, New York, NY, Doubleday (1990), p.10.

5. Willis Barnstone, ed, Part 1, Creation Myths, "The Creation of the World," *The Other Bible: Ancient Alternative Scriptures*, New York, NY, HarperSanFrancisco (1984), pp. 29–38.

6. Rev. Dr. Leslie Rumble, M.S.C. and Rev. Charles Mortimer Carty, Vol. 2, *God, Radio Replies*, St. Paul, MN, Radio Replies Press. Imprimatur, John Gregory Murray, Archbishop of St. Paul (1940), p. 22 #37.

7. Ranke-Heinemann, p. 94.

8. Rumble and Carty, Vol. 2, "The Dogmas of the Church, " p. 148 #611.

9. D.F. Miller, C.SS.R., *How to Conquer the Most Common Sin of Impurity*, Liguorian Pamphlets, Redemptorist Fathers, Liguori, MO (1962), pp. 7-8.

10. Rumble and Carty, Vol. 2. "The Church in Her Moral Teachings," p. 241 #988, p. 242 #990.

11. Laura Flanders, "Dr. Joycelyn Elders: Marijuana, Masturbation and Medicine," *The Nation*, http://www.thenation.com, October 20, 2010.

12. USCCB, *Fundamental Challenges in the Nature and Purposes of Marriage*, Section 1, Contraception, pp. 19, 20

13. Rumble and Carty, Vol. 3, "The Church in Her Moral Teachings," p. 278 #1156.

14. Ibid, p. 281 #1167.

15. Ranke-Heinemann, Chap. 25, "The Nineteenth and Twentieth Centuries: The Age of Birth Regulation," pp. 294-295.

16. "Bishop notes that vasectomies and tubal ligations are mutilations of the body," http://www.catholicnewsagency.com, Oct. 27, 2010.

17. "Castrati History," http://www.essortment.com.

18. Ranke-Heinemann, Chap. 17, "The Heightened Campaign Against Contraception ('Unnatural Sex') and Its Legal Consequences in the Church, from the Middle Ages to the Present," p. 197.

19. Ranke-Heinemann, Chap. 20, "The Council of Trent and Pope Sixtus the Momentous," p. 254.

20. Ranke-Heinemann, p. 298.

21. Rumble and Carty, Vol. 2, p. 250 #1024.

22. See http://blogs.reuters.com/faithworld/2010/11/21, "Pope Breaks Ice on Catholic View on Condoms."

23. Ranke-Heinemann, Chap. 17, p. 196.

24. Maureen Dowd, "Bishops Play Church Queens as Pawns," *The New York Times, Sunday Review, April 29, 2012, p. SR11.*

25. Ranke-Heinemann, p. 199.

26. Atheists For Human Rights and Jerold M. Gorski, Esq., Brief Amicus Curiae in support of Michael A. Newdow, Respondent, vs. Elk Grove Unified School District and David W. Gordon, Superintendent, March, 2004.

27. Msgr. Charles M. Mangan, "Married Couples Who Intentionally Chose Sterilization For Contraceptive Purposes And Lasting Repentance," Introduction, Catholic Online, http://www.catholic.org, 1/25/2004.

3

DUMB AS A ROCK: THEOLOGY AND NATURE'S SEXUAL DIVERSITY

"If writing the demands of the Book of Leviticus into the Constitution is not a state-church separation issue, then I don't know what is."

—Randall Tigue, constitutional law attorney

Granting civil rights to lesbian, gay, bisexual, and transgender people (LGBT) has long horrified authoritarian religions. For centuries, armed with a Bible that calls homosexuality an "abomination," they have established laws that marginalized and persecuted sexual minorities, and criminalized their sexual behavior. Since the 1970s in the United States, a gay rights rebellion against these laws has achieved repeal of most of them in the face of opposition that included violence and murder. In 2003, the U.S. Supreme Court finally declared unconstitutional one of the last major types of discriminatory law, the criminalization of homosexual sex (sodomy) in its *Lawrence v. Texas* ruling.[1] The decision reversed the *Bowers v. Hardwick* lower court ruling that upheld Georgia's statute prohibiting oral and anal sex by either homosexuals or heterosexuals. The statute had used a "community consensus" on morality to deny a right to privacy. *Lawrence* rejected the idea that majority perceptions can justify the denial of rights for a minority.

In *Lawrence*, Justice Anthony Kennedy, supporting reversal, noted that centuries of majority hatred of homosexuality based on religious views had been the driving force behind discrimination against homosexuals. Justice Sandra Day O'Connor, also supporting reversal and noting the element of hatred said, "We have consistently held, however, that some objectives, such as a bare desire to harm a politically unpopular group, are not legitimate state interests. When a law prohibits such a desire to harm a politically unpopular group, we have applied a more searching form of rational basis review to strike down such laws under the equal protection clause."

But despite the *Lawrence* ruling, discrimination persists. Gays and lesbians can be fired because of their sexual orientation in 29 states, and it's worse for transgender people, who can be fired in 35 states because of their sexual orientation. As a result, LGBT people often hide who they are for fear of losing their families, friends, or jobs. In many school districts, LGBT students are bullied and harassed with impunity.

One of the worst forms of abuse is the bullying of gay teens in high school, driving all too many of them to suicide. Here's an example of the religious right's barbaric manner of dealing with this form of persecution: In 2011 the Republican-controlled Michigan senate passed "Matt's Safe School Law." It was an anti-bullying law, but it exempted religion-motivated bullying from prosecution. Ironically, the bill as originally proposed was a response to the 2002 suicide of a gay teen who had been bullied by his classmates for being gay. Although the intent of the bill was to penalize such behavior, the Republicans modified it to exempt religion-based bullying. The Republican-passed version of the law "allows harassment by teachers and students as long as they can claim their actions are rooted in a 'sincerely held religious belief or moral conviction.' Those who truly believe homosexuality is wrong, for example, are free to torment classmates consequence-free."[2]

Strong opposition from Democrats caused the bill's sponsor, Republican senator Rick Jones, to reconsider it. He allowed that it "'may not be perfect,' but believed it to be 'a step in the right direction.'" In 2012 in Minnesota, the same barbarism was exhibited when an anti-bullying school policy was deemed by religious right opponents as "unfair to students with conservative values."[3]

In many states, opponents of homosexuality are attempting to deny lesbian and gay couples the right to adopt children or become foster parents.[4] In Minnesota, a gay couple with children is treated differently under the law with regard to obligations, rights, taxes, benefits, etc., from an identically situated straight couple with children. The state actually has 515 statutes that discriminate against committed domestic partners, including same-sex couples.[5]

Same-Sex Marriage and the Culture War

There is no rational basis for religion-based hostility toward homosexuality. Of course, the religion-based views of one Christian religion are not the same as those of another, though all are based on the Bible. Liberal religions tend to take a humane approach, choosing the Bible's "love" verses, while the conservative religions seem to prefer the equally mandatory "kill" verses. Some have tried the middle road of loving the sinner while hating the sin by being socially tolerant. Others have gone further, deciding that God loves everyone, and have ordained gay clergy and married same-sex couples.

Now, with laws against sodomy declared unconstitutional, same-sex marriage has moved to the political front lines in the culture war. So far, only six states and the District of Columbia have legalized same-sex marriage: Connecticut, Iowa, Massachusetts, New Hampshire, New York, Vermont, and DC. Most other states have banned it by law or constitutional amendment, and there are ongoing efforts to ban it in the remaining states. This issue is not likely to go away any time soon.

In 2000, California, voters passed Proposition 22, which banned same-sex marriage. Prop 22 ultimately went to the state Supreme Court, which, in 2008, ruled that same-sex marriages were constitutional based on: 1) the state constitution's equal protection clause; 2) marriage being a civil right; and 3) the state having no compelling interest in prohibiting same-sex marriages. As a result, about 18,000 same-sex couples got married. This set off a campaign to prohibit same-sex marriage by constitutional amendment, so Proposition 8 went on the ballot and was passed. This was challenged in turn and this time the state Supreme Court ruled that Proposition 8 was constitutional because: 1) being a constitutional amendment, its provisions automatically became constitutional; 2) equal protection didn't apply because only the word "marriage" was relevant and domestic partnerships were not affected; and 3) not being retroactive, existing same-sex marriages were not affected.[6]

The State of California, despite having its officials named as defendants, had refused to defend the constitutionality of Proposition 8 and left the defense to the religious zealots who had started the petition drive. This placed the religious motive for the enactment front and center, and supporters of same-sex marriage then filed a separate lawsuit on federal constitutional grounds rather than state constitutional grounds. Their case went before federal district court Judge Vaughn Walker who ruled in 2010 that Proposition 8 was unconstitutional, with the Ninth Circuit Court of Appeals affirming the decision in 2012. Judge Walker's reasons for his ruling (as well as those of the Ninth Circuit Court) demolished all the supposedly "secular" arguments against same sex marriage, finding "no rational basis" to oppose it.[7] Walker noted how weak the arguments were for opposing same-sex marriage. He cited all of them and concluded:

> The court provided proponents with an opportunity to identify a harm they would face "if an injunction against Proposition 8 is issued." Proponents replied that they have an interest in defending Proposition 8 but failed to articulate even one specific harm they may suffer as a consequence of the injunction. . . . Proponents had a full opportunity to provide evidence in support of their position and nevertheless failed to present even one credible witness on the government interest in Proposition 8.[8]

With these controversial state and federal rulings in place, the only place left to go is the United States Supreme Court. What is important here is that, if the Supreme Court rules against Proposition 8, the effect could be to legalize same-sex marriage nationwide. Meanwhile, the Court is expected to rule in 2013 whether the existing federal law—the Defense of Marriage Act—defining marriage as between one man and one woman is constitutional. Whether it recognizes marriage as a civil function with a secular rationale or a theology-based function whose religious traditions should govern society remains to be seen. The current makeup of the Court does not inspire confidence in a secular-based ruling. However, one thing working for advocates of same-sex marriage is that the opponents have found it impossible to come up with arguments that make sense that don't include "Because God says so." The Supreme Court might not be willing to so blatantly repudiate the First Amendment's Establishment Clause. One can only hope.

Sexuality and "Natural Law"

Arguments for denying sexual minorities the same rights the heterosexual majority takes for granted are based on Bible-based religious doctrine, along with a religious interpretation of "natural law" (whatever that might be). Fundamentalists, Catholics and Mormons take it as a given that this "law" has produced males and females for reproductive purposes. Therefore, all sexual activity must be limited to male-female copulation and anything else is unnatural. The Protestant fundamentalists, Mormons, and the U.S. Catholic bishops have mounted a ferocious campaign to outlaw same-sex marriage based on this religious view of natural law. Here is the rationale, from the United States Conference of Catholic Bishops' 2009 Pastoral Letter:

> Marriage is a unique union, a relationship different from all others. It is the permanent bond between one man and one woman whose two-in-one-flesh communion of persons is an indispensable good at the heart of every family and every society. Same-sex unions are incapable of realizing this specific communion of persons. Therefore, attempting to redefine marriage to include such relationships empties the term of its meaning, for it excludes the essential complementarity between man and woman, treating sexual differences as if it were irrelevant to what marriage is.

> Male-female complementarity is intrinsic to marriage. It is naturally ordered toward authentic union and the generation of new life. Children are meant to be the gift of the permanent and exclusive union of a husband and wife. A child is meant to have a mother and a father. The true nature of marriage, lived in openness to life, is a witness to the precious gift of the child and to the unique roles of a mother and father. Same-sex unions are incapable of such a witness. Consequently, making them equivalent to marriage disregards the very nature of marriage.

> Jesus teaches that marriage is between a man and a woman. "Have you not read that from the beginning the Creator 'made them male and female' . . . For this reason a man shall leave his father and mother and be joined to his wife, and the two shall become one flesh" (Mt 19:4-6).

> . . . Today, advocacy for the legal recognition of various same-sex relationships is often equated with non-discrimination, fairness, equality, and civil rights. However, it is not unjust to oppose legal recognition of same-sex unions, because marriage and same-sex unions are essentially different realities. "The denial of the social and legal status of marriage to forms of cohabitation that are not and cannot be marital is not opposed to justice; on the contrary, justice requires it" [quoting from the Catholic Church's 2003 Congregation for the Doctrine of the Faith publication No. 8, "Considerations Regarding Proposals to Give Legal Recognition to Unions Between Homosexual Persons"]. To promote and protect marriage as the union of one man and one woman is itself a matter of justice. In fact, it would be a grave injustice if the state ignored the unique and proper place of husbands and wives, the place of mothers and fathers, and especially the rights of children, who deserve from society clear guidance as they grow to sexual maturity. Indeed, without this protection the state would, in effect, intentionally deprive children of the right to a mother and father.

. . . [T]he Church teaches that homosexual acts "are contrary to the natural law. They close the sexual act to the gift of life. They do not proceed from a genuine affective and sexual complementarity. Under no circumstances can they be approved" [quoting from the Catechism of the Catholic Church, No. 2357].

. . . The legal recognition of same-sex unions poses a multifaceted threat to the very fabric of society, striking at the source from which society and culture come and which they are meant to serve. Such recognition affects all people, married and non-married, not only at the fundamental levels of the good of the spouses, the good of children, the intrinsic dignity of every human person, and the common good, but also at the levels of education, cultural imagination and influence, and religious freedom.[9]

This pastoral letter makes many alarmist claims, but provides not one example from real life of the destruction same-sex marriage supposedly wreaks. Not even a hypothetical example. So now that we have read these dire predictions that the workings of natural law, religious freedom, and civilization as we know it would be destroyed in some mysterious way by same-sex marriage, let's visit reality, an area with which the bishops seem quite unfamiliar.

The Varieties of Sexual Orientation

The case for equal rights (including same-sex marriage) for sexual minorities stands on much firmer ground than Bible verses and papal pronouncements. The basic problem with the religion-based arguments is misunderstanding of what is meant by "natural law." A toxic stream of wrongheaded ideas has spewed forth from that misunderstanding, causing needless suffering, hateful acts, and punitive laws. Natural law is not something handed down by a creator god, as religious opponents of same-sex marriage assume. There is no "lawgiver" involved. Natural law, in the only real sense of the term, is simply a description of how nature works, as best we can understand it from observation, experimentation, and testing. And what does all this observation, experimentation, and testing tell us? Nothing at all that is even close to the religious assumptions. It tells us that homosexuality is just one of the more harmless ways nature works. It is not contrary to natural law, but part of it. Religion has no relevance here.

Further deepening the religious confusion is an assumption that the way nature works reflects a purpose. Therefore, since heterosexual sex sometimes produces offspring, that is nature's purpose. This idea prevails because a great many people are scientifically illiterate, thanks to fundamentalists' attacks on science in the schools, and the consequent dumbing down of the science curriculum. Fundamentalists attack evolution, denying its massive factual support, and try to replace it with "intelligent design," which is simply relabeled creationism, and is in no way a scientific theory. (It's unfalsifiable; it makes no testable predictions.)

Nature is nothing if not prolific and varied. Changes wrought by evolution have produced an assortment of sexual and gender variations and orientations. In humans (and maybe other species), both sexes have observable physical characteristics of the other sex, although usually only the parts for one sex are developed. But physical manifestations of sex are not the only options nature has produced. Often enough, there are psychological variations too, and they direct one's sexual behavior. The body may be configured for one sex while the brain is configured for the other. The result is that some people are transgender, meaning they don't conform to the expected behavior patterns of their sex. Transgenders can be any orientation because gender identity and sexual orientation are not the same. Some are simply crossdressers. Some are transsexual, meaning their brain configuration tells them they are one sex, even though their bodies are of the opposite sex. Some transsexuals have sexual reassignment surgery because of this.

And then there are those with Klinefelter's Syndrome. It is said to affect about one in 1,000 boys. These boys have three sex chromosomes (XXY). Since girls are XX and boys are XY, someone who is XXY is physically a male but infertile, while genetically being both male and female. Such boys can and do have girlfriends, but can be psychologically drawn to female behaviors. They are in reality two sexes in one. If such boys want to marry, which sex should they be able to partner with?

Some states try to deny the right to change one's sexual configuration to conform to one's core identity on the grounds that one has to keep the genitalia one is born with. (Why? Who knows?) But what if a baby is born with male and female genitalia, and both are about equally developed? It happens. Doctors used to ask the parents which gender they preferred and would then remove the unwanted parts. However, as these babies grew, sometimes the selected sex did not match an obvious psychological orientation toward the other sex. So now they wait a few years until the child's gender-expressive behavior tells them which parts to remove.

Here's a true sex-mixup story I know about first-hand. (I've changed only the names.) It should give the Vatican fits trying to work it into their mystical views of sexuality, sexual orientation, anatomical complementarity and who gets to marry whom: When Glen and George met, both were males presenting themselves as women. Psychologically they were essentially females trapped in male bodies. They wanted to get married, but same-sex marriages were not allowed, so George had sex reassignment surgery and became legally Georgia. Glen and Georgia were then able to get married, since they now had the Vatican-approved opposite-sex anatomical complementarity. Then Glen had surgery and became legally Glenda. The result is that Glenda and Georgia are now a legally married female couple that started out as a male couple (although presenting as females), then became a male-female couple before finally becoming the female couple they always wanted to be, thanks to surgery that put their physical and psychological makeup in sync. All is well.

As for what the law says about having sex reassignment surgery to bypass prohibitions against same-sex marriage, it probably depends on the state. For Glen/Glenda and George/Georgia, who live in Minnesota, there is no problem. In 2012, in a case challenging the right of a transgendered female to coverage on her husband's employer-paid health care plan, a federal district court judge ruled that coverage could not be denied. He noted that the law prohibiting same-sex marriage did not apply and the sex change was irrelevant because "Minnesota law recognizes a married person's sex when the marriage takes place."[10]

Such simple, logical reasoning is not likely to come any time soon from the Vatican's theologians. Their attempts to figure out what nature's God is up to when it plays mix-and-match with gender identity, and medical science can end the confusion with a little genital reconfiguration, should be interesting to watch. No doubt the Vatican will deal with this entirely mystical non-problem in whatever way causes the most misery for people whose bodies and brains don't match up sexually.

It wouldn't be theology as we've always known it to decide there is no harm in letting one's core psychological orientation prevail as long as no harm is done. It could, in fact, even be theologically demanded. After all, if there is a soul, where would it be located? In the brain! You can amputate or transplant or redesign or artificially replace almost any other part of the body, but you cannot do that with the brain. If it goes, you go. And if there is a soul in there, it goes too. Therefore, if the brain knows its body is really the opposite sex or if it feels sexually oriented to the same sex, then that's the way it is and the only thing to do is adjust the body (and society's expectations) to match. Sex reassignment surgery? Fine! Same-sex marriage?

Why not? Some churches may raise doctrinal objections and insist that what appears between the legs at birth is ultimately defining and must stay that way. But it's not the business of government to enforce those doctrines.

Sexuality: Nature's Shotgun Approach to Species Survival

There is nothing wrong with this sexual mixing and matching other than the prejudicial treatment of LGBT people. It's just what nature does. Nature has no purpose, only consequences, some of which we perceive as good, some bad, depending on their effects on us. Sexuality, driven by evolutionary processes, is not rigidly heterosexual, as can be observed throughout the animal kingdom. Every form of sexual attraction is out there. It may even be that pedophilia is a natural variation. However, that involves a coercive power relationship that harms children, so, natural or not, our laws prohibit it, just as rape—apparently another natural inclination—is prohibited. We simply have to resist and reject some behaviors to which nature mindlessly inclines us. Homosexuality is not one of them, since it does no harm. Sexually transmitted diseases don't count. They occur because human contact transmits disease. We pass on diseases by breathing in another's vicinity, by shaking hands, by a mother kissing her baby. Sexual contact is just another means of transmission.

Because heterosexuality produces offspring, heterosexual orientation predominates in the gene pool. Although the sex drive for homosexual couples does not produce offspring, there is still the emotional bonding that often accompanies sexual relationships—a good thing by itself in terms of social stability and harmony. As consequences go for humans, this has probably worked well if we can assume that prehistoric homosexual childless individuals were free to help raise the children of heterosexuals. Children need watchful care at all times, so the extra help surely aided our species' survival. Until humans figured out where babies came from, sex was naturally directed by sexual orientation solely because it was enjoyable. Why would it not be? Once paternity was understood, the picture changed drastically.

Although the history of marriage shows many forms and rationales (including same-sex marriage), an overriding reason for its institutionalization was male interest in controlling women to ensure a prolific, no-guesswork paternity and, therefore, inheritance, economic aggrandizement, and ruling authority. Women became men's property, as noted in the Ten Commandments, and enforced, until recently, by all religions, and even today by some religions. Women were treated legally as men's property in the United States until around the time of the Civil War. Being in love didn't become acceptable as a sole reason for marriage until some decades later. As recently as the 1970s, divorces were difficult to get unless one could prove adultery. Being abused didn't count. I remember well the cottage industry that developed around staging fake adulterous encounters so a divorce could be granted. Those staged encounters didn't fool anyone, but the letter of the law was upheld, so no questions were asked.

The Bible says Solomon (the wisest of all kings, according to 1 Kings 10:23) had 700 wives and 300 concubines (meaning sex slaves). Where was the one-man, one-woman tradition then? With such exploitation of women now illegal, marriage essentially legalizes a sexuality-based bond without regard for procreation. Reproductive interests have never been the sole justification for marriage in any case. Deliberately childless marriages take place for any number of reasons—financial concerns, physical problems, a need for companionship, even immigration status or the need for health insurance.

Some religions are convinced that same-sex marriage would destroy the institution of marriage. It's hard to see how. The interests of religion and government are different (or should be where state and church are separate), so religions can set their own rules about whom they will marry. Religion is primarily concerned with rituals and such things as sexual behavior, religious affiliation, and procreation and indoctrination of children. Government is concerned with issues beyond procreation, such as mutual financial and personal responsibilities, inheritance laws, medical care, visitation rights, child custody (not limited to heterosexuals), and so on. Given this, it is socially advantageous to provide the legal benefits of marriage for loving, committed couples, whether gay or straight. Government has no compelling interest in being selective about the sexual orientations of those it marries for socially valid reasons. Those orientations are natural, and if one kind tends to produce children and the other doesn't, so what?

Anatomical Complementarity

Religious arguments against same-sex marriage tend to center on anatomy. Their position, put badly, is that since male and female genitalia fit together, and fitting them together often results in offspring, that must be its sole purpose. And because there are offspring, there must necessarily be marriage. Because there is marriage, government has the duty to oversee and protect that arrangement, limiting it to one man and one woman. (Lots of non sequiturs here.) Here's what Archbishop John C. Nienstedt, of the Archdiocese of St. Paul and Minneapolis wrote in a letter to the editor. He claimed he was just defending reality, not his religious position. The Catholic Church, he said, "does not seek to impose its own beliefs on others . . . . The reality we are defending predates any religion or government. It finds its logic in the complementarity of the human anatomy, as well as the male/female psyche and in the propagation of the human species." [11]

What he meant by the male/female psyche in this context is anyone's guess. If it's the emotional aspect of sexuality, that psyche seems to be operating rather nicely for same-sex couples as well. As for anatomical complementarity, people of all sexual orientations have found that there is more than one route to complementarity. If nature was purposeful and wanted sex to be limited to one form of male-female complementarity, all these other options wouldn't be available—some of them useful in preventing unwanted propagation. One is tempted to think that maybe nature actually is purposeful and finds it useful in natural-selection terms to provide a variety of sexual work-arounds to enable us humans to control this whole sexual orientation/anatomical/psyche/propagation business to our advantage.

And speaking of sexual purposes, I don't recall ever reading any Vatican pronouncement about the clitoris. Unlike the penis, which has three distinct and useful purposes, the clitoris has only one—pleasure. It has no complementarity function. Yet there it is, conforming fully to natural law, doing nothing but providing the one thing that has historically made the Vatican nervous—sex-related pleasure. No wonder the Vatican is silent on this. Perhaps the Catholic bishops should study a good sex manual and a few books on sexual evolution before they expound on a topic about which they are so obviously dumb as a rock.

On the fundamentalist side, the Rev. Elden Nelson, a Lutheran minister from Plymouth, Minnesota, in reference to a proposed amendment to the Minnesota state constitution that defines marriage as between one man and one woman, says:

There is nothing discriminatory about the Minnesota Marriage Amendment, nor is it a political matter. Neither is it intended as an offense against any individual or group. Rather, it is a moral and ethical matter that finds its basis and answer in the infallible, inerrant and inspired word of God. [12]

How that squares with the First Amendment's "Congress shall make no law concerning an establishment of religion" clause he does not say. Those propagating these views always assume that the only relevant part of the First Amendment's religion clause is "Congress shall make no law . . . prohibiting the free exercise thereof." That invariably is interpreted by fundamentalists, Mormons, and the Catholic Church as allowing religions to do whatever they wish, with the support of government, however much that destroys the religious freedom of others.

What It's Like to Be in Marriage Limbo

One view of the same-sex marriage controversy is that the matter could be settled by simply designating marriage as between one man and one woman and creating domestic partnerships that are essentially contractual arrangements for same-sex couples. However, there is no way domestic partnerships can be legally equitable without them being a carbon copy of the marriage laws, so why call them something different? What's in a name? Nothing, unless the names confer different rights and responsibilities. Domestic partnerships do that. They confer lesser assurances of equity than marriage, in which everything is automatic, no contracts needed.

Project 515 in Minnesota has compiled a list of the 515 Minnesota laws that work to the disadvantage of same-sex couples in domestic partnerships in ways marriage never does. (If it is this bad in a state as historically liberal as Minnesota, it can't be much better anywhere else.) Below are Project 515 accounts of some of the harmful fallout from this inequity. The stories are true, as are the names except where otherwise noted.[13]

Trying to Teach Life's Lessons to Our Children. (Names have been changed.) When Lisa, Susan and their 6-year-old daughter Paige moved to a new city, they chose to bank with Susan's employee credit union. Wanting to teach their daughter good savings habits, they took Paige with them to open their new accounts and chose to establish one for Paige.

Lisa and Susan completed the required banking forms and were then informed that they could not open a joint account because they were not married. In addition, they could not open an account for Paige, they were told, because Lisa, not Susan, was Paige's legal parent. This credit union carried the employer's name, logo and colors in their signage and advertising. The employer had a strong nondiscrimination policy, and about 20% of its employees were not heterosexual. Yet, when Lisa and Susan protested, they were informed that the banking policies were set by the credit union board of directors, not the employer.

To set a good example for Paige, Lisa met with the manager and voiced her concerns about the policies and the lack of alignment with the employer. She expressed her disappointment and humiliation when the credit union rejected them and their daughter as clients. After they left, Paige became very angry and frustrated, holding on to her piggy bank and refusing to give anyone her money.

"Would this also be the policy if an employee who was a grandparent, aunt or uncle wanted to open an account for a child?" Lisa wondered. "If an employee wanted to open a joint account with a brother or sister, would they be refused?"

Sometimes Planning and Legal Work Aren't Enough. Tim Reardon is a prudent man. When he and his partner Eric decided to have a child through a surrogate, they made certain all the legal documents were in order. They already had a partnership agreement, executed before their commitment ceremony in 2001. They had drafted powers of attorney, health care directives, and every document they could within the restrictions of the law to be certain their relationship to one another and their future children was clear and protected.

Yet when Tess was born in 2003, Tim and Eric waited for a year to get a judge's order for a birth certificate because the state insisted on DNA testing for proof of paternity. The cost, both monetary and emotional, was enormous. Adding to the emotional burden was a serious health challenge. Three months after Tess's birth, Eric was diagnosed with a malignant brain tumor. The family life Tim and Eric had dreamed of was thrown into chaos. Tim and Eric returned to their attorney to be certain their paperwork was in order. It had become imperative that Tim was clearly named the person to "call the shots" upon Eric's death.

Four years later, when Eric was to go from the hospital to a hospice residence, a social worker conducted a financial eligibility screening to determine if Eric was eligible for funds to offset the cost of the hospice residence not covered by either insurance or Medicare. The hospital business office wanted to include Tim's earnings in the calculation of "household income." "They wanted to recognize our relationship when it was financially in their best interest," Tim said. Tim refused. When Eric died a short time later, Tim was informed that the medical examiner would not recognize Tim's relationship to Eric.

To make matters worse, the cremation society did not consider Tim next of kin, with the right to make decisions about Eric's remains, even though Tim showed administrators a power of attorney document, a health care directive, and Eric's will, all clearly naming Tim as the decision maker. Only with the consent of Eric's mother and father was Tim ultimately allowed to sign the cremation society's paperwork.

"I felt so violated and angry that at this most vulnerable moment of life, they would not acknowledge our relationship," Tim said. "All our planning didn't mean anything to these people. Eric's wishes didn't mean anything. This never would have happened to a legal spouse. All it takes is one challenge from a person with an issue or different belief system, and the cost to us in money, time and emotions is enormous—because we have no recourse in the legal system. Any legally married spouse is automatically recognized as next of kin and is granted that right by law with no papers, no lawyers, and no need to prove their relationship at life's most vulnerable moments—the law protects them from such insult."

Fighting to Keep One's Home. (Names have been changed.) Jane's partner Carol was diagnosed with a terminal illness late in 2004. By the time the disease had progressed to the point that Carol required full time care, she had already spent most of her assets on medical bills. Carol applied for and was placed on medical assistance, which provided her with around-the-clock care in the final months of her life.

Following Carol's death, the state placed a lien on her home—the home she had shared with Susan for more than 15 years. By law, the state had the legal power to enforce the lien and recover the money it spent for Carol's medical expenses. Jane was faced with the prospect of selling her home to pay off the state.

However, had Jane and Carol been married, Minnesota law would have protected the home. Current law provides that the state cannot enforce a medical assistance lien on the home of the person who received aid if the person's spouse still lives in the house. In these cases, the state must wait until after the spouse has died before it can recoup money from the home's equity.

No Secular Justification

Laws that support unverifiable religious views of sex and marriage have no place in a secular society. They should be nullified as unconstitutional, and some have been, but progress is slow. It does seem, however, that laws discriminating against sexual minorities are on the way out, due to the tenacious political organizing of LGBT people and their supporters. Public opinion is increasingly on their side. Same-sex marriage may be the last battle in the sexual-orientation phase of the culture war. Arguments raised by the Catholic Church and religious right arguing for defining marriage as only between one man and one woman are weak to the point of being ludicrous. None of them make any secular sense. All are based on religious dogma tied to an intractable ignorance of human sexuality. If the religious right zealots had any understanding of how evolution works, they would know that human sexuality as it actually exists (with LGBT people) is a prime example of "natural law"—a natural outcome of the evolutionary process.

To sum up, here is a list of 11 religious arguments against same-sex marriage, in no particular order of validity (since they have none) followed by the view from the real-world:

1. *Marriage has always been about procreation so we are not mistreating homosexuals by not allowing same-sex marriage.* Our ancestors were wrong about many things, such as slavery and subjugation of women (which marriage facilitated, of course). We abandoned their ideas because they led to mistreatment of subjugated men and women for no worthwhile purpose. We are now abandoning the mistreatment of homosexuals for the same reason.

2. *Our sexual organs exist for procreation by a male and a female. Any other use is unnatural.* Our sexual organs (the external ones we control) perform several functions, only one of which is procreation. The penis has three functions: urination, pleasure, and procreation. The clitoris has only one function: pleasure (interestingly, the only function common to both sexes). Homosexuality squares with all of these functions, including procreation, which can be, but not necessarily, achieved indirectly through sperm donation.

3. *If the human sex drive is not controlled by marriage, limited to male-female couples for procreation, it will be misused in destructive, immoral ways.* The human sex drive, being stronger than needed for procreation (thus suggesting its primary purpose for humans is pleasure), can indeed be misused. It is more extravagantly misused by heterosexuals, especially in sexual exploitation

of women, but can be misused by homosexuals as well. Controlling one's sex drive is a common issue for everyone, regardless of orientation.

4. *Homosexuality, if it becomes acceptable, will harm society by leading to its degradation.* Homosexuality has existed in all societies at all times, sometimes accepted, sometimes not. What society has it ever harmed? None. It has never been prevalent because it involves only a small percentage of the population. It can't be caught and can't be taught because it's a natural orientation, just like heterosexuality.

5. *If same-sex marriage becomes legal, what's to stop polygamous and polyamorous people—even dog lovers and who knows who else—from demanding marriage rights?* Probably nothing, but neither now nor throughout history has there been any sign of a widespread interest in such relationships. Same-sex couples feel the same pull of love as opposite sex couples. They value the same personal and emotional commitment that marriage can provide heterosexual couples. There is no sign of any such commitment operating among the other groups (with the exception of a relatively few polyamorous people), and certainly no interest in organizing a political movement around it.

6. *Homosexuality, even if appearing to be harmless, exacts a spiritual cost that can lead to perdition. We should not be enabling that fate.* Some religious people may believe homosexuality leads to "perdition" (whatever that is), but that is no basis for discriminatory laws against homosexuals. All such laws are a destructive, unconstitutional establishment of religion with no secular justification whatsoever. The Book of Leviticus may have a place in some churches, but there it should stay. It does not belong in our laws.

7. *Same-sex marriage will destroy the institution of marriage.* Religious people often make this argument, but have yet to provide a single concrete example of such destruction. They always fall back on abstractions. Divorce destroys heterosexual marriages all the time, but we allow it because, for one thing, it's none of the government's business, and for another, forcing incompatible couples to stay together only brings pain and misery from which no good ever comes. Does the availability of divorce encourage the dissolution of marriages? Perhaps, but this has nothing to do with same-sex marriages. Perhaps the feared destruction is that of religion's control over marriage as a sacred institution ordained by God to license a couple to have sex so they can increase and multiply. If so, so be it.

8. *Marriage is rooted in religious beliefs and cannot be cut off from that.* No one is cutting marriage off from religious beliefs. Religions are free to set their own rules for marriage and to marry or refuse to marry whomever they will. But there is religious marriage and secular marriage, and they have different standards. Religions marry people for their own religious reasons, and governments marry people for their own secular reasons. Generally, the only

marriages the state does not allow are those that are coercive or harmful. So, for example, an age of consent is required, and inbreeding by close relatives is not allowed (though if pregnancy is impossible in some cases, why not?).

9. *Children need a mother and a father.* Yes, but people who did not produce them in the traditional biological way can and do raise happy children. They may have adopted them, used a surrogate mother to bring them to birth, or conceived them by artificial insemination. The only thing that matters is that children grow up in a caring environment with one or more people who love them and help them become productive, responsible adults. Same-sex orientation has never been a hindrance to good parenting, just as heterosexual orientation has never been a guarantee of it.

10. *If homosexual relations are natural, what is wrong with adultery, pedophilia, and bestiality if they are also natural behaviors?* Yes, those behaviors are probably natural for those who engage in them, but we need to prohibit only those that are harmful. Adults can deal with the harmful effects of adultery on their own. Pedophiles, however, will have to find a way to control that tendency or we will continue to lock them up to ensure the safety of children. As for bestiality, we'd have to check with the beast in question as to any harm done. To most of us, bestiality is just disgusting (or possibly hilarious), but again (as with pedophilia) one runs into the problem of consent—both practices are by their nature nonconsensual. As for homosexuality, there is nothing harmful about it when it's between consenting adults.

11. *If same-sex marriage is approved, there will be harmful civil consequences for those whose religious beliefs cannot allow them to accept it.* Yes, there will be consequences—just as there were consequences when civil rights laws were passed. No doubt there were town clerks who lost their jobs when they refused to marry mixed-race couples. No doubt religious adoption services found they could no longer discriminate against mixed-race couples. No doubt there were parents distressed when their children were exposed to public school classes about racial equality and justice. All because traditional views about race had been overturned by law. But that is the price some people have to pay when they can no longer inflict their irrational beliefs on others. Just as society has survived and improved in the absence of punitive racist laws, so will it survive in the absence of punitive marriage laws.

---

1. *Lawrence v. Texas*, 123 S. Ct. 2472; 156 L. Ed. 2d 508; 2003 U.S. LEXIS 5013, (2003).

2. Laura Hibbard in The Huffington Post, www.huffingtonpost.com/2011/11/04/michigans-matts-safe-schools-law-allows-bullying_n_107649.

3. Maria Elena Baca, "Q&A: Parent group raises school issues," *Minneapolis Star Tribune*, Jan. 15, 2012

4. Human Rights Campaign mailing, Feb. 2012. See www.hrc.org.

5. "Unequal Under the Law: 515 Ways Minnesota Laws Discriminate Against Couples and Families," published by Project 515, October 2007. See www.project515.org.

6. See http://rationalwiki.org/wiki/Perry_v_Schwartzenegger for a lengthy account of the Proposition 8 controversy.

7. Dahlia Lithwick, "A Brilliant Ruling." See http://www.slate.com/articles/news_and_politics/jurisprudence/2010/08/a_brilliant_ruling.single.html.

8. *Perry v Schwartzenegger*, No. C 09-2292 VRW, United States District Court, N.D. California, Northern Division. Aug. 12, 2010.

9. "Marriage: Love and Life in the Divine Plan," A Pastoral Letter of the United States Conference of Catholic Bishops, Chapter 2, Same-Sex Unions, issued by USCCB, Nov. 17, 2009. To order a copy of this statement, please visit www.usccbpublishing.org and click on "New Titles."

10. Dan Browning, "Health plan can't deny wife coverage due to sex change," *Minneapolis Star Tribune*, April 5, 2012.

11. The Rev. John C. Nienstedt, "Gay Marriage: Church defends reality for the common good," *Minneapolis Star Tribune* opinion page, Oct. 8, 2011.

12. The Rev. Elden Nelson, letter to the editor, *Minneapolis Star Tribune* opinion page, Feb. 21, 2012.

13. "Unequal Under the Law," op cit.

4

WOMEN AND RELIGION:
AN ABUSIVE RELATIONSHIP

*"[Mother Teresa] was not a friend of the poor. She was a friend of poverty.
She said suffering was a gift from God. She spent her life
opposing the only known cure for poverty, which is the
empowerment of women and the emancipation of them from
a livestock version of compulsory reproduction."*

—Christopher Hitchens, *The Missionary Position:
Mother Teresa in Theory and Practice*

It is impossible to talk about religion-based laws without discussing the people most severely victimized by them—women, half the world's population. They are the childbearers, so you'd think that would count for something in terms of decent treatment, but it doesn't. Largely if not entirely because of that primal function, women have been the object of male dominance, abuse, and social control throughout history and across almost all cultures. With some exceptions, women have existed as men's property from the time people figured out where babies came from. Was subjugation of women considered the best way to relieve male anxiety regarding paternity? To establish unquestioned heirs? It seems likely, but who knows for sure?

Regardless, women traditionally have been culturally limited to bearing children, and not allowed to do much else. The social reforms of the 1960s did begin to remove that limitation, however haltingly. Although "women's lib" was ridiculed routinely, increased higher educational opportunities received support—by attaching those opportunities to motherhood. I often heard the argument in those days that an educated woman would be better able to raise children to be productive citizens. That always reminded me of the story of Moses, who was allowed to lead his people to the Promised Land, but for some arbitrary reason was condemned to see it only from afar and never go there himself.

When sex discrimination was included in the Civil Rights Act of 1964 as a last-minute amendment, it was greeted with laughter. Sen. Howard K. Smith, a Virginia Democrat and an opponent of the Civil Rights Act, proposed it. His motives were unclear. There was speculation that he thought his amendment would kill the bill; however, he had always been a strong supporter of the Equal Rights Amendment, so perhaps (as others speculated) he only wanted to embarrass fellow Democrats from northern states who opposed women's rights in deference to male-dominated, sexist, labor unions. But the Civil Rights Act passed, and additional protections for women's rights followed. Whether they'll continue to hold is uncertain, given the misogynistic aspects of the culture war.

Religions seem always to have played on and reinforced misogynistic prejudices, assuming the right to control women's childbearing function as a social necessity, with no consideration given to what women themselves might want or need. Irrational—even punitive—views of women have become so embedded in theology and in our laws that one could argue that controlling women's sexuality and childbearing role has been the primary purpose of most religions. The contrived justification for such control is the Bible; and some of its interpreters go even further than it does:

Be fruitful and multiply. (Genesis 1:28)

Unto the woman he said, I will greatly multiply thy sorrow and thy conception; in sorrow thou shalt bring forth children; and thy desire shall be to thy husband, and he shall rule over thee. (Genesis 3:16-God's punishment of Eve for seducing Adam into eating the forbidden fruit)

You shall not covet your neighbor's house; thou shalt not covet thy neighbor's wife, nor his manservant, nor his maidservant, nor his ox, nor his ass, nor anything that is thy neighbor's. (Exodus 20:17)

Women will be saved through childbearing. (1 Timothy 2:15)

No gown worse becomes a woman than the desire to be wise. Men have broad and large chests, and small narrow hips, and are more understanding than women, who have but small and narrow chests, and broad hips, to the end they should remain at home, sit still, keep house, and bear and bring up children. (Martin Luther, in "Table Talk")

Married life presupposes the power of the husband over the wife and children, and subjection and obedience of the wife to the husband. (Pope Pius XI, *Casti Connubii*)

"However we may pity the mother whose health and even life is imperiled by the performance of her natural duty, there yet remains no sufficient reason for condoning the direct murder of the innocent." (Pope Pius XI, *Castii Connubii*)

"Man was made to rule, woman to obey." (Augustine, *De Genesi*)

"[I]n divine matrimony man receives by divine institution the faculty to use his wife for the begetting of children." (Aquinas, *Summa Theologica*)

This is all mythical nonsense, of course, but the restrictive and demeaning attitudes toward women reflected in these passages remain much the same today around the world. Only in recent times, particularly since the 1960s, have patriarchal cultures and the religions that support them been forced in some places to loosen their control of women. These pockets of enlightenment, where women are free to make their own social, educational, economic and childbearing decisions, are the secular democracies.

The Last Stand

But not all of them. In the United States, the fight to maintain control of women continues, carried on by the Catholic hierarchy, the Mormon hierarchy, and Protestant fundamentalists. This fight has become increasingly fierce, although it's concentrated primarily in one area. Control of women is no longer about opposing women's right to vote or get an education or pursue a high-level career or (to some extent) practice birth control—religious misogynists have lost those battles. What is left now is their last stand: women's right to abortion, to have the ultimate control over their own bodies. The Catholic-fundamentalist-Mormon coalition will not concede that right.

In 1973, the U.S. Supreme Court issued its *Roe v. Wade* decision, and on November 20, 1975 the United States Catholic bishops, acting in defense of papal authority, issued their "Pastoral Plan for Pro-Life Activities."[1] It signaled the start of the culture war, and within a few years drew in Protestant fundamentalist allies—notably the Moral Majority, founded by Jerry Falwell and Paul Weyrich in 1979—acting in defense of biblical authority. The Pastoral Plan was not a reflection of either group's desire to "save innocent pre-born babies"—as the hysterical anti-abortion rhetoric would have it. Catholic-dominated countries in Latin America (where abortion is illegal) have abortion rates much higher than in the United States,[2] yet there is no campaign to stop them. Before *Roe v. Wade*, there were clandestine abortion clinics all over the United States, and doctors willing to do abortions in their offices. I knew about them and knew how to find them, as did most savvy women who were willing to ask around, yet there were no Catholic or Protestant campaigns to stop them (other than an occasional dustup somewhere by a vote-pandering politician). The reason is that they were illegal. And that is all the anti-abortion movement cares about, as will be explained below.

The following quotations expose the fundamental, governing rationale for the bishops' Pastoral Plan: the protection of the Catholic Church as an institution and the credibility of the pope as the infallible representative of God on Earth. The quotations are from *The Life and Death of NSSM 200: How the Destruction of Political Will Doomed a U.S. Population Policy,* by Stephen D. Mumford.[3] This highly readable book spells out in great detail the plans and strategies the United States Catholic bishops implemented to bring about the culture war that has fragmented our society.

The book begins by describing the failed efforts of the Nixon and Ford administrations to implement the recommendations of National Security Study Memorandum 200 (NSSM 200) for controlling population growth. NSSM 200 detailed the security threat to the United States of uncontrolled global population growth. It urged efforts to free women economically and socially through education, and to make family planning options available to them. It emphasized that population growth could not be controlled if abortion was not among those options. Mumford carefully documents the Catholic bishops' efforts to derail the Study. They were successful, and the study was shelved permanently by the Reagan administration. Because of Mumford's thorough documentation—including reproduction of original texts—his book is arguably the most important ever written on the cause of the culture war and the social-economic-political dysfunction that has ensued. Consider the following:

> In his book, *Persistent Prejudice: Anti-Catholicism in America*, published by *Our Sunday Visitor* [the leading Catholic newspaper at the time] in 1984, Michael Schwantz summarized the position of Catholic conservatives on the abortion issue: "The abortion issue is the great crisis of Catholicism in the United States, of far greater import than the election of a Catholic president or the winning of tax support for Catholic education. In the unlikely event

that the Church's resistance to abortion collapses and the Catholic community decides to seek an accommodation with the institutionalized killing of innocent human beings, that would signal the utter failure of Catholicism in America. It would mean that U.S. Catholicism will have been defeated and denatured by the anti-Catholic host culture." (p. 124)

In April 1992, in a rare public admission of this threat, Cardinal John O'Connor of New York, delivering a major address to the Franciscan University of Steubenville, Ohio, acknowledged, "The fact is that attacks on the Catholic Church's stance on abortion—unless they are rebuffed—effectively erode Church authority on all matters, indeed on the authority of God himself."

It is important to note here that, as Mumford says, laws outlawing abortion ". . . need not be enforced to meet the needs of the Vatican. The Vatican requires only that the civil law not conflict with canon law. Then papal authority and civil authority are not pitted against one another. It is only legal abortion that threatens papal authority." (pp. 310–311)

I encountered this view myself several years ago when I was deep into organizing for abortion rights here in Minnesota. The anti-abortion man leading the anti-choice forces told me that if abortions were outlawed the Church would have no interest in enforcing the law because all it cared about was having the law validate Catholic doctrine.

And for that we have been dragged through decades of social and political chaos with no end in sight. Even birth control, long considered a basic, settled right, again became a major controversy in 2012 with the presidential candidacy of Rick Santorum, staunch Catholic, father of eight, and a reputed member of Opus Dei, a secretive, authoritarian Catholic society.

Mumford describes how the problem of papal infallibility and institutional authority surfaced in 1964 when Pope Paul VI authorized the Papal Commission on Population and Birth Control to see if there was a way to approve contraceptive use. (p. 126) The Commission met until 1966 without finding a way to do this consistent with Catholic doctrine. The commission's lay members voted 60 to 4 in favor of approving contraceptive birth control, and the clerical members voted 9 to 6 in favor. Even though it undermined papal infallibility, the commission's majority voted that way "because it was the right thing to do." (p. 124) However, the minority (which included Karol Wojtyla, who became Pope John Paul II) prevailed to such an extent that Pope Paul VI, in his 1968 encyclical, *Humanae Vitae*, reinforced the condemnation of abortion and contraceptive birth control as well as his claim to infallibility. Here is an excerpt from the minority report:

> If it should be declared that contraception is not evil in itself, then we should have to concede frankly that the Holy Spirit had been on the side of the Protestant churches in 1930 (when the encyclical *Casti Connubii* was promulgated), in 1951 (Pius XII's address to the midwives), and in 1958 (the address delivered before the Society of Hematologists in the year the pope died). It should likewise have to be admitted that for a half a century the Spirit failed to protect Pius XI, Pius XII, and a large part of the Catholic hierarchy from a very serious error. This would mean that the leaders of the Church, acting with extreme imprudence, had condemned thousands of innocent human acts, forbidding, under pain of eternal damnation, a practice which would now be sanctioned. The fact can neither be denied nor ignored that these same acts would now be declared licit on the grounds of principles cited by the Protestants, which popes and bishops have either condemned or at least not approved. (quoted by Mumford, p. 126)

In other words, the Vatican found that it had dug itself into a hole and decided the only way out was to keep on digging. This would not be a matter of concern—or even noteworthy—if *Humanae Vitae* applied only to Catholics (most of whom have ignored it). However, in the Vatican's worldview, *Humanae Vitae* applies to everyone, and governments have the duty to enforce its view of morality. Monsignor John A. Ryan, in his 1940 book, *Catholic Principles of Politics*, explains the matter:

> If there is only one true religion, and if its possession is the most important good in life for States as well as individuals, then the public profession, protection, and promotion of this religion and the legal prohibition of all direct assaults upon it, becomes one of the most obvious and fundamental duties of the State. For it is the business of the State to safeguard and promote human welfare in all departments of life. (quoted by Mumford, p. 114)

The Power of a Living Fossil

Any rational, thoughtful person would want to dismiss such an absurd, arrogant claim out of hand, but that would be unwise. As Mumford explains in detail, the U.S. Catholic bishops have such a high level of organizational expertise, political shrewdness, public relations skills, and talent for negotiating alliances with religious-right fundamentalists that they have now brought those "state duties" alarmingly close to realization.

This is truly bizarre. The Catholic Church has no real power, only a perceived power because of its 2,000-year history, ostentatious papal encyclicals, impressive cathedrals, colorful rituals, magnificent music, and priceless works of art. Or perhaps it's the Vatican's seemingly bottomless pockets and ability to make common cause with Protestant extremists. A Feb. 21, 2012, fundraising letter from Americans United for Separation of Church and State noted this:

> The Pew Forum on Religion and Public Life released a study last year [2011] that showed lobbying expenditures by religious groups have increased about fivefold since 1970, with $390 million now shelled out annually. Most of these groups are ultra-conservative and are working around the clock to convince politicians to make their theology the law of the land.[4]

When the bishops announced a new lobbying group in 2011, religious right activists were ecstatic. Tony Perkins, president of the Family Research Council, wrote, "I welcome their renewed commitment to the fight before us. We are united in the fight for faith, family and freedom."

One evidence of this "conviction" was that the Catholic bishops spent $26.6 million in 2009 lobbying Washington. Of the top 15 groups the Pew Form lists, 10 are religious right organizations or are aligned with the Catholic hierarchy.

Yet all the evidence from surveys and church attendance shows that most Catholics have little or no interest in papal restrictions on sexual matters, and they dismiss the pope's pronouncements. Almost every Catholic I know fits this description. They remain Catholic out of habit or because they think of the Church as a social welfare service that feeds the hungry and shelters the homeless (see Chapter 8 for what is really going on) or because they love the pageantry or for other personal reasons. Catholics will turn out in massive numbers to see the pope, listen to him rant about abortion and birth control, then go home and guiltlessly engage in all kinds of non-doctrinal, essentially harmless, sexual and reproductive "sinful" behavior.

So what explains the political power of the Catholic Church? Single-minded dedication and organizing ability, which can outweigh almost any majority opinion. Mumford explains it in describing the Church's initial failure to get a Human Life Amendment passed:

In September 1991, Catholic activist William Bennett, former Secretary of Education, and other Catholic "conservatives" announced the formation of Catholic Campaign for America. Creation of this organization even 20 years ago would have been unthinkable. For nearly 200 years, Protestants have warned that the Vatican plans to create such organizations in the U.S. and that American democracy was threatened. One needs only listen to what these Catholics are saying now to understand that the strategy Stephen Settle described in the *National Catholic Register* is being implemented—and to recognize that this minority, with its "stamina, smarts and perseverance" intends to impose papal law using any means necessary and to "co-opt" our democratic institutions. (p. 172)

Although Catholics are no longer a reliable voting bloc, politicians seem to tremble at the thought of opposing the bishops' imperious anti-abortion demands. None of them have the courage to stand up for the victims of religious tyranny. Oh, some of them speak legalistically, and almost apologetically, of defending *Roe v. Wade* as the law of the land. But none of them, as far as I know, defend the women that ruling is supposed to protect. Their support of reproductive rights is too *pro forma* to inspire confidence. What might be the impact on how women (and the men who love them) vote if a candidate said something like, "Of course I support *Roe v. Wade*. I support it because I respect women. They're childbearers, but they're not a public utility for us to regulate. I respect their intelligence and their ability to know what's best for themselves and their families. They don't need me or any legislative body to make their personal decisions for them." Sounds like a vote-getting speech to me.

The Problem with Roe v. Wade

Roe v. Wade was a bad ruling because it regulated the timing and circumstances under which abortion is permitted. It thus assumed what societies have always and everywhere assumed: that women, as society's childbearers, are a community resource, a public utility to be controlled and regulated. Granted, *Roe v. Wade* did end the criminalization of abortion that existed in almost all states, thus saving the lives of several hundred women a year who otherwise would have died of botched illegal abortions. And its three-trimester regulatory system was hardly restrictive. It was nothing more than what women had always worked out on their own through common sense and need.

The Supreme Court should have declared the law *Roe v. Wade* challenged as unconstitutional on the basis that abortion is not the government's business; it is a medical matter involving a woman's bodily functions to be resolved between a woman and her doctor. Instead, by creating a totally unnecessary regulatory structure, the Court opened the door to all the modifications, restrictions and bureaucratic hoops to jump through that regulations invite, and that we have today, with more on the way. The Court's ruling that the Constitution implied a right to privacy consistent with the right to abortion was weak, since governments invade one's privacy all the time, in many ways. A better ruling—along with upholding a woman's right to bodily autonomy in medical matters—would have invoked the First Amendment's prohibition of an establishment of religion, since the history of opposition to abortion centers around theological notions about "ensoulment" as defining when life begins. Unfortunately, the Court's ruling said, though by implication only, that women's autonomy stops where their childbearing function begins; therefore they are—yes—a public utility in need of government regulation.

The Equal Rights Amendment failed in 1985 precisely because opponents hammered away that it would give women autonomy and therefore the right to be in control of their own bodies, and therefore the right to abortion. The practical effect of *Roe v. Wade* and the defeat of the ERA has been to open the way to making women slaves of the state where an unwanted or disastrous pregnancy is concerned.

The Pastoral Plan for Pro-Life Activities

Mumford's book provides the complete text of the bishops' plan, including its "unsanitized" version. It describes strategies for manipulating government processes at all levels, for creating political action units at all levels, for recruiting members of Catholic professional, business, and civic associations, for forming "pro-life" organizations in every parish in every city and county in the nation, and for recruiting Catholic writers and intellectuals to promote the "pro-life" agenda. The plan has been largely successful as can be seen from the mounting restrictions on access to abortion.

The 1976 Hyde Amendment started the legislative brutality by ensuring there would be no federal funding for abortion for poor women on Medicaid. Further legislation ensured that poor women in rural areas have virtually no access to abortion even if they can afford it. Servicewomen serving on a military base are denied the right to abortion even in cases of rape or incest, and even if they pay for it themselves. There are onerous waiting periods (to forestall a "hasty decision"—though any woman facing a traumatic pregnancy doesn't think of anything else after a missed period). There are parental notification requirements (never mind that some parents get physically violent when their teenage daughter informs them she is pregnant). There are informed-consent requirements (including a law passed in Texas in 2011 that would imposed a rape-like requirement that doctors insert a probe in the woman's vagina to provide her with a video image of the fetus—in case she is too dumb to know what pregnancy is; a near-identical proposal in Virginia failed in 2012). All of these obstacles and humiliations, and others the anti-abortion zealots dream up, are unnecessary, intrusive, busybody measures to force women to bend to their will—and there are far more than can be kept track of easily or covered in this book. In 2009, because of the bishops' interference, President Obama was forced to remove abortion coverage from his health care reform plan. Abortion clinics have been forced to close because they can't afford the extensive, completely unnecessary, hospital-like remodeling mandated by anti-abortion legislative "regulations." It goes on and on.

Origins of the Religious Right

The bishops' plans for developing ecumenical activities with conservative Protestant organizations were well calculated and effective. Their strategy was guided by Virgil Blum, a Jesuit priest and founder and first president of the Catholic League for Religious and Civil Rights. Mumford writes:

> [Blum offered the bishops] a set of well thought out guidelines which capitalized on centuries of experience of Jesuit manipulation of governments. (p. 155)

> . . . Blum recognized early on that "ecumenism" would be an essential weapon to counter the criticism certain to come with the blatant involvement of the bishops in making public policy. He saw that constant defense of the Catholic bishops by Protestant leaders, in the name of "ecumenism" was critical. In hindsight, he was obviously correct. Protestant leaders have served as tools of the Catholic bishops to blunt criticism, by branding such criticism as anti-Catholic or anti-freedom of religion and thus un-American. Protestants with good intentions were used like pawns to advance papal security interests at the expense of this country's. (p.160)

Almost everyone assumes the religious right (notably the Moral Majority) was founded exclusively by Protestant fundamentalists. It wasn't. Paul Weyrich, a conservative Catholic, co-founded the Moral Majority with Jerry Falwell. Other conservative Catholics were key figures in the founding of the religious right in the late 1970s and early 1980s. They included Pat Buchanan, National Conservative Political Action Committee co-founder Terry Dolan, religious-right fundraising guru Richard Viguerie, Eagle Forum founder Phyllis Schlafly, and Operation Rescue founder Randall Terry. In fact, right-wing Catholics (and, lurking behind them, the Catholic bishops) were arguably more important to the founding of the anti-gay, anti-choice religious right than their Protestant counterparts (Jerry Falwell, Pat Robertson, Ralph Reed, et al.). Mumford makes a good argument that without the Catholic bishops and their Pastoral Plan for Pro-Life Activities—not to mention the many leading Catholic figures of the religious right—there would be no anti-abortion movement and no culture war.

From "Miracle of Life" to "Sniveling Welfare Cheat"

After the religious right's political takeover of Congress and most state legislatures in the 2010 mid-term elections, the push for suppression of reproductive rights moved into what can only be called a "shock and awe" phase. The Guttmacher Institute created a chart giving an historical perspective on the number of abortion restrictions enacted from 1985 to 2011. It's a J-curve like the one for population growth. The horizontal line, although quite jagged, is fairly constrained until 2011; then it shoots straight up from around 200 to 300 restrictions to nearly 1,000 in one year. Yes, religious-right legislators introduced 1,000 bills in 2011 at the state and federal levels that would further restrict or deny women's right to abortion and to contraceptives (that would prevent the need for abortion).[5]

One-thousand! That was out of about 40,000 bills of all types and does not include the many bills that give increased preferential treatment to religion. Every possible restriction, criminalization and humiliation of women was in those bills. One even required miscarriages to be criminally investigated. (In Iowa, a pregnant woman was arrested for falling down a flight of stairs—she had called 911 for help—on suspicion that she might have been trying to induce a miscarriage.) Another bill protected murderers of abortion doctors from prosecution. Another defined rape as such only if the woman was physically beaten and had the wounds to prove it—thereby putting statutory rape, rapes at knife point, date-rapes, etc. in the "get out of jail free" category. One bill denied federal funding for training doctors in how to perform abortions, even though such medical knowledge is necessary when a pregnancy threatens a woman's life. There were several state-federal fetal "personhood" amendments (part of a nationally organized campaign). There were TRAP bills (Targeted Regulation of Abortion Providers) that have already shut down several abortion clinics that couldn't afford the full hospital-level modifications mandated by the bills. The National Organization for Women (NOW) newsletter for September 2011 reported that "During the healthcare reform debate, Senator Jon Kyl of Arizona objected to including prenatal and maternity care in the basic benefits package by saying, 'I don't need maternity care. So requiring that in my insurance policy is something that I don't need and will make the policy more expensive.'" Well, yes, since women get pregnant all by themselves, why should the costs be shared by men? All of the above exemplifies the from-another-planet mindset that has created a dysfunctional political system.

Why are there so many bills hostile to women's welfare and why are they so similar from state to state? It is not a coincidence. It is organized. It's called "blueprint legislation."[6] For some time, national organizations have crafted bills to be introduced by supportive legislators around the country. The most prominent such group is ALEC, the American Legislative Exchange Council. It has provided legal language for many bills, most notably for voter suppression laws (labeled voter-ID laws in right-wing sales pitches, "papers please" laws such as Arizona's SB 1070, and "stand your ground" gun rights laws —"shoot first and ask questions later").

Similar to ALEC in strategy, but unknown to the general public, is AUL—Americans United for Life.[7] That group comes up with almost all of the anti-woman bills, and the fingerprints of the Catholic bishops' Pastoral Plan for Pro-Life Activities are all over it. A Unitarian minister founded AUL in 1971 (before *Roe v. Wade*), and its purpose then was only to hold intellectual discussions on the pros and cons of abortion. After *Roe v. Wade*, in 1975, it was completely reorganized as a legal entity designed to find ways to overturn *Roe v. Wade*. As in so many anti-abortion groups, Catholics hold leadership positions in it, and the Pastoral Plan informs its activities. At this writing, the most visible Catholic leaders of AUL are Charmaine Yoest and Abby Johnson,[8] who led its attacks on Planned Parenthood and the Obama health care plan.

Of course, the most absurdly abusive bills go nowhere, but many others get passed, though some face legal challenges.[9] Examples: A bill was passed in Arizona and upheld by a federal judge that makes it a crime for doctors to perform an abortion after 20 weeks counting from the start of the last menstrual period (realistically, that's 18 weeks into pregnancy). The judge bought the argument that the fetus can feel pain by then and ignored medical testimony to the contrary. There just isn't enough cognitive development by then to feel anything.[10]

In July, 2012, a federal district judge, John Kane, in Colorado ruled that a Catholic business owner did not have to comply with the Obama healthcare mandate to provide his employees with insurance coverage for birth control. The judge noted that numerous religious organizations had been granted exemptions, so why not commercial businesses with religious owners?[11] (See Chapter 7 on taxes.) As well, in 2012, the Arizona legislature passed a bill allowing doctors to conceal information from patients about possible birth defects to keep women in the dark and thus forestall possible abortions. On July 24, 2012, in Missouri, the Eighth Circuit Court of Appeals in St. Louis ruled that a South Dakota law allowing doctors to lie to patients about the risks of suicide following an abortion is constitutional. It seems the Court thought the law didn't unduly burden a woman's abortion decision, that it supported the free speech rights of doctors, and the intent of the law was informative. This despite testimony that no such risk exists, and the clear legislative evidence that the law was passed precisely to hinder a woman from having an abortion.[12]

Then there is Plan B, the so-called "morning after" pill that prevents pregnancy if taken within 72 hours after unprotected intercourse. After years of conflict between knowledgeable scientists who presented abundant evidence for the pill's safety for over-the-counter (OTC) distribution, and religious right opponents who insisted with no factual evidence whatsoever that 1) the scientists were wrong and 2) the pill was an abortifacient, it was approved for OTC sale to girls and women 17 and older. Only girls 16 and younger still needed a prescription. In 2011, when further studies had shown the pill was safe for all females of childbearing age, the Food and Drug Administration (FDA) approved it for OTC sales across the board—it could go on the shelves with all the other birth control products.

Normally, when the FDA approves a medication, that is the end of it. However, contrary to all past practice, Health and Human Services Secretary Kathleen Sebelius stepped in and overruled the FDA.[13] This was almost certainly a political decision designed to avoid a controversy with the religious right in the runup to the 2012 election.

Part of the stated opposition to OTC sales was that there might be harmful side effects for girls as young as 11, an age group that had not been studied regarding Plan B. Yet, many common OTC medications—such as aspirin, Tylenol and cough syrups—have all kinds of side effects, sometimes fatal (read their labels), but can be bought OTC by pre-teen children (who have not been studied regarding side effects). For vulnerable young girls, who can be so easily seduced into an unwise sexual encounter or are the victims of incest, how does the potential side effect of, say, a headache from taking Plan B compare with the potential side effects of a pregnancy from not taking it? Yet, in the religious right's view, nothing can be allowed to interfere with a potential fetus's "right to life."

Some religious rightists even claim that Plan B induces promiscuity.Really? Contraception is not exactly cheap when used regularly. Although it can be free at some clinics, Plan B costs between $25 and $60 at pharmacies. As one sexual health activist said, "The cost is one reason why it is plan B, not plan A." Regarding promiscuity, here is what an ob/gyn doctor friend told me: "Even a $9 pill prescription costs $108 a year, which is $540 for five years, getting into the range of what an IUD costs. Besides, a lot of OTC contraceptives are prescribed for non-contraceptive reasons, at times even for a woman without a uterus. All contraceptives should be OTC. No prescription is needed for getting pregnant, after all, and any OTC [drug] is less dangerous than pregnancy."

With so much hostility to abortion, one would think there would be strong legislative support for family planning programs and widely available and cheap contraceptives. What better way could there be to greatly reduce the need for abortions? Pro-choice organizations have repeatedly tried to introduce legislation to this end, but have been opposed every time by anti-choice lobbyists.

But Protestant religions generally have no objection to birth control, so what is the problem? The Catholic bishops, of course, the organizing force behind the religious right. For them, birth control is an evil on the level of abortion.

In contrast to the relentless campaign to restrict contraception, and then save the resulting fetuses at all costs, there has been no compensating legislative push to do anything for the children born as a result of anti-choice laws. The same legislators who want to force every pregnant woman to carry to term also advocate tax and spending cuts that reduce or eliminate programs that provide children with good nutrition, health care, education and, in general, all the social support needed to turn them into productive adults.

The overall legislative theme has seemed to be "reproduce and abandon" as that precious little "pre-born baby," a "miracle of life" while in utero, gets transformed by birth into a "sniveling little welfare cheat" (as one particularly apt political cartoon put it).

A Politically Generated Person

Since 2010, the religious right has conducted a campaign for "personhood" amendments to state constitutions and the U.S. Constitution. Generally, the wording is some variation of this: "The life of each human being begins with fertilization, cloning or its functional equivalent, at which time every human being shall have all the legal and constitutional attributes and privileges of personhood." Such a constitutional amendment would outlaw all legal abortions forever. (Illegal ones with all their lethal potential for women would, of course, take their place.)

Well! Whoever first said there's nothing new in the world didn't reckon with the overheated imaginations of religious ideologues. No society anywhere has ever defined fertilized eggs as people. They've all had sense enough to wait to see if a person actually develops. Usually this is at birth because a lot of personhood-obstructing mishaps can occur during nine months of gestation. Not even the Bible treats fetuses as persons. Not even the Catholic Church did until recently. For centuries, it held a variety of views about abortion related to when "ensoulment" (the Church's criterion for personhood) supposedly took place. At one time it was at 40 days gestation for males and 80 for females. (It evidently took females longer to become human.) At another it was at "quickening" (about five months gestation), when the woman could detect the reflexive fetal movement. Before those times abortion was OK. The only consistent position taken by the Church over the centuries was that abortion was wrong if it was a cover-up for the sin of having engaged in non-marital sex.[14]

The discovery of DNA gave the anti-abortion crusade a new argument (not a good one, just new): since a fertilized egg has DNA it must be a person! Of course every cell in one's body carries DNA and, with the possibility of cloning, any one of those cells could be made into a person. This means that when we shed skin cells (which we do constantly), we are sending zillions of potential "pre-born babies" to their deaths. St. Augustine (fifth-century Church father), despite the overall flat-Earth level of his thinking, was smarter than today's Church dimwits:

> The law does not provide that the act (abortion) pertains to homicide, for there cannot yet be said to be a live soul in a body that lacks sensation when it is not formed in flesh and so is not endowed with sense.[15]

Let's see what theology's politically generated person looks like. Fertilization begins the process of cell division. At that point the "pre-born baby" is a cluster of undifferentiated cells no bigger than the period at the end of this sentence. Yet the Church sees a person there. That is major delusion indeed—or, more likely, politically motivated institution-saving desperation.

But what about that heartbeat so endearingly called to our attention on "pro-life" billboards? Yes, a heartbeat can be detected at about two-months gestation, but it's only from a two-chambered heart—the lizard level of development. A real person's heart has four chambers. But what about brainwaves, suggesting some cognitive development? Yes, they can be detected very early, but they don't suggest anything. As a medical doctor friend informed me: "All 'brainwaves' means is 'living tissue,' not thoughts. The anti's [anti-choice zealots] are ignoramuses."

Abortion before the third trimester never kills a baby—it only keeps a baby from forming by stopping the gestational process. The "ingredients" haven't yet come together sufficiently to form anything viable. It takes time for that process to produce an actual person, and that doesn't happen until the third trimester. By that time, it's almost always a wanted pregnancy, so if something goes wrong it is heartbreaking for the would-be parents. If the fetus has to be removed, delivery can be induced or a Caesarian performed. There is no need for an abortion except in rare and desperate life-or-death cases when that is the only rational, humane option. It's a medical matter that no legislature is competent to be involved in. Religion-based laws forbidding these so-called but misnamed "partial birth" abortions force doctors to use procedures that could endanger the woman's life or health or future childbearing ability for no useful purpose.

Personhood, defined as "from the moment of fertilization," could limit fertility treatments. There could be criminal charges if an embryo doesn't survive. Couples would be forced go to other states for fertility treatments to avoid restrictive statutes. All pregnancies would be forced to be carried to term regardless of rape, incest, maternal health problems or severe birth defects. There are annually in the U.S. tens of thousands of pregnancies started by rape (5% of rapes start a pregnancy). For example, a 1996 estimate in PubMed (www.ncbi.nlm.nih.gov/pubmed) was 32,101. This is out of hundreds of thousands of rapes.

Many contraceptives would be outlawed, including the morning-after pill and the IUD, because anti-abortionists ignorantly insist that they are abortifacients. Miscarriages would be criminally investigated and would require both birth and death certificates. What about inheritance laws?

Think about that—and a whole host of other laws now based on real personhood—and then try to fit a politically generated person into them. You would have a legal mess to end all legal messes.

No rational person believes a cluster of undifferentiated cells is a person. Ask yourself: If a building was on fire and you could save either a baby or a container of frozen embryos, which would you save? The answer is always the baby. But maybe not. When I was in Catholic school, the nuns told a story to emphasize the sacredness of the Eucharist (the consecrated Host—God himself!): A church had caught fire and the priest rushed in to save the Host displayed on the altar for adoration. In saving it, he died. The nuns held this priest up as a hero for sacrificing his life to save the Host. It wouldn't surprise me if, given the absurdity of theological imaginings, had there also been a baby to be saved, the Host would have taken priority.

Despite the reverence for fetal tissue, church funerals are not held for fetuses, although sometimes there are burials. One woman I know miscarried at two months and held a priest-attended burial. Although I was a devout Catholic at the time, I did have limits to my credulity—enough to ask what she used for a coffin, a small matchbox?

Then there was the fetal tissue obsession of devout Catholic Rick Santorum, a former U.S. senator and presidential candidate. His wife miscarried at 4½ months and the family (including three children ages 6, 4 and 1½) treated the fetus to hugging, kissing and a private mass. (I don't know about the coffin, but a large matchbox would do.)

This story resonated with me, since I also experienced a late miscarriage and wonder if Mrs. Santorum's was like mine: massive hemorrhaging, severe shock, unconsciousness, not breathing, husband running red lights racing to the hospital, doctor telling me I was lucky to have made it, etc. What miscarried was a bloodclotty blob the hospital simply disposed of. I certainly had no interest in hugging and kissing it.

But what did this trip through politically generated personhood land mean to that fetal "person"? Nothing. Cognitive development sufficient for some level of sentience does not occur until the third trimester. If a problem arises then, it is a medical issue for medical professionals to deal with, not politicians. Meanwhile, throughout the gestational process there has been only one claimant to real personhood—the woman, fully cognitive, fully sentient. What does personhood mean to her?

What It Means to Be a Real Person

Frances was a real person, a very pretty 22-year-old blonde. She lived next door to me when I was 10 years old. One weekend she went out of town and came back dead. It was the first funeral I ever went to. They said she died of obstruction of the bowels from eating peanuts on the train. I later learned Frances actually died of a botched abortion and that, in those days, doctors would give the cause of death as obstruction of the bowels to save the family from embarrassment.

Vera was a real person too. She was my best friend when she and I were devout Catholics trying, with little success, to make the rhythm method ("Vatican roulette") work. We had names for the "medications" required—"Sulfadenial" and "Noassatol." Vera had a blood condition that caused cerebral palsy or death in a fetus unless it could be delivered early in the third trimester before the condition took hold. Vera's first child had a severe case of cerebral palsy. Every pregnancy after that, she delivered by Caesarian section to try to save the fetus, but every fetus died. Vatican roulette was a failure as usual, and Vera went through six of those uterine surgeries. During the seventh pregnancy, her uterus ruptured, blood got into her lungs, and she drowned in her own blood, in the ambulance, on the way to the hospital.

Vera's was the second funeral I attended. Vera thought that if she practiced birth control she would go to hell. But it was her heartbroken husband and a child in need of constant care who were put in hell, the real one created on Earth by inhumane doctrines that good, trusting people—real people—are conned into believing, and no one is allowed to question publicly, because that would be "religion bashing."

In no other business can an organization get away with brutalizing people so severely and yet have its behavior not only treated with respect and placed beyond question, but be given grants, subsidies, government contracts, and tax exemptions besides.

Not to be left out of the gullible (aka "good, trusting people") category, I (also a real person) will mention one of my real-person experiences as a devout—therefore often pregnant—Catholic. (I found this story to be intensely boring to anti-abortion people when I told it a couple of times, thinking it might generate some understanding. It did not.)

One of my pregnancies went very wrong (as opposed to only partially wrong in others) when, at about the fifth month, I started filling with fluid.

Doctor's diagnosis: It was a sign of defective fetal development. What kind or how bad he couldn't say. I was carrying 40 pounds of fluid, and it created tremendous pain. No abortion of course, since I was still a devout Catholic at the time and obviously a slow learner, having learned nothing from those funerals I'd attended. To make a long story short, at about the eighth month of this horrendous mentally and physically traumatic pregnancy, the doctor decided there was no point in me continuing to be miserable for what would most likely lead to nothing, so he induced labor.

The baby was a girl, a sweet little thing with red hair, looking good despite weighing only four pounds. Well, that was just on the surface. Her intestines hadn't formed and were mostly a fibrous mass. Her esophagus was solid instead of hollow. She couldn't eat. It took her a few days to starve to death. But, hey, she did get baptized, and isn't that the most—the only—important thing? Certainly the anti-abortion religious zealots would say so. Most people abhor sadism, but it seems that, in the world of dogma-driven religion, it is sacred.

Trying to avoid getting pregnant has always been difficult for women, and that's made even more difficult by archaic, theology-based laws that deny women autonomy. As recently as the 1970s, a woman who wanted a tubal ligation had to get her husband to sign off on it. If he wouldn't sign, too bad. Here's what it was like. The *Minneapolis Star Tribune* on Oct. 9, 2011, had an article titled "Minnesotans look back on 1968." Among the people it profiled was Carol Connolly, a peace activist. The article reported:

> Connolly was also busy raising her six kids. "I tried using the rhythm method," she said. "It didn't work." A few years later, after giving birth to an eighth child who died, Connolly wanted to get a tubal ligation, "but in those days the husband had to sign off on that." John [her husband], a staunch Catholic, was initially reluctant, but eventually agreed after consulting with medical professionals.

Yes, that's what we had to put up with. I had one friend who wanted a tubal ligation but the doctors refused to do it because (as my friend said) they assumed they knew better than she did what she wanted. She finally got her tubal by very forcefully threatening a lawsuit. My frequently pregnant friends and I had the experience of doctors refusing to do a tubal unless we were at least 35 years old and/or had five children. One friend even faced and survived a life-threatening pregnancy her doctor had warned against; but he would not do a tubal until that 5 and/or 35 "rule" kicked in for her. Doctors always seemed to think that, because we were women, we surely must want lots of kids. (Now you know where the baby boom came from.) No, we didn't, as should be obvious by the way the birth rate dropped like a rock when the pill became available.

We had a saying: "Before they're born you wouldn't give two cents for them; after they're born you wouldn't take a million bucks for them." In those days of large families, Vatican roulette, and unreliable contraceptives, miscarriages were welcomed, even hoped for, definitely envied, and never regretted—at least in my post-World War II blue collar working class environment. (Hysterectomies too. We regarded them as trading in a baby carriage for a playpen.) Life can get cheap when there's too much of it and you have little or no control over your fertility. It's the way the world is for real persons—or was in those days. The baby boomers changed all that with their rejection of anti-birth control dogma and acceptance of the improved and more reliable contraceptives. (Even priests were reported to be advising people in confession to "follow your conscience.") Couples, including Catholics, spaced their children, and family sizes dropped drastically. The dark humor that had once expressed our fertile helplessness was gone. Baby showers became joyful occasions instead of the make-the-best-of-it acceptance of fate they once were. But now the Catholic bishops with their Pastoral Plan for Pro-Life Activities are determined to return us to the 1950s, under the guise of concern for microscopic, politically generated "persons"—but in reality concern for the Catholic Church's power and (most importantly) institutional survival.

Abortion providers have stories to tell about real persons, too. They are not like the ones just described where there was no way out. They are stories of taking control of one's own life. Anne Nicol Gaylor, administrator of the Women's Medical Fund, Madison, Wisconsin reports the following. It typifies what faces poor women in need of abortions. (Wisconsin is one of the many states that will not cover abortions for poor women under Medicaid.)

> Through July 31, 2011, the Women's Medical Fund helped 347 Wisconsin girls and women pay for abortions. Far too many of these were victims of rape, both by an acquaintance and a stranger—or ex-husband in one case. Several women the Fund helped were carrying grossly abnormal fetuses. Others included a heroin addict, two in rehab for other substance abuse, a girl with serious epilepsy, a woman about to be evicted, and a woman with a 3-year-old requiring special care since birth, still on a feeding tube. The oldest woman helped in 2011 was 44, the youngest was just 13, an 8th-grade honor roll student.

An early abortion in Wisconsin now costs about $500. Although the typical woman needing help in paying for an abortion is in her 20s, unmarried with two children, in 2012 we heard from more patients in their 30s, many with sizable families. In many cases these are women whose health providers are Catholic clinics and hospitals that have denied women the tubals they asked for. Why do we allow our tax dollars to go to such sexist, medieval institutions?

Informed Consent: Fiction versus Reality

Anti-abortion laws always include the requirement for "informed consent." That is, a woman seeking an abortion is required to listen to a script detailing (rare and sometimes untrue) possible complications of an abortion, listen to the fetus's (lizard-level) heartbeat, watch a sonogram showing (non-volitional reflexive) fetal movements, and hear details of a fetus's development. These are designed to dissuade the woman from aborting the pregnancy.

But if informed consent is so important for an abortion, why is it not even more important for pregnancy and childbirth? After all, those are inherently life-threatening conditions, and doctors routinely approach the onset of labor as a disaster waiting to happen. Yet the anti-abortion zealots never show any interest in informing a woman about the problems she could face during pregnancy. None are trivial. They are prevented or managed to the extent possible only with good medical care. They are the reason for that care and why, without it, throughout history, death in childbirth has been (and in some countries still is) common. They are the reason obstetrics is a medical specialty and why its malpractice insurance premiums are the highest in the medical field.

There are many things that can go wrong: anemia, major birth defects, blockage of the birth canal, breech birth, eclampsia, ectopic pregnancy, fistulas, hemorrhage, high blood pressure, late-miscarriage hemorrhaging, pernicious vomiting, placenta previa, post-partum depression, post-partum fatal blood clots, toxemia, and more. All are serious, many are life threatening. None are of such a nature that treatment should be subject to legislative or religious control.

There's also the well known but not normally life threatening "morning sickness" that actually can last all day, every day, and is no fun. (I know—been there, done that; plus I've experienced several other things on the above list.) In addition, pregnancy-related economic, and social problems can be disastrous to a woman's ability to control her destiny. Nothing has a greater impact on her than childbearing. No one else can take on her physical, emotional, economic, and social burdens (certainly not the self-righteous busybodies who promise a year's supply of diapers to women who decide against abortion). And because no one else can do this, no one else has a right to decide for a woman whether she should terminate a pregnancy.

The Road to Hell

But what about that "reverence for life" mantra that so frequently marks anti-abortion rhetoric? Let's visit this particularly vacuous theological landscape for a moment and see what meaning that term might have. Here is an anecdote from Cecil Bothwell's book, *Whale Tales*. It speaks for itself:

It was 1981 and I and my then-partner Susan were working in Arizona as house parents for a program to help mainstream developmentally disabled—mentally retarded—kids. The house was brand new, having been constructed by a wealthy doctor for the benefit of two of his children who were among our seven charges.

One truly memorable client was "Donna" (not her real name). She was 19 years old with language skills at about a three-year-old level. She was angry and violent. Left alone with "Lynn" (another child) she would invariably dump her out of her wheelchair and laugh at the younger girl's inability to regain her seat. She repeatedly tore the heads off of Lynn's dolls and once grabbed me from behind as I drove the crew to school in nearby Prescott in our household passenger van. Donna was very strong and was choking me as I wrestled the vehicle to the apron.

She was given to disrobing in the boys' restrooms at the high school where she was being "mainstreamed," and by multiple accounts she was very sexually active in that situation, attracting a willing crowd of young partners. So we "progressed," to the extent that progress was possible, going through the motions of teaching language and life skills to a household full of young adults with no prayer of learning language or life skills.

The crowning irony of that period involved Donna. Thanks to her sexual activity her parents had authorized a birth control pill prescription and she'd been taking them for four years (when she didn't spit them out). But she reacted violently to medical examination and didn't ever experience menstruation during the months that we were her caretakers. Based on the advice of her doctor, who suspected tumors, and with her parents' consent, we scheduled Donna for a hysterectomy. Wrong. Her caseworker intervened, insisting that Donna was an adult, had a right to parent, and that we were interfering with that basic human right. Oh, indeed. She would be a great parent. Maybe tear the head off her baby? But we were legally outgunned at the requisite hearing. Donna was granted continued fertility.

In the decades since I have occasionally pondered how the parents of young men in that high school would have felt about their sons lining up to have at it with Donna, perhaps gracing them with a grandchild or, for that matter, how those now middle aged men might feel about their first sexual encounters with a too-compliant mentally deficient woman. In those pre-AIDS days they probably didn't pass around anything terminal, but there's little doubt that "safe sex" didn't figure in her picture. I still wonder from time to time whether Donna ever enjoyed the great satisfaction of parenting and whether any resultant baby survived. I fully understand the legal and ethical arguments concerning forced sterilization and the idea that we are all endowed with inalienable rights, but it seems clear that there have to be rational exceptions to any rule. Good intentions really do sometimes only pave the road to hell.

My take-home lesson from that home-parenting year was that pre-natal diagnosis of severe mental issues and the availability of abortion-on-demand are one incontrovertible blessing of modern medical science and politics. None of the clients [we] tended that year had any remote prospect of living even semi-independent lives. Only the doctor's children enjoyed any measure of parental support (in that he built and partly financed the house) and even for those there was no meaningful family interaction. Families had abandoned the rest to state care, which, whether in large facilities or group "homes," amounted to warehousing. To the extent that giving over such fundamentally damaged children to state care was a painful choice, the families certainly suffered. But what enduring good was served by the entire effort? And how could anyone consider abandonment of a child to state caretakers to be more ethical than abortion?[16]

Babies born with severe defects are a sad thing and society has a moral obligation to take care of them and help them achieve whatever is possible. But when a fetus is known to be severely damaged or parents know they carry a genetic mutation that is almost certain to produce a damaged fetus, it's cruel to require such a life to be sustained, especially when the people who must bear the physical, emotional and economic consequences feel they cannot handle it. There is no decent, humane reason to force this on anyone. Usually it is religious belief that dictates this, against all humane considerations. But when does the religion that forces this on others ever step up to support severely damaged children in any meaningful way? That is left to the parents to the extent they are able, and to the larger community through tax-supported services. The "reverence for life" religions, of course, don't even help by paying taxes.

But what about the families who accept a pregnancy they know will result in a child with serious birth defects, and who then raise it with love and selfless care? One can only applaud their humanitarian instincts—until they say that such children teach us to be compassionate, and by losing them to abortion we lose what they could have offered us. Now think about that. They are saying that for us to be compassionate we must deliberately allow children to be born with severe physical and/or mental limitations that neither their selfless caretakers nor anyone else would choose for themselves. What kind of reasoning is it that says others must be allowed to suffer so we can show compassion? This is wrong.

No Secular Justification

The obsessive drive to control women's reproductive decisions is neither pro-life nor moral. It is, in fact, nothing short of moral depravity. It relegates women's status to less than that of a corpse. A corpse has far more autonomy. You can't take its organs without the deceased's prior consent or the consent of the spouse, close family members or attorney for medical decisions. A living woman's body, if she is pregnant (and even before, through contraceptive limitations), is controlled by government regulations. Nothing about this can be justified from a secular, human-centered perspective.

What would happen if there were no laws regarding abortion other than those that cover general medical practice? Women would terminate pregnancies that were disastrous for them as the situation required—almost all during the first trimester, some in the second trimester for medical reasons, and very rarely in the third trimester for truly severe medical reasons where no other option could be humanely or practically justified. What valid (i.e., humanitarian) secular reason exists for overriding the woman's decision and forcing motherhood and all its lifelong ramifications on her? There are none. There is only the theocratic religious desire to have sectarian dogma enforced and validated by our legal system. No one is harmed by leaving a woman free to have an abortion. The fetus neither knows nor cares. A few women may regret their abortions, but they should take this up with the clergy who guilt-tripped them, not their legislators. As for society, far more damage is done, in terms of social welfare costs and dysfunctional families, by prohibiting abortion than by allowing it. Only abortion for sex selection is socially harmful when it is done to avoid having girl children in societies that devalue and mistreat girls. But the problem is patriarchal sexism and the solution must address that.

Where are the churches when it comes to bearing the social costs of unwanted children—so often due to religion-based restrictions on access to contraceptive birth control? The objection by Catholic, Mormon, and fundamentalist churches to reality-based sex education, contraception, and abortion is well known. The costs are not. In 1991, the Minnesota Women's Consortium published an analysis of the public cost over a five-year period of one unintended pregnancy and birth in Minnesota. The costs included counseling, prenatal care, the Women-Infants-Children (WIC) nutrition program, childbirth, the Aid to Families with Dependent Children (AFDC) program, food stamps, medical assistance for mother and child, public health nurse, and the Head Start pre-school program. The total came to $58,446.48. The report noted that there were 55 pregnant girls in one St. Paul high school in February 1991. The calculated five-year cost to the taxpayers for those girls and their babies was $3,214,530.00. This analysis has not been updated since 1991. However, since then, according to the Federal Reserve Bank of Minneapolis, the consumer price index has risen by 71%, which would bring the estimated five-year cost to taxpayers to well over $5 million.

Although some teenagers get abortions, many others end up on welfare. In January 2010, the Guttmacher Institute (www.guttmacher.org) published a study titled, "U.S. Teenage Pregnancies, Births and Abortions: National and State Trends and Trends by Race and Ethnicity." It showed that, nationally, 750,000 teenagers became pregnant during 2006, with a potential need for financial support and social services lasting several years. The percentage getting abortions varied by state, from over 50% in New Jersey, New York, and Connecticut to less than 15% in Kentucky, Arkansas, South Dakota, Oklahoma, and Utah. (The lower percentages are almost certainly due to the near impossibility of getting an abortion in those states.) Every year, approximately another three-quarters of a million teenagers get pregnant. Taxpayer-funded, religion-based abstinence training in high schools (in lieu of reality-based sex education) has not worked.

There is much vapid anti-abortion talk about promoting a "culture of life" while calling anything that offers control over one's fertility a "culture of death." Yet, without fertility control, our species, like every other species that reproduces beyond what its environment can sustain, will go extinct. Revering life (whether out of honest sentiment or political power mongering) is fine in the abstract, but what about reality? Women are born with perhaps 100,000 eggs in their ovaries. Only one egg is discharged per month from about age 12 to 45. Men produce sperm by the millions. Does it really matter which egg and sperm connect? And to whom? Why should it matter to legislators and total strangers if a woman ends a disastrous pregnancy? Yet many people (even some atheists) feel they have a right to decide whether a woman should abort a pregnancy. What makes it their business?

Maybe it's a primitive tendency toward fertility worship, a probably subconscious feeling that women, as a scarce reproductive resource, must not be free to end a pregnancy of their own volition. How else to account for even some atheist men saying they are pro-choice, "but abortion bothers me" or "there should be some restrictions." (Those who make such comments usually fear they might have been aborted, so perhaps such comments are a reflection of the basic instinct for survival—but one badly in need of a shot of rational thinking.) And so there is little objection among the general public to restricting a woman's reproductive freedom, however much it limits or destroys her wellbeing and whatever potential or ambitions she may have beyond being a mother. Male suppression of abortion rights and contraception is the ultimate in misogynistic control.

Women's opposition to contraception and abortion rights exemplifies the passive slave mind at work, instilled in them through thousands of years of being someone's property (sometimes through abduction and rape). It's arguably an expression of the "Stockholm Syndrome," an adaptive behavior of captives who bond with their captors. In extreme forms, this means women doing anything to curry favor with their masters, whether they be imaginary gods or men in power positions whose political or economic support they want and think they need. Or, it may be that these women really do think they and all other women are airheads incapable of making rational, ethical decisions about disastrous pregnancies, and that women need legislators and clergy to make their decisions for them.

Religions have capitalized enormously on these human propensities by getting fertility-worshipping concepts inserted into our laws regardless of the social costs. But there is no future for humanity, only extinction, in this archaic religious worldview. How women are treated is critical to the survival of the human species, yet they have been more mistreated than any other group throughout history. If the world's pro-natalist religions (not just Catholic conservatives, Mormons, and Protestant fundamentalists) have their way, the prospect for human survival is bleak. We are adding 80 million people a year to the planet. By 2100, world population will reach 10 to 14 billion if nothing stops it. Of course, something will. Earth can sustain only so many people and at some point the consequences of over-population will become evident and frightening enough to override any and every form of opposition to birth control and abortion. We can only hope the override won't be draconian and a catalyst for genocidal wars.

The following statement by John Seager, president of Population Connection, a grassroots population organization, is instructive:

> The Guttmacher Institute finds that 222 million women around the globe want to avoid pregnancy but have no modern contraception. Providing the current level of contraceptive use in the developing world costs $4 billion each year, while saving $5.6 billion. If the world invested $8.1 billion per year, we'd see 54 million fewer unintended pregnancies, 26 million fewer abortions, 21 million fewer unplanned births, 79,000 fewer pregnancy-related deaths and 1.1 million fewer infant deaths—and we'd save an additional $5.7 billion. Contraception pays for itself. Giving women the power to control their own futures is the solution, but powerful interests stand in the way. House Republicans have fought at every turn to prevent access to contraception. And at the Rio + 20 United Nations Conference, the Vatican was successful in removing references to gender equality and reproductive rights from the final document.[19]

To forestall an overpopulation-generated apocalyptic future requires confronting beliefs about sex and women's rights. Free, educated women do not overpopulate. Therein lies the solution, but it must be worldwide. At the very least: 1) Develop foolproof, easy-to-use contraceptives and distribute them free or at low cost worldwide; 2) Make abortion safe, available and affordable; 3) Make education freely available to women; 4) Remove barriers that prevent women from learning job skills and becoming self-supporting.

These were essentially the recommendations of NSSM 200, disastrously rejected due to pressure from the U.S. Catholic bishops. They will continue to be rejected as long as political control remains effectively in the hands of religious institutions that oppose contraception and abortion, aided by patriarchal societies that encourage men to equate "manhood" with having numerous children, and by developed countries fearful of being called "elitist" if they suggest that Third World countries cooperate in population control.

Besides population-growth control, there is another civilization-saving benefit to ending the mistreatment of women. Stephen Pinker writes about this—the general decline in violence through the ages in all areas of life—in *The Better Angels of Our Nature*, regarding one of his sources:

> Potts and his coauthors argue that giving women more control over their reproductive capacity (always the contested territory in the biological battle of the sexes) may be the single most effective way of reducing violence in the dangerous parts of the world today. But this empowerment often must proceed in the teeth of opposition from traditional men who want to preserve their control over female reproduction, and from religious institutions that oppose contraception and abortion.[17]

Pinker notes how women's empowerment and increasing influence have been an important factor in the decline in violence he documents. None of this violence-reducing empowerment has come from authoritarian, theocratic religions. It has come in spite of them.

At some point the fawning, pandering, social-political charade that is propping up archaic, morally depraved beliefs about women as social property will become so abhorrent to thoughtful citizens that we'll finally tell the religious emperors they have no clothes, and be done with them.

---

1. Stephen D. Mumford, *The Life and Death of NSSM 200: How the Destruction of Political Will Doomed a U.S. Population Policy. Center for Research on Population and Security*, 1996.

2. See http://www.guttmacher.org/pubs/journals. The overall abortion rate for Latin America is 37 per 1,000 women of childbearing age. For the Caribbean it is 50, for Central America it is 30, for South America it is 39. (Data are from 1995 but more recent figures show little change.) For North America, where abortion is legal (though not easy to access), the rate is 22 per 1,000.

3. Mumford, op cit.

4. Barry W. Lynn, Executive Director, Americans United for Separation of Church and State, fundraising letter, Feb. 21, 2012.

5. Factcheck.org/CBSNews/http://www.guttmacher.org/pubs/gpr/15/1/gpr150114.html.

6. Sarah Seltzer and Lauren Kelley, "Meet ALEC's Equally Despicable Anti-Choice Cousin-AUL. posted April 10, 2012 at http://alternet.org/story/154947/meet_alec%27s_equally_despicable_anti-choice_cousin.

7. See history and purpose at http://en.wikipedia.org/wiki/Americans_United_For_Life, posted April 17, 2012.

8. Erin Gloria Ryan, "Meet the Group Behind All Those Crappy Ultrasound Laws" under "Roe v World" at Jezebel.com, posted March 8, 2012, and Benjamin Mann, "Abby Johnson's new memoir UnPlanned" at http://www.catholicnewsagency.com/news/abby-johnson-reveals-details-of-pro-life-turnaround-and-catholic-conversion.

9. See the lengthy list of assaults in "The War on Women's Reproductive Rights," http://www.politicususa.com/en/the-dirty-thirty-year-end-edition.

10. Bloomberg News, *Washington Post*, July 31, 3012.

11. Terry Baynes, "Catholic Business Owners Win Temporary Halt to Obama Birth Control Mandate," Reuters news service, July 27, 2012, published in the *New York Times*, July 31, 2012.

12. *Planned Parenthood v. Mike Rounds*. U.S. Court of Appeals Case No. 09-3231 and No. 09-3233 and No. 09-3362,, U.S. District Court for the District of South Dakota - Sioux Falls.

13. Gardiner Harris, "Plan to Widen Availability of Morning-After Pill Is Rejected," *New York Times*, Dec. 7, 2011. Also: Daniel J. DeNoon, "Plan B: Sebelius Overrules FDA, Nixes Sale Without ID," *Medscape Pharmacists News*, Dec. 7, 2011.

14. Jane Hurst, "Abortion in Good Faith: The History of Abortion in the Catholic Church." Catholics for A Free Choice, Washington D.C. 1981.

15. Ibid.

16. Cecil Bothwell, *Whale Tales*, pp. 68–70, Brave Ulysses Books, Asheville, NC, 2010.

17. Steven Pinker, *The Better Angels of our Nature: Why Violence has Declined*, Viking Press, New York, 2011, p. 688.

5

THEOLOGY-BASED HEALTHCARE

"We have legalized the ability for medical professionals to honor their religion and their conscience over law. We have legalized anarchy."

—Niles Ross, former pharmacist and
retired pharmaceutical industry professional

Of all the topics covered in this book, none have the potential to compromise your health and wellbeing—even determine whether you live or die—like religion-driven health care. And you can't easily escape it because you are unlikely to know where the pitfalls lie. Even if you do know, you may not be able to decide where an ambulance takes you.

Most people are aware that Catholic hospitals will not perform abortions or provide birth control services for religious reasons; but there's a lot more to it than that. Much more. Children suffer needless pain, become disabled, spread contagious diseases, and die of medical neglect because the laws say faith healing is healthcare. Medical personnel may legally refuse to provide standard—even life-saving—medical care if it is contrary to their religious beliefs. Your health insurance coverage may shift in unpredictable ways from secular to religious control. Reality-based sex education is prohibited in some places, and critically needed contraceptives, such as the morning-after pill, are kept as inaccessible as possible—especially for young girls who need them the most. Even reproductive technology to achieve wanted pregnancies is compromised by restrictions. End-of-life decision making is constrained by the religious beliefs that only God can determine when you die, and that "suffering is the kiss of Jesus," as Mother Teresa said.[1] And, of course, stem cell research (see Chapter 6) that promises new ways to treat or even eliminate many diseases continues to founder on the rocks of legally sanctioned mystical beliefs about protoplasmic "personhood."

Every one of these restrictions is based entirely on theological concepts. All of them could be challenged as state-church violations, especially when religion-based providers are tax exempt and government funded. However, even if the entire health care system was privatized and taxed, we would still be up against the laws that establish "conscience" exemptions. They override all other laws. They override your humanity, your right to control your own body, your right to live and your right to die—all to support religious beliefs many find barbaric.

Conscience Exemptions Trump All Other Laws

Conscience exemptions may sound like a laudable human rights concept, but they are a major roadblock to health care based on your own needs rather than someone else's religion. As so often happens, there are unintended consequences of good intentions. These exemptions were, in part, a response to the post-World War II Nuremberg Trials and the Nazi defense that "I was just following orders." Conscience exemptions were seen as a way to legally protect people from being forced to commit atrocities. Such exemptions made "I was just following orders" no longer a legitimate defense, and placed individual conscience as a barrier against unjustifiable, inhumane orders. (This is the rationale for these exemptions; the real reasons are different, as we'll see.)

Unfortunately, such well-intentioned exemptions became, paradoxically, a protection for those who refuse to provide objectively justifiable and humane medical care—even what is otherwise considered the minimum acceptable standard of care—that does not conform to their religious beliefs.

The 1973 *Roe v. Wade* decision legalizing abortion was the catalyst for the first national conscience exemption in the United States (some states already had them). Immediately after that decision, Sen. Frank Church, from Idaho, introduced an exemption bill that passed 92 to 1.[2] It protected private hospitals that were receiving federal tax support through the Hill-Burton Act and government programs (such as Medicare and Medicaid) from being required to provide reproductive services that did not conform to the religious beliefs of those providing the services. These services have come to include abortion, contraception, sterilization, and referrals to other providers, as well as some fertility treatments and the use of stem cells. Many states followed with their own conscience exemptions and some pharmacies have allowed "pharmacists for life" to refuse to fill prescriptions for contraceptives. The only protection for patients was an informed consent clause that prohibited medical personnel from giving fraudulent information about a procedure they refused to do, such as claiming harmful side effects for the procedure. This, unfortunately, has not worked well, as fear-mongering has continued to deter patients from seeking needed reproductive health care. (See the discussion of "Plan B" in Chapter 4.)[3] In some states, religious-right legislatures have passed laws requiring that false information be presented to patients.[4] Arizona has taken this even further, with a 2012 conscience-exemption law allowing physicians to conceal information from pregnant patients and their partners about possible birth defects.

With conscience exemptions it is sometimes not so much the medical facility as the personnel working there who create the problems. The following is a personal account by a medical professional, Niles Ross:

> Suppose there is a hospital that is non-sectarian, and performs abortions. Individual OB-GYN physicians are not obligated to perform them, even if the "hospital" performs them. Each individual health professional—doctor, nurse, pharmacist, X-ray technician—has his or her own individual religious- and conscience-directed right not to perform a procedure.

> In 1970 I was working in what was my final job as a pharmacist. I was working in a private, non-profit, non-sectarian hospital in New York state. At that time New York State legalized abortion, prior to the United States Supreme Court doing so.

> The chief administrator of the hospital made a tour of every single department. He walked into the pharmacy and stated (this is paraphrased): "Starting Monday, this hospital will perform abortions. We are open 24-hours a day, and we will perform abortions as needed. If there is any pharmacist who cannot dispense the drugs [used during abortions], let your supervisor know, and you will be exempt from that. However, we *are* open 24 hours a day, and the drugs *will* be dispensed 24 hours a day."

> So, way back then, the conscience exemption was well known and alive and well. It happened that we had two Catholic pharmacists. Neither of them expressed objection, and they did dispense the drugs. This alleviated a big potential problem. We had only one pharmacist on the night shift—a Catholic. He preferred the night shift and, of course, we all preferred that he preferred it. Had he voiced objection, the entire shift system would have collapsed. Nothing happened, but it could have. So, the issue is not only with institutions, but also with individuals. The chain of providers involved in your exercising your right to have procedures you need is only as strong as the

weakest link, and that is the conscience exemption. (This was very evident in the Nancy Cruzan "right-to-die" case as specific nurses objected to care that was other than "keep her alive into infinity.")

Certainly, there are pockets of the country where religion-controlled, non-Catholic hospitals and health care providers are also part of the problem. Religions other than Catholicism do play a special role in healthcare. But Catholicism bears the brunt of this discussion because of the number of Catholic hospitals.

I am now living in Iowa. My personal physician is an employee of a Methodist hospital. He is fine with my living will, but he may not be able to honor it. This is why: The Methodist hospital has a "hospital within a hospital" for very ill, long-term patients (severe burn patients, for example), and specially trained physicians work in that part of the hospital. The hospital gets those physicians from a medical contracting company that supplies specialists to hospitals all over the country The contracting company is Catholic.

The Methodist hospital, as an institution, will honor my living will. However, there is no Methodist hospital treating me. There are only physicians, and nurses, and pharmacists, and X-ray technicians. Therefore, the conscience exemption can make things very difficult. A patient cannot interview every single health care provider. The inpatient, particularly, is subject to the religious whims of whomever shows up at his or her bedside. Even with the strongest health care advocate—and my lawyer is—that health care advocate cannot be there every single moment. (Note the above discussion of 24-hour abortion availability—hospitals treat on a 24-hour day.)

If I'm dying, it will not help me even if my lawyer threatens legal action at the very moment the health care provider decides to plunge some device into me to keep me alive. A valid Supreme Court ruling in my favor is of no use to me.

What this comes down to is that a medical facility and/or its conscience-driven staff members can refuse to perform a legal—even necessary—procedure if it is against their religious beliefs. They can even refuse to tell you of its availability elsewhere. And there may be nowhere else to go if you are in an HMO or an employer-provided health care plan that limits you to a single facility, or if you live in a rural area where you have no choice of facilities. And there is not a damn thing you can do about this.[5]

The issue Niles Ross raises is serious. Conscience exemptions have created veritable chaos in medical care, with patients vulnerable to whatever religious belief drives the medical caregiver at hand. Further, if a patient dies or is otherwise harmed by irrational conscience-driven refusal to provide treatment, the hospital and/or its staff cannot be sued. Oh, they can be sued for malpractice, but there is no such thing as conscience malpractice in the medical field. Cut off the wrong leg and you're in trouble, but let a woman die rather than perform a life-saving abortion and you're home free.

Obviously, the consciences of others can sometimes be dangerous to your health. Yet there are no standards for what constitutes a legitimate conscience exemption. There should be, and the standards should be secular and evidence based, with the patient's desires and needs given priority. No one's conscience should be given the power to deny the morning-after pill to rape victims, or permit medical neglect of a child to satisfy the parents' faith healing beliefs, or deny physician aid in dying to end irremediable suffering, or compromise the treatment of any of the other diseases and conditions some religions believe must be subject to theological control, however inhumane and unwanted the result for the patient.

For the hopelessly ill and suffering person, the medieval mindset has come full circle. The rack of the Inquisition is now one's deathbed. Still in the name of religion. Still just following orders—from God.

Here's a test case for setting conscience exemption standards: In 2009, Sister Margaret McBride, an administrator at St. Joseph's Hospital and Medical Center in Phoenix, Arizona, authorized an abortion as the only way to save the life of a woman in her 20s who was eleven weeks pregnant and near death from pulmonary hypertension.[6] Catholic doctrine forbade the abortion, as spelled out in the U.S. Conference of Catholic Bishops' "Ethical and Religious Directives for Catholic Health Care Services" that governs healthcare in Catholic hospitals in the United States.[7] Bishop Thomas Olmsted of the Roman Catholic Diocese of Phoenix excommunicated McBride, claiming her action was a source of scandal for the Church. The diocese also ended the hospital's affiliation with the Church.

Since my beliefs are human centered, it's hard for me to see this as punishment. I would think both McBride and the hospital would want to say, "Good riddance." But the pull of religious belief is strong for many people. McBride and the hospital were heroic in rejecting that pull so they could save a life. McBride was, in fact, given an award by a Catholic lay group called "Call to Action."

The hospital president, Linda Hunt, defended McBride's actions, saying, "If we are presented with a situation in which a pregnancy threatens a woman's life, our first priority is to save both patients. If that is not possible, we will always save the life we can, and that is what we did in this case." Bishop Olmsted said the mother's disease (with death nearly a 100% certainty, according to the doctors) "needed to be treated. But instead of treating the disease, St. Joseph's medical staff and ethics committee decided that the healthy 11-week-old baby should be directly killed." Noooo, it was not a "healthy 11 week-old baby." It was a fetus at two-and-a-half months gestation—approximately an inch-and-a-half long, weighing a quarter of an ounce—still unable to breathe and impossible to save under any circumstances.

But such are the emotional word games that infuse anti-abortion propaganda. No such sympathy-seeking language is ever used to describe the very much alive and sentient young women whose lives the church hierarchy considers disposable.[8] Instead, that hierarchy recites a constant litany condemning women who supposedly have abortions "for birth control" and "for convenience."

So, the question is, which conscience-driven action operating at St. Joseph's Hospital should realistically be classified a conscience exemption: McBride's, for saving the young woman's life, or Bishop Olmsted's, for wanting to sacrifice the woman's life to save an unsavable fetus, just to uphold his Church's "sanctity of life" (for fetuses only) theology and avoid an abortion "scandal" for the Church? As the law stands now, both saving the woman for demonstrable humanitarian reasons and letting her die for irrational theological reasons are conscience-driven actions. Accepting both as valid leads to medical chaos. The solution is to apply the exemptions only to actions that are evidence based, demonstrably humanitarian, and supportive of the patient's wishes.

Hospital Mergers and Secular versus Religion-Based Care

The economics of hospital management have led in recent years to a proliferation of hospital mergers and acquisitions to gain greater market share and achieve cost efficiencies. Trouble arises when a hospital is controlled by the Catholic Church. In these circumstances, Catholic theology must prevail and all staff in the merged institutions must agree to adhere to the "Ethical and Religious Directives for Catholic Health Care Services." They apply to everyone, Catholic or not. Here is what the Directives say about such mergers, taken from Part Six, "Forming New Partnerships with Health Care Organizations and Providers":

69. If a Catholic health care organization is considering entering into an arrangement with another organization that may be involved in activities judged morally wrong by the Church, participation in such activities must be limited to what is in accord with the moral principles governing cooperation.

70. Catholic health care organizations are not permitted to engage in immediate material cooperation in actions that are intrinsically immoral, such as abortion, euthanasia, assisted suicide, and direct sterilization.

71. The possibility of scandal must be considered when applying the principles governing cooperation. Cooperation, which in all other respects is morally licit, may need to be refused because of the scandal that might be caused. The diocesan bishop has final responsibility for assessing and addressing issues of scandal, considering not only the circumstances in his local diocese but also the regional and national implications of his decision.

72. The Catholic partner in an arrangement has the responsibility periodically to assess whether the binding agreement is being observed and implemented in a way that is consistent with Catholic teaching.[9]

This means that, if the only hospital near you is Catholic or in a Catholic-secular partnership, you're in trouble. No contraceptives, no abortion (or even a referral for an abortion) even if your life depends on it, no removal of a life-threatening ectopic pregnancy (but see Chapter 2 for an interesting exception), no prenatal diagnosis if there is any hint that it may lead to an abortion, no vasectomy or tubal ligation, no morning-after pill even if you've been raped, no in vitro fertilization or other doctrinally off-limits fertility technology (see Chapter 2), and no aggressive end-of-life pain remission. Here is what the Catholic bishops say about that, from Part Five of the Directives, "Issues in Care for the Seriously Ill and Dying":

61. . . . Since a person has the right to prepare for his or her death while fully conscious, he or she should not be deprived of consciousness without a compelling reason. Medicines capable of alleviating or suppressing pain may be given to a dying person, even if the therapy may indirectly shorten the person's life so long as the intent is not to hasten death. Patients experiencing suffering that cannot be alleviated should be helped to appreciate the Christian understanding of redemptive suffering.[10]

If you can't understand why suffering is good for you, too bad. And we all pay for this "Christian understanding of redemptive suffering." Because Catholic hospitals are tax exempt, everyone else's taxes are higher; to add insult to injury, hospitals get federal funding—supplied, of course, by the taxes we pay. Therefore, a hospital that refuses to provide a standard service for doctrinal reasons is getting paid by the taxpayers for doing nothing. There is no recourse for the patient. Hospitals can't be sued if they have a clause in the admitting documents (who reads them?) mandating arbitration in case of disputes, and a 2011 Supreme Court ruling upheld such clauses.

Defunding Family Planning Programs

Nothing is more central to a woman's life than the ability to control her childbearing. And it often seems that nothing is more central to authoritarian religions' belief systems than to prevent her from doing that. The *Roe v. Wade* decision has been the focal point of the religious right's vendetta against women from the day the ruling was announced on August 22, 1973. (This is covered in more detail in Chapter 4.) Their determination to take control of childbearing out of women's hands seems to know no bounds. The religious right's inability to overturn *Roe v. Wade* entirely has led to endless restrictions on obtaining an abortion—as well as restrictions on the availability of contraceptives that would reduce the need for abortions. (See Chapter 2 for the theology-based connection.)

Since the introduction of President Obama's healthcare reform legislation, Planned Parenthood has had a target on its back. "'Taxpayers should not be subsidizing the abortion industry,' said Elizabeth Graham, the director of Texas Right to Life."[11] No matter that performing abortions is a very minor part of what Planned Parenthood does. Mostly Planned Parenthood provides a wide range of fact-based family planning services, screening for cancer and various gynecological diseases, and testing for sexually transmitted diseases (STDs). Planned Parenthood has provided these services at very low cost to low-income women who need them most.

Planned Parenthood is not alone in being targeted by religious-right legislators. According to Niles Ross, the many community health centers around the country have suffered severe cutbacks in funding from the Center for Disease Control, just when their services are needed most. Any "cost-saving" here is fantasy. We all pay dearly in many ways for a rise in unplanned pregnancies, unwanted births, communicable diseases, and untreated medical conditions.

Prior to passage of the Affordable Care Act ("Obamacare"), the Catholic bishops and their allies in Congress forced President Obama to eliminate coverage of abortion. In 2012, he agreed to conscience exemptions for strictly religious entities, which IRS calls the "integrated auxiliaries" of churches. That left the female office workers and housekeepers who staff them out of luck—and money. The cost of oral contraceptives varies but adds up over time. The IUD—although good for several years—costs $800 to $1,000 up front. Other methods are comparably expensive. Worse, most of these medications and devices are also used for non-contraceptive purposes—so that's out, too. Obama sensibly insisted that religion-controlled facilities, such as hospitals, colleges and social service agencies that serve the general public, be covered. (There are 600 hospitals and more than 200 colleges controlled by the Catholic Church, plus numerous social service agencies, such as Catholic Charities—all tax exempt and funded largely by the taxpayers through government grants and contracts. There are hundreds of thousands, perhaps millions, of employees in these hospitals and social service agencies and about 900,000 students in the colleges, all with widely varying religious beliefs, and 98% of the Catholics among them use or have used contraceptives.)[12]

Not good enough, the bishops said. They insisted that their "religious freedom" (the "freedom" to force their beliefs on those millions of religiously diverse employees and students) was under attack. So Obama backed down again, somewhat. He said all Catholic-run organizations would be exempt from providing contraceptive coverage, but the insurance companies would provide it instead, still at no cost to patients. That would have left the bishops' medieval "conscience" clear for public relations purposes.

Still not good enough, the bishops said. Even this very separate and indirect contraceptive insurance coverage was too much of an infringement on their religious liberty. Almost immediately, a private company in Colorado, Hercules Industries, whose owners happen to be Catholic, made the same claim, and a judge issued a temporary restraining order to prevent "imminent irreparable harm."[13]

Since then, religious right legislators have tried to protect such "religious liberty" at the expense of everyone else's freedom by amending the health care bill to allow employers and health care insurance providers to exclude any coverage they consider to be immoral or in violation of their religious beliefs. If they'd succeed, where would this end? Could coverage be denied for any sex-related condition some employers considered immoral or simply contrary to their religious beliefs? HIV testing? Childbirth for unmarried women? How about blood transfusions (Jehovah's Witnesses) or almost all medical care (Christian Scientists)? There would be no end to the religion-generated chaos.

Senator Roy Blunt (R-MO) introduced an amendment to institutionalize such chaos, but the U.S. Senate voted to table it on March 1, 2012. The vote was 51 to 48, which was frighteningly close on such a potentially destructive law. It appears that the controversy will end up at the Supreme Court. The Court has already expanded religious exemption privileges in employment discrimination lawsuits, so it's probably a good bet that the Court will rule in favor of the bishops.[14] Our Constitution is no protection. (See Chapter 1.)

Faith Healing Laws

The only organization dedicated to protecting children from faith-based medical neglect is CHILD, Inc. (Children's Healthcare Is a Legal Duty). It was founded by Rita and Doug Swan, former Christian Scientists, whose 18-month-old son died of meningitis when the Swans relied solely on prayer to heal him. The tragedy brought reality home to them and they have since worked relentlessly to repeal laws that validate faith healing as legitimate health care. These laws exist in many states as a result of Christian Science lobbying.

The Swans publish a newsletter that reports on their legislative efforts and on cases of child mistreatment, suffering, and death when parents rely solely on prayer for healing. (To get it, contact CHILD at www.childrenshealthcare.org.) The newsletter is heartbreaking as well as infuriating.

When CHILD began its work, Nebraska was the only state without a religious exemption in its child abuse or neglect laws, thanks to the legislative initiative of Senator Ernie Chambers.[15] To date, CHILD has succeeded in removing religious exemptions in six states: Hawaii, Oregon, Massachusetts, Maryland, South Dakota and North Carolina. Two other states, Mississippi and West Virginia, have no religious exemptions from immunizations. Only Mississippi allows a religious exemption from metabolic testing. (This simple pinprick of a blood test on a newborn can indicate the presence of a condition that causes mental retardation if not treated quickly, yet Mississippi permits parents to refuse it for religious reasons.) The worst states are those with a religious defense to manslaughter or negligent homicide charges. They are Ohio, Iowa, Idaho, Arkansas, and West Virginia.

Other states have an unsatisfying mix of exemptions and non-exemptions. For example, Washington state requires parents to provide "medically necessary health care" as part of its criminal mistreatment law. However, it then says, "It is the intent of the legislature that a person who, in good faith, is furnished Christian Science treatment by a duly accredited Christian Science practitioner in lieu of medical care is not considered deprived of medically necessary health care or abandoned." Astonishingly, this says in effect that Christian Science prayer is equivalent to medical care. In defense of the Washington state legislature's overall sanity, if not due diligence, this exemption was added secretly in a conference committee's reconciliation of house and senate healthcare bills. It was then accepted by the legislature with no indication that most legislators were aware of the addition. Sadly, the secretly added exemption was used as a defense by a couple who let their son die slowly and horribly of a ruptured appendix in 2009. They were members of the Church of the Firstborn and claimed the law's exemption for Christian Science should apply to them also. The parents were convicted of manslaughter, but ended up getting probation.[16]

One has to wonder how any state could allow this barbaric abuse of children. I found out how this happened when a faith healing death in Minnesota spurred me to become a lobbyist for CHILD as they challenged Minnesota's faith healing laws. Below is the story. It is discouraging.[17]

What It's Like to Challenge Faith-Healing Laws

"We have a statute that says that?!" That stunned comment by a legislator was one of the few rational responses I got when I began what I thought was a no-brainer lobbying campaign on behalf of CHILD to repeal Minnesota's faith healing statutes, which exempt faith healing parents from prosecution for medical neglect of children. What should have been a simple task became a five-year slog through mind-numbing legislative cluelessness and timidity.

It started in 1989 and ended with very little success in 1994. The project was a response to the death from diabetes of 11-year-old Ian Lundman when his Christian Science mother and stepfather relied solely on prayer to treat his illness. I was joined in the lobbying effort by CHILD member Steve Petersen, who worked diligently, and by George Erickson, also a CHILD member, with assistance from the American Civil Liberties Union-Minnesota.

Rita Swan warned me not to expect much from liberal legislators, although one would think they would be supportive. I found that both the liberal left and the conservative right were more concerned with protecting parents' religious freedom than the lives of children. There were exceptions, of course, as illustrated by the above quotation. The liberal legislator I'm quoting was horrified that statutes existed saying faith healing is legitimate healthcare. I did get two of the top ranking liberal Democratic legislators to sponsor our bill to repeal the statutes. Senator Jane Ranum sponsored it in the senate, and Representative Phil Carruthers did the same in the house. They were tenacious. We also had the support of Sen. Bill Luther (later elected to Congress, now retired from public life), who helped with lobbying and witnesses' testimony.

Rita and Doug brought witnesses to testify about the tragic consequences of statutes that give parents permission to let their kids die by relying solely on prayer. Ian Lundman's biological father, who had been living in another state, came to testify, carrying his son's baseball glove. His testimony—and many others'—was wrenching, but did no good. Compassion and common sense went out the window when religion came in the door.

For example, Rita was asked to describe Christian Science beliefs. She was professional and gave an unemotional, straightforward, textbook account of the belief system. (That system consists of not admitting that disease exists. The "treatment" for an illness is a prayer that refuses to acknowledge the illness, for only by acknowledging it can it come into existence.) The legislators listened, and then one of them accused her of bashing religion! One legislative staff member said to me, "Well, doctors don't cure everyone either." (No, but their track record sure beats a system that denies illness exists.) The ignorance (much of it willful) was astounding.

I saw the medical examiner's photos of Ian's body. He was extremely emaciated, like a corpse dragged out of a Nazi extermination camp. Yet, when Ian's grandmother testified, she said, "I was with Ian the day before he died, and he looked just fine to me." No doubt he did. Her religion had so deadened her to reality that she could not allow herself to see what was in front of her, and so she didn't.

Our bill had to get through two committees, one chaired by Senator John Marty and one by Senator Allen Spear. Both could not bring themselves to infringe on the beliefs of well-meaning Christian Science parents ... Not even when one Christian Science woman pleaded with legislators to keep in place the faith healing statutes because, if they repealed them, she would not be allowed to let her child die. This astonishing statement did not seem to horrify the legislators at all. That children in faith healing families were being denied the equal protection of the law regarding medical care seemed not to concern them. Of course, neither committee recommended passage of our bill.

Our sponsors, Senator Ranum and Representative Carruthers, tried very hard to get something useful passed. In the end, against opposition from legislators determined to protect religious beliefs, they achieved a partial victory when faith healing parents were required to report a sick child. How those parents could do that without acknowledging that the illness exists, I have no idea, but at least they were made accountable—for reporting.

The political power of this small religion is astounding. Christian Science has too few members to affect the outcome of an election, yet legislators readily accede to the church's requests for preferential treatment. For example, Congress granted the Christian Scientists a special copyright extension of 75 years in 1971—the copyright would have run out in 1973—for the Christian Science bible, *Science and Health.* This is the only time the government has ever granted a special copyright extension. (In 1987, a federal district court ruled it unconstitutional under the Establishment Clause.) And such preferential treatment doesn't end with statutes. Christian Science lobbyists approach insurance companies and ask for coverage for their prayer "treatment" based on the exemption statutes. And they get it. Then they go back to the legislators for stronger exemptions based on the insurance coverage. And they get it. During the 2009–10 debate on health care reform, they came close to getting the law to cover prayer "treatment." That provision was removed after pressure from CHILD members, but attempts to include it at the state level continue, as state governments develop essential benefits packages.

As part of the federal Affordable Care Act, the government offers states a number of plans from which they can select a "benchmark plan." This is a template to be used by a state's insurance carriers. At least one of the policies each carrier offers must be identical to the benchmark plan. One of the plans on offer is the Federal Government Employee Health Association Plan. It includes coverage for Christian Science prayer "treatments." Colorado has already chosen it as one of its three plans. The governor has been lobbied by the Christian Science Church to choose it as its benchmark plan. With 50 states choosing plans, it is highly probable that payment for prayers will be part of a good number of state plans. Not many people will pay attention to this, and not many legislators will stop to think how this state validation of prayer as medical care will encourage faith-healing parents to rely solely on it, with inevitable tragic results.[18]

Then there are the Christian Science nursing homes. They provide only basic custodial care. They don't take temperatures or do anything else that might suggest a disease exists. Yet patients get this care at no cost through Medicare, whereas they would have to pay several thousand dollars a month for custodial care in any non-Christian Science facility. This is because Medicare covers only care that requires skilled nursing services—except for Christian Science facilities.

Christian Science did suffer a temporary setback in 1997 when U.S. Attorney General Janet Reno opposed tax support for Christian Science nursing homes. Another temporary setback came when a federal court ruled that Medicare-Medicaid payments for Christian Science nursing homes were "unconstitutional, invalid, unenforceable."

However, Christian Science advocates in the U.S. Senate continued to seek tax-funded faith healing, and in 1998 they prevailed. In 2000, CHILD lost the battle entirely when the Supreme Court ruled that faith healing is "a subset of medical care." Both the 8th and 9th Circuit Courts of Appeals have upheld Medicare funding for Christian Science nursing homes and the U.S. Supreme Court has refused to hear those cases. So, absurd as it is, yes, we have statutes mandating taxpayer funding for faith healing, and at the same time statutes exempting from prosecution those who allow children to die because of it.

End of Life Decision-Making

You may think you have a right to make your own end-of-life decisions—after all, who knows your situation better than you? Well, there are people who are sure they know better, and they are determined that their "know better" attitude be enshrined in law—that you must be forced to follow their dictates. Here's that "know better" attitude spelled out in the "infallible" (even though entirely speculative) doctrines of the U.S. Catholic Bishops' "Ethical and Religious Directives for Catholic Health Care, Part Five, Issues in Care for the Seriously Ill and Dying":

> The truth that life is a precious gift from God has profound implications for the question of stewardship over human life. We are not the owners of our lives and, hence, do not have absolute power over life. We have a duty to preserve our life and to use it for the glory of God, but the duty to preserve life is not absolute, for we may reject life-prolonging procedures that are insufficiently beneficial or excessively burdensome. Suicide and euthanasia are never morally acceptable options.[19]

So, you see, you don't own your life, the bishops do, and you just have to take their word for it that they are authorized by God, through the pope, to dictate the conditions of this ownership. They think suffering is good for you in a spiritual way, and they will do their best to see that the laws of the land force you to suffer, even when you're in hideous pain with no prospect of recovery. Fortunately, the laws are changing, but we still have a long way to go before our end-of-life decisions become our own and not the bishops'.

Not too long ago, there were seldom any end-of-life decisions to make. Nature made them for us. Pneumonia was once called "the old man's friend" because it ended a suffering person's life fairly quickly. Then came medical advances that led to the control and even the cure of many diseases, but sometimes had the unintended consequence of allowing one's dying to be extended with an endless array of often-unwanted life-support equipment and medications.

For the chronically ill and suffering, release into death was impossible because our laws denied that physicians could reasonably have a duty to help their patients die when it was no longer possible to help them live. Organizations promoting the right to physician-assisted dying began forming. Some people took matters into their own hands by assisting a suffering loved one's death. Some were prosecuted for this, but sympathetic juries tended to go light on punishment. In the 1970s, Derek Humphry, a British journalist, helped his cancer-ridden wife die peacefully. He escaped prosecution and went on to organize the Hemlock Society (now called Compassion and Choices) to work for the right to physician-assisted dying. Other groups followed. Humphry has since published a best-selling book, *Final Exit*, which describes methods of self-deliverance.

In the 1990s, Dr. Jack Kevorkian, a Michigan pathologist who was known for supporting voluntary euthanasia (Greek for "good death"), opened up public debate on the issue in an attention-getting way. He developed a "death machine" that ensured a quick, painless, self-administered death from inhaled chemicals. Dr. Kevorkian advertised his services and charged no fees. He never lacked for volunteers, assisting about 130 desperate people during a ten-year period. After defying many legal attempts to stop him, he was finally arrested after appearing on the CBS Television show, "60 Minutes." On that episode he showed a videotape he had made of the self-deliverance of Thomas Youk. Although the death was clearly voluntary, wanted, and rational (as attested on the video by Youk himself), Dr. Kevorkian was charged with second degree murder and the delivery of a controlled substance. He was tried in 1999 and sentenced to 10–25 years in prison but released after eight years. He died an unassisted death of natural causes in 2011.

An HBO movie, "You Don't Know Jack," accurately dramatizes his stubborn insistence on the right to die on one's own terms, and his willingness to break the law and pay the price for forcing the issue to public attention. Dr. Kevorkian had hoped to have his murder conviction go to the U.S. Supreme Court for a ruling on its constitutionality. The Court refused to hear the case, but Dr. Kevorkian did succeed in raising public awareness of this issue and, consequently, increased public acceptance of a physician-assisted death. Along with that increased awareness came an increase in membership in organizations advocating physician aid in dying. Most such organizations worked to change state laws, but one—Final Exit Network (FEN)—focused on helping people perform self-deliverance (to the extent the law allowed), because the needs of the suffering, incurably ill were urgent and it would be years before the laws changed—if they ever did.

The Supreme Court had ruled earlier that states could experiment with "death with dignity" laws, although getting state legislators to allow physician-assisted dying has been almost impossible. The issue is clouded by a great deal of religion-instigated fear-mongering propaganda about slippery slopes and Nazi-like euthanizing of disabled people. To date, only Oregon, Washington and Montana have death-with-dignity laws. The people of the first state out of this box—Oregon—had to vote for their Death with Dignity Act twice, once to pass it and then to vote down the opponents' proposal to repeal it. The repeal was defeated 60 to 40 percent. Then U.S. Attorney General John Ashcroft (a religious-right zealot) tried to kill the Oregon law by threatening to prosecute doctors under the federal Controlled Substances Act. The Supreme Court ruled against this 6-3 on the basis that medical practice is traditionally regulated by the states. The Oregon approach, with its popular appeal, successful implementation, and problem-free track record made it easier for other states to follow, although only two others have, and with resistance from authoritarian religions all the way.

On November 4, 2011, the state of Georgia arrested and held for prosecution four volunteers from Final Exit Network on a charge of assisting a suicide. This assistance amounted to nothing more than giving advice and emotional support to someone who wanted to self-deliver, who was mentally competent, and whose medical condition had been verified as serious, debilitating, and irreversible. In addition to arresting the four volunteers, the state froze Final Exit Network's assets and persuaded law enforcement authorities in Arizona, Maryland, and Ohio to raid the homes of other Network volunteers and confiscate their computers and records. No surprise so far.

Then there was a surprise. It came in February 2012 when the Georgia Supreme Court ruled that Georgia's law prohibited physician-assisted dying only when it involved a publicly advertised offer to provide that service, as in Dr. Kevorkian's case. As long as the physician had not made such public announcements and the assistance was kept confidential, physician aid in dying was a private family matter and legal. The only thing the Final Exit Network volunteers could be charged with was talking to their client—and that was free speech protected by the Constitution.

So there it stood, but not for long. As expected, the Georgia legislature acted quickly to pass a restrictive law that would be constitutional. Attorney Robert Rivas explained it in the Spring 2012 Final Exit Network newsletter:

> The ruling opened for Georgia the opportunity to enact a law criminalizing assisting in a suicide, like those of many states. The General Assembly of Georgia set out to pass such a law at lightning speed, compared to their usual snail's pace, and Georgia lawmakers thanked the Catholic Conference and Georgia Right to Life for their help in hurriedly drafting the new statute. . . . The draft defines "assist" as "the act of physically helping or physically providing the means" to commit suicide. This definition, clearer than defining words in other states, would protect Final Exit Network's volunteers from being charged in future Georgia cases. . . . In contrast, the laws of some states are obtuse when they prohibit "aiding" or "assisting" in a suicide. Some state laws provide definitions that are downright hostile or threatening to FEN's mission. Minnesota, for instance, makes a criminal of anyone who "intentionally advises, encourages, or assists another in taking the other's own life," language that would be unconstitutionally overbroad if it is interpreted to prohibit FEN from providing information, education, and emotional support to members in the hour when they most need it.

Yes, indeed, and that is exactly what happened here in Minnesota. In May 2012, Final Exit Network and four of its volunteers were indicted on 17 counts of assisting the suicide of a 57-year-old Twin Cities woman who self-delivered in 2007.[20] She was in great pain from an irreversible, untreatable condition, and left a letter explaining her determination to end her agony. She called on FEN for information and guidance, which they provided. FEN will probably have to spend thousands of dollars defending its right to extend compassion to those who ask for it, need it and desperately want it. Somehow this is considered criminal. The person or persons who called in the police, obviously preferring to see this woman suffer as long as possible, will not be charged for invading her privacy and dishonoring her desire to die on her own terms. Only those who cared about her enough to help her will be dragged through the court system.

Meanwhile, other laws impede one's right to die with dignity. People who self-deliver without a doctor's help can certainly do so, but there are insurance laws that can make it impossible without the survivors' being penalized financially. Also, emergency medical personnel are required by law to revive a person who is clearly trying to self-deliver, but has not yet succeeded. Tattooing "Do Not Resuscitate" on your chest is no protection. Only a medical form for that, signed by a doctor, and readily at hand for the paramedics, will work.[21]

No Secular Justification

Where is the secular justification for laws that deprive individuals of the right to control their own medical decisions? And what is a valid conscience exemption? Unfortunately, those who follow their consciences sometimes do awful things. Anti-abortion zealots murder doctors and nurses who dare to provide abortions. Faith-healing believers let their children die of medical neglect.

Our legislatures have passed conscience-exemption laws to ensure that "I was just following orders" (the Nazis' defense at the Nuremburg trials) is no longer a defense. Yet now, for end-of-life procedures, we can be subjected to torture at the hands of others who are just following their personal religious beliefs. When does the conscience exemption become not only barbaric but absurd? Anti-abortion "pharmacists for life" refuse to dispense birth control pills (that reduce the need for abortion). Muslim cab drivers refuse to pick up passengers at airports if they are carrying liquor or are accompanied by service dogs. Christian cab drivers refuse to drive women to abortion clinics. Can a Jew or Muslim refuse to work with pork—even as a cashier ringing up sales? What about a Hindu required to sell slaughtered beef?

Conscience exemptions should apply only if demonstrable harm results from not following one's conscience. That was the intent of conscience-exemption laws following World War II and Nazi medical experiments on Jews, and it should remain the sole intent. Otherwise, should grocery store checkout counters post signs that say, "Muslim checker on duty. Please do not bring pork products through this line?" Should medical personnel wear color-coded name tags identifying them as currently giving treatment only according to their particular doctrine, regardless of the patient's needs? Should hospitals post signs at admission desks spelling out the treatments they will refuse to give for doctrinal reasons? Should patient admission sheets specify that they are not to be seen or treated by any medical personnel whose color-coded name tag indicates they will be denied treatment for their condition? Why should we have to accommodate mystical, unverifiable beliefs at all?

If such beliefs are so important to some believers that they cannot do the required job, they should find a different job. The United States would do well to adopt the position of the health ministry in Norway. Faced with "conscience" demands, it has refused to budge. As their Secretary of Health, Robin KŒss, said, "If you're a pacifist, you can't work as a police officer. If you refuse to perform a blood transfusion, you can't be a surgeon. If you deny a patient contraception or a referral for an abortion, you can't be a general physician."[22]

As for hospitals, none of them, whether or not owned or affiliated with a religious organization, should be permitted to deviate from the medical standard of care. Saying, "That would have gone against my conscience," should be no protection from failing to follow medical care standards. If a church wants to own or manage facilities for adults that do not conform with the medical standard of care, let it do so at its own expense and without pretending that it provides standard medical treatment.

Similarly, why treat faith healing as legitimate health care? It has been demonstrated over and over again that prayers for healing don't work. As Anne Nicol Gaylor, founder of Freedom From Religion Foundation, says, "The cemeteries are full of people who prayed not to die."

Is there any rational reason to defund Planned Parenthood or any other reality-based family planning service? The motivation for such defunding is based purely on religious beliefs about the "ensoulment" of fertilized eggs and the "personhood" of embryos and fetuses, and that any sexual activity that interferes with the possibility of pregnancy is immoral. (See Chapters 2 and 4.) These beliefs and their underlying doctrines are neither rational nor practical, even for a society that is entirely Catholic, much less for a religiously pluralistic nation like the United States.

Some birth control opponents would not restrict sale of contraceptives, but would deny taxpayer support for insurance that provides contraceptives free with no co-pays. They object to funding sexual pleasure that does not allow for childbearing. Leaving aside the idiotic theology-based notion that there is something wrong with non-childbearing sexual pleasure (see Chapter 2), is there a secular justification here? Hardly. On the contrary, wider use of contraceptives would save lives, mostly because pregnancy itself carries risks of death. In addition, many women have health, financial, or social problems that make pregnancy unwise or even potentially disastrous. The economic costs to taxpayers of such pregnancies and their complications can be substantial in terms of direct costs, lost income, and disability payments. And then there are the massive costs to society of the nutrition, housing, medical, and educational expenses of children who are the result of unwanted pregnancies. Taxpayer funded contraceptives are by far the cheapest insurance against such outcomes.

In any rational view, free contraception would seem to be a necessity. Clearly, nothing but misery comes from government policies that reduce the availability and affordability of family planning services. (And let's not even get started on the horrifying prospects of further overpopulating an already overpopulated world.)

End-of-life decision-making should be a civil right. There is no rational, secular underpinning for laws denying this right. They are based solely on doctrinal beliefs that suffering has spiritual merit and that only some imagined god can determine when one's life is to end. Our bodies belong to us, not to the church and not to the state. The role of government should be only to ensure that the person requesting a physician assisted death is mentally competent, not being coerced, has considered the decision thoroughly, and is suffering from an incurable condition that is unbearable for that person. And tattooing "Do Not Resuscitate" on one's chest should be all the instruction paramedics need.

Reality and personal autonomy must be determining factors. Religion-based health care denies both, based as it is on unverifiable magical thinking. It should have no place in our secular laws.

Postscript: Death with Dignity

I am including the following story because Annie Chase would have wanted me to, and because it is satisfying to see that the human species really does include people like Annie—grounded in reality, intelligent, decent, caring, and thoughtful, who know how to live and how to die, and who bring meaning and purpose into a meaningless universe.

Annie Chase (born 1946), is now, in her words, "one lucky stiff," after achieving her self-deliverance on Monday, March 8, 2010. Annie wanted her story told to encourage more open discussion of the right to a self-directed death. She began writing her thoughts in January 2010 and completed them with an audio recording as her failing eyesight made using a computer difficult. Her last recording was on March 8, as she prepared her self-deliverance. She gave her written and recorded materials to me to condense and compile into what became a 32-page booklet: *My Purpose Driven Death: How I Became One Lucky Stiff*. The following is an excerpt. Because of religion-based laws Annie had to die alone to avoid legally jeopardizing those she loved. At least she knew her family and friends were with her in their thoughts.

HELLOOOO FROM THE "OTHER SIDE"! Annie Chase here. As I write this I am pretending to speak from the Great Beyond. No afterlife is involved, just a literary construct to help me address a topic I've found is difficult to discuss because it involves unpreventable sadness and loss. The topic is Death. Because many people are not at ease discussing either their own death or someone else's, they miss the opportunity to shape their final stage of life to their own desires and ethics, and to convey their wishes to those who love them. This is a sad but preventable loss.

From my perspective, I could see death's necessary inevitability as part of the terrible, wrenching beauty of life. The choice isn't whether to die. No one is exempt from that One-Death-Per-Birth rule. I am that lucky stiff who got to choose some of the specific features of the experience. I wanted to make it a fulfilling, consciously enacted final stage of the only life I would ever have. Metaphorically speaking, I didn't want my approaching union with the debonair Mr. Oblivion to be solemnized in a hasty 2 a.m. shotgun wedding, with a few glum family members in their bathrobes looking on. I didn't want my one-and-only death to be a forcible abduction by a barely-glimpsed stalker who sneaked up and conked me on the head before dragging me off to his rude hovel.

I got inklings that my life's "best if used by" date was becoming gradually decipherable, like the fortunes that float murkily up to the little window in a Crazy 8-Ball oracular device. In 2005, after years of occasional, sudden and puzzling symptoms, I was diagnosed with Wegener's Granulomatosis, a degenerative disorder similar to lupus. When in an active phase, it can flare up in sporadic, unpredictable periods of debilitating fatigue, dizziness, joint pain and weakness; extreme sensitivity to light, noise, heat and cold; rapidly-growing and randomly appearing tumors; and sometimes, as in my case, loss of sight. About a year ago, the unmistakable signs of rapid reduction of my visual capacity made it necessary to consider whether to continue To Be or Not To Be. I also had to decide how soon I must act or how long I could safely wait to do so, since I would need my eyes to research and carry out my exit plan.

I owned my body. As long as I was of sound mind, and acting of my own volition in my own behalf, and as long as I was not endangering anyone else in the process, no one but me had the right to decide anything about what I did or didn't do with that body of mine. I was single and fiercely independent, with no one reliant on me for support. Beginning with my life-long, voracious appetite for books, almost all the activities that were meaningful to me depended on the use of my eyes. I had no willingness to re-learn every small, daily survival skill to live as a non-sighted person, bereft of reading and art and dance performances and fall color and unfettered mobility. That was my decision, and mine alone to make. Others may choose a different destiny, and I had nothing but the greatest admiration for those who found fulfillment in dealing courageously with a debilitating disease or physical impairment. They deserve full support, respect and love.

In recent years, some people had begun talking openly about end of life options, including the right to die and the recent availability in some states of medically assisted death. That was a start, but it didn't cover what I wanted to avoid-suffering, loss of control over my body and life circumstances or allowing some outside "expert" or a panel of them to dictate the terms of my experience of the all-important last stage of my life. I wanted practical information and a dependable method of ending my life. The book *Final Exit* by Derek Humphry was invaluable—straightforward, simple and reassuring. It offered several dignified procedures and explained why some methods many people (including me) first called to mind were not good at all. I recommend that everyone obtain that book. How in the world could the right to die not be a basic human right? I saw how badly the right-to-die movement was needed but, of course, there was a huge oppositional movement that said only God gets to strike us down or take us home to his eternal loving bosom, or both.

In May of 2009, it became clear that I was losing my sight and it was time to plan it being my last trip around the sun. As I peeled away the onion layers of accumulated possessions, I also simplified my finances. I turned most of my valuable things and accounts into cash. I knew how much I needed to live on for the remaining time. Wow! I was rich! It turned out that being rich didn't have anything to do with how much money it was. It was the sense of ease and freedom because I had more than I needed. What I had enough for was to make the money and treasured possessions emblematic of almost another form of immortality. My resources went a long way and covered a lot of needs when it was divided into chunks of a few hundred, or a thousand, or in a couple of cases, even a few thousand dollars, all directed to helping—to having the joy of helping—mostly younger people get a better start.

It turned out to be so much fun. What bliss, what freedom, an absolute sense of being on a total lark! A hugely enjoyable part of my life began at that point. I started cherishing everything, thinking in terms of the last trip around the sun. I started looking at the seasonal things I was enjoying and experiencing for the final time. Everything from the last ride on one of the best roller coasters at Valley Fair. . . . the last time I would see the fall leaves change color. . . . the last time I would eat a Colorado peach. . . . the last really good watermelon. . . . the last Michigan cherry.

When I realized the plan needed to go ahead there was a tiny bit of relief because I realized that I'd made this plan and it was mine and I really did want to be able to carry it out and I really did want it to be an emblem of what can happen if you take matters into your own hands. I knew I was down to about the last month that I would be here. I had to make some decisions—about my son, for example. He had not wanted to hear much about this. His body language told me he was resistant to the information that I was going to be leaving, but I wanted to consciously have those last parts of my time with him. I decided to tell him the specifics of the plan, but not the day and time.

One of the most wrenching things for me was on the day I carried out my plan. My son had stayed with me the night before. We had talked about it and I knew he at least accepted the reality of what I was going to do. He hadn't fully accepted that it was entirely necessary, but he seemed to be OK with it. We got up that morning, my last day, and I needed to pretend it wasn't my last day, and I needed to not break down when (I thought) he's blissfully unaware that his mother is hugging him for the last time.

There were some sad things—unavoidably sad things—but even those sad things were so much easier to handle when I was deciding to handle them. What is true is that everybody who is born will die. And what is true is that, during the time between the being born and the dying, our lives and the lives of everybody around us can be profoundly affected by our smallest actions, our smallest decisions, our smallest little meannesses and holding back, our smallest acts of kindness and generosity. They all matter. They all matter so much. And, realizing what a precious incredible privilege it was to have a human form, to be in human form-though painful as hell-I wouldn't have missed it for anything.

During the last two weeks I realized it was time to tell more people. It was an emotional last two weeks because people were breaking down and crying, and I was breaking down and crying for them-for them-in their sorrow. And yet, for me, a healing sort of detachment had begun to set in. I felt more keenly than ever-although it had been a factor during all that last year-my freedom. I realized I didn't need to be concerned about anything that was going to happen. I knew I was engaged in the pain of other people's having to release me, but I felt released, I felt wonderfully released with each such encounter.

MARCH 8, 2010. Now I've finished talking as a disembodied spirit from the "great beyond." This is me now. This is me, Annie Chase, on my last day of life at about a quarter to 5 in the afternoon on March 8, 2010. I woke up this morning, ate a light breakfast and prepared for what I would be doing in the evening. In about another hour I'm going to eat a light meal so I have something on my stomach, nothing too heavy. I'm going to write a letter to my grandson in the next hour or so, telling him how much he's been a bright light in my life, and telling him I hope he is not angry at me for not making clear when our final goodbye was.

Now I'm down to the last few hours of my time here on Earth. I have a certain anticipation, a little bit of apprehension, kind of a fluttery feeling in my stomach. It's a little bit like the time my sister kept barring me with her arm from getting on the roller coaster until we could be in the very front seat. I'm in the very front seat of this roller coaster. It hesitates at the top of the hill so I can have a last look out over the whole sun drenched, shimmering active world of this amusement park. I look around and I see I've already been on the Laugh in the Dark ride. I've already gone in the Fun House and looked at myself in a whole bunch of—I hope—distorting mirrors. I've been scrambled on the Scrambler ride. I've been caught in the grip of the Octopus ride.

I've been saving the roller coaster for last. The biggest thrill. The wheels on the front of this roller coaster are just about to go over the little bump at the very top of the hill. I know that as it starts to plunge down and gather speed I will surrender to it. I'll surrender to the free fall. At the end of the free fall will be—nothing. Nothing. David Byrne's song about heaven said, "Heaven is a place where nothing happens." I'm not scared. I'm not scared of that kind of nothing. I know that nothing really is not something. . . . Love to you all.

(Annie's booklet, *My Purpose Driven Death,* is available for $5 ppd. from Atheists For Human Rights, 5146 Newton Ave. N., Minneapolis MN 55430).

1. Quoted in *No Greater Love*, Becky Benenate, Thomas Moore, and Joseph Durepos, editors. New World Library, Novato, California, 2002.

2. See www.thepublicdiscourse.com/2012/04/5306/

3. http://www.cbsnews.com/2100-50036_162-2718947.html.

4. Michels KB. Xue F. Colditz GA. Willett WC., "Induced and spontaneous abortion and incidence of breast cancer among young women; a prospective cohort study." archives of *Internal Medicine*, 2007 Apr 23; 167(8):814-20, abstract online at http://www.ncbi.nlm.nih.gov/pubmed/17452545.

5. Nancy Cruzan was 25 years old when a car accident on Jan. 11, 1983, damaged her brain severely, leaving her in a persistent vegetative state. Her parents wanted to remove life support and allow her to die, but the state of Missouri intervened in opposition with a court ruling, assuming it had a priority interest that encompassed the sanctity of life and its prolongation. The case went to the U.S. Supreme Court, which supported Missouri's contention that convincing evidence that a comatose person wanted life support removed. On Dec. 14, 1990, the case went to a Missouri circuit court for review after three people came forward with the convincing evidence needed. The court then ruled that life support could be removed. This was done and Cruzan died on Dec. 27, 1990. Source: "Courts and the End of Life-The Case Of Nancy Cruzan, http://www.libraryindex.com/pages/3143/Courts-End-Life-CASE-NANCY-CRUZAN.html.

6. Amanda Lee Myers, "Arizona hospital loses Catholic status over surgery to end woman's pregnancy," Associated Press, Dec. 21, 2010, and Rob Boston, "Medical Emergency: Catholic Hospitals Usurp Patients' Rights," *The Humanist,* March-April 2011.

7. United States Conference of Catholic Bishops, "Ethical and Religious Directives for Catholic Health Care Services," Fifth Edition, USCCB, Nov. 17, 2009.

8. Examples of the medieval theology for this: In *Casti Connubii*, Pope Pius XI said, "However we may pity the mother whose health and even life is imperiled by the performance of her natural duty, there yet remains no sufficient reason for condoning the direct murder of the innocent." Not to be outdone, the Lutheran Philip Melancthon (Martin Luther's associate), said (quoted by Madalyn Murray O'Hair in Women and Atheism: "If a woman weary of bearing children, that matters not. Let her only die from bearing, she is there to do it." (Fortunately, most Lutheran churches have given up on this misogynistic view.)

9. United States Conference of Catholic Bishops, op cit.

10. Ibid.

11. Thanh Tan, texastribune.org, "Planned Parenthood Struggles After State Budget Cuts," *New York Times*, www.nytimes.com, October 15, 2011.

12. Catholics for Choice (http://www.catholicsforchoice.org). Also: Katha Pollitt, "Bishops vs. Women: Which Side is Obama On?", *The Nation*, Nov. 30, 2011, reprinted on the Catholics for Choice web site.

13. http://www.lawweekonline.com/2012/07/judge-blocks-contraceptive-coverage-mandate-for-colorado-company/

14. Robert Pear, *New York Times*, "Obama: No exemption on rule for birth control," reprinted in the Minneapolis *Star Tribune*, Jan. 21, 2012, p. A3.

15. See "Sen. Ernie Chambers, a Solo Act in Negraska" at http://www.npr/templates/
story/story.php?storyId=5170002 and "Ernie Chambers poised for another swing at the
Legislature" at http://journalstar.com/news/local/ernie-chambers-poised-for-another-...
and "Nebraska State Senator Sues God" at http://newsone.com/nation/associatedpress3/
nebraska-state-senator-sues-god/

16. Rita Swan, "Washington State parents sentenced in teen's faith death," published in the
No. 1, 2012 newsletter of Children's Healthcare Is a Legal Duty (CHILD). See http://www.
childrenshealthcare.org.

17. Reported in detail over the time span of the case in the newsletters of Minnesota
Atheists, *Secular Nation* (now *Secular World*), published by Atheist Alliance Intl.
(now Atheist Alliance of America), and in "Running in Place," a history of the atheist
movement from the 1980s to 2010, published by Atheists For Human Rights (AFHR). All
publications are archived at AFHR headquarters, Minneapolis, MN.

18. Swan, Rita, CHILD letter to members, August 23, 2012.

19. United States Conference of Catholic Bishops, op cit.

20. Katie Humphrey, "Legal fight looms in suicide case," *Minneapolis Star Tribune*, May 15,
2012, p. B1. Maricella Miranda, "Right-to-die group indicted in 2007 Apple Valley death,"
St. Paul Pioneer Press, May 15, 2012, p. 1A.

21. See http://finalexit.org/chronology_right-to-die_events.html. See also a Pew Forum
on Religion & Public Life article, "The Right-to-Die Debate and the Tenth Anniversary of
Oregon's Death with Dignity Act" by David Masci, Oct. 10, 2007, at http://pewresearch.
org/pubs/609/right-to-die.

22. "Doctors can't opt out of abortion duties: ministry." Published: 14 Feb 2012 at http://
www.thelocal.no/page/view/doctors-cant-opt-out-of-abortion-duties.

6

No Right to Know:
Science, Education & Free Expression

You shall know the truth and the truth shall make you free.

—Gospel of John 8:32

What is truth and how can we know it? The only reliable way is by being open to new ideas, verifying the credibility of their sources, applying the scientific method of rigorous and repeated observation, testing, and peer review, always allowing that additional facts may require some changes in our understanding.

The vast majority of people in developed countries have abandoned religion-based claims about how the world works. Except in certain fundamentalist circles, the Earth is no longer flat, nor is it the center of the universe. Diseases are no longer caused by demons, and natural disasters are not expressions of God's wrath. The most contentious notions still with us are about zygote personhood, genital complementarity, and the fanciful biblical story of creation. All are front-burner political issues and will remain so until the realization sinks in that these are sectarian religious concepts that have no place in the laws of our secular government.

Every religion looks at the world and at human behavior and makes claims. But based on what? On subjective assumptions and imaginative fantasies about supernatural realms and deities that are impossible to verify, even if they weren't mutually as well as internally contradictory. Throughout history, objective investigations of religious claims have always disproved them. Despite this, deity-dependent religious beliefs have become so embedded in our society that they are rarely questioned. Politicians routinely run for office claiming deeply held religious beliefs that supposedly attest to their moral principles. Yet no one dares examine those beliefs in a public discussion. Pointing out the bizarre doctrinal underlay of so many of our harmful laws, or questioning why religion is sacrosanct and supposedly worthy of taxpayer subsidies, is called "religion bashing." The truth that would set us free from harmful laws and policies is lost in a dense fog of self-censorship and phony outrage. Because of this, education and scientific research continue to be compromised by ideologies whose self-serving goal is indoctrination, not education.

Scientific Knowledge and Education

Ever since Charles Darwin proposed the theory of evolution, proponents of the biblical creation story have waged a relentless battle to keep evolution from being taught in public schools. With courts consistently ruling against the teaching of creationism, religious fundamentalists have tried to get it into science classes by renaming it "intelligent design," hoping to disguise its biblical foundation through reference to an unspecified designer. (Guess who.) Since that approach also has failed, they have been trying to weaken acceptance of the theory of evolution by having textbooks designate it as questionable, the (false) implication being that scientists are divided or are unsure of the theory's validity. In Tennessee in 2010, the legislature passed a bill allowing students to challenge the theory of evolution and also climate change without being penalized academically. (This, needless to say, places religious dogma and know-nothing assertions on the same level as science.) Essentially the same legislation has passed in Florida, Texas, Missouri, Kentucky, Oklahoma, New Mexico and Louisiana. Although, due to Supreme Court rulings, these laws go nowhere, they still cause considerable damage by inciting controversy and costing taxpayers money in the states' legal defense of these sure-to-lose bills. As a consequence of this religious hysteria, some science teachers discuss evolution reluctantly and minimally or not at all to avoid stirring up controversy. As a result, the United States ranks poorly in scientific literacy. As *Church & State*, the newsletter of Americans United for the Separation of Church and State, reported in its July–August 2011 issue:

> Polling data has consistently shown soft support for evolution in the United States. A Gallup poll issued late in 2010 found that 38 percent of Americans backed what might be called "theistic evolution"—the idea that humans developed over millions of years from less advanced forms with guidance from God. An additional 16 percent said they believe in development over time with no input from God. The remaining 40 percent backed creationism and

said they believe "God created human beings pretty much in their present form at one time within the last 10,000 years or so.[1]

To put those figures in perspective, the United States ranks next to last in support of evolution among 34 countries, only slighter better than Turkey, which ranked last in a survey by *Science* magazine.[2] In regard to scientific literacy in this area, the top dozen countries are Iceland, Denmark, Sweden, France, Japan, United Kingdom, Norway, Belgium, Spain, Germany, Italy, and The Netherlands. The dozen at the bottom of the barrel were Slovak Republic, Poland, Austria, Croatia, Romania, Greece, Bulgaria, Lithuania, Latvia, Cyprus, United States, Turkey. You might be wondering how the United States could rank that low. Consider that, for the 2012–2013 school year in Louisiana, Governor Bobby Jindal signed a bill into law that allows school voucher money to be transferred from public schools to Christian fundamentalist schools whose "science" curriculum suggests that the Loch Ness Monster actually exists. It supposedly is a dinosaur that was tracked by a submarine and caught by a Japanese fishing boat. One wonders what Turkey must be teaching to beat that one to earn its bottom-of-the-list booby prize.[3]

Despite this embarrassing ranking and Supreme Court rulings that creationism by that or any other name is a religious belief and therefore cannot be taught in public school science classes, the battle continues with the fundamentalists coming up with ever more creative and confusing disguises for creationism. This is reflected in the fact that 60 percent of biology teachers in public high schools are already reluctant to teach evolution in a straightforward way.[4]

One of the serious problems with creationist attacks on evolution is that all science is thereby attacked. To question evolution is to deny the facts of physics, chemistry, geology, astronomy and all the rest, because all are related.

Scientific Knowledge and Stem Cell Research

Stem cell research holds the promise of curing Parkinson's disease, diabetes, spinal cord injuries, and other afflictions, but religion-based laws restrict it severely. Why? Because of the belief that an embryo, a microscopic cluster of cells, is a real human being, a person with an immortal soul. (See chapters 2 and 4.) Destroying these nearly invisible specks is called murder. This is human imagination run amok, while sick people pay with their health and their lives. Would finding useful alternatives to embryonic stem

cells resolve the controversy? Perhaps, but with the unacceptable consequence of establishing a precedent of allowing religious beliefs to interfere
in benign, beneficial scientific research.

As with attacks on teaching evolution, opposition to stem cell research
compromises the future of science and scientific research in the United
States. In South Korea, a global center for embryonic stem cell research
is attracting scientists from other countries (including the United States)
who don't want to deal with irrational and pointless restrictions on their
work.[5] The center has been accepting thousands of applications from of-
ten-desperate people willing to participate in tests of stem cell treatments.

The bottom line with stem cell research is that it has the potential to produce effective and, more to the point, very lucrative treatments. And that
financial appeal may eventually override religious mysticism. Consider the
business community's response to an "anti-cloning" bill introduced in the
Minnesota legislature in May 2011. The Republican CEO of a global implant company put it this way:

> I'm concerned about the ambiguous language in the bill. This whole thing
> started as a way to prevent reproductive cloning. I agree that reproductive
> cloning is not appropriate under any circumstances. But I'm concerned the
> same bill could also ban therapeutic stem-cell research . . . potential cures
> for Alzheimer's, diabetes or even certain cancers. . . . I would one day like
> to move [our] research office to Minnesota to join the rest of our U.S. op-
> erations, . . . but this proposed bill makes me nervous about the future of
> biologic research in Minnesota.[6]

Scott Fischbach, the head of the anti-abortion organization Minnesota
Citizens Concerned for Life, quoted in the same article, said in response:

> The bill says researchers should not kill life to create it. There's nothing am-
> biguous about this. We're not focused on 12 jobs in California. I represent
> 70,000 Minnesota families, and they all work and play in Minnesota. Here
> in Minnesota, we respect life. We don't kill each other in pursuit of a dollar.
> The scientific research industry wants to do whatever it wants to do. They
> want no bounds.

Researchers at the University of Minnesota agreed with the business
community, noting that the bill would inhibit work on regenerative medicine and even "criminalize" it. The bill went nowhere, but efforts to restrict
the research continue. How the controversy resolves may depend on who

can scream the loudest. There are thousands of sick people who might not think use of stem cells is the same as individuals "kill[ing] each other in pursuit of a dollar." Just as there are abortion opponents who picket clinics, then bring a daughter in to have an abortion because it's a different story when it's their own family, there are opponents of stem cell research who conveniently welcome a cure derived from stem cells when they need it for themselves.

A good example is provided in a story published in the *Washington Post* about Timothy Atchison, a 21-year-old Alabama man who faced lifelong paralysis from injuries suffered in a car accident. He volunteered for a test using embryonic stem cells to see if they could repair his spinal cord. The results have been promising and Atchison is regaining some movement. Because of his religious beliefs, he had always opposed abortion and stem cell research—until stem cells offered him a way to improve an otherwise greatly restricted future. It's a different story now. He said these cells were suddenly "different." They were leftover from fertility treatments, weren't going to end up in someone's uterus, would probably be thrown away, etc., etc. He explained it all:

> I am adamantly against abortion in any form. It did cause me some search-ing and researching biblically what is the proper answer. I don't really see a baby's life was destroyed for this to take place.[7]

So much for embryonic personhood, which indeed is not mentioned in the Bible. (But then, neither is abortion in any restrictive way.) As the *Post* article noted:

> Atchison's story reveals provocative insights into one of the most closely watched medical experiments, including what some may see as an irony: that a treatment condemned on moral and religious grounds is viewed by the first person to pioneer the therapy, and his family, as part of God's plan.

More of God's mysterious ways, no doubt. Now, if only Atchison could get pregnant . . . .

Abstinence-Only Sex Education: Lies and Wishful Thinking

In October 2011, Andy Kopsa, who writes for AlterNet, posted the re-sults of research he had done on abstinence-only sex education programs 2011. As one would expect, his research (and virtually all studies on absti-nence-only "education") showed that these programs do not work, despite all the taxpayer money funneled into them. According to Kopsa, the United States has wasted $1.5 billion over 15 years funding abstinence-only sex education programs. President George W. Bush backed these worse-than-useless programs with his Community Based Abstinence Education grants. President Obama tried to get rid of this waste of taxpayer dollars, but Congress included $250 million for failed abstinence-only programs in the Affordable Health Care Act. Here are some details from Kopsa's lengthy report:

> Study after study has revealed the ineffectiveness of abstinence-only programs in reducing the number of teen pregnancies and reducing the spread of disease. According to the Journal of Adolescent Health, virginity pledges, a staple of abstinence-only programming, not only did not decrease occurrences of teen STDs, but actually resulted in pledge-takers not seeking medical attention once infected, leading to an increased possibility of transmission.

> . . . I have covered two abstinence-only groups in the past year: Project SOS in Florida and WAIT (Why Am I Tempted?) Training, now known as the Center for Relationship Education (CRE), based in Denver. I investigated their methods, connections and over $14 million combined in federal and state grants [they received].

> The group's [SOS's] founder, Pam Mullarkey, . . . says God described Project SOS in its entirety to her over the course of five evenings. And, like so many other ab-only programs, SOS was cited for peddling erroneous medical information in its curriculum and relying on shame and fear as means of instruction.

> During an assembly in a Colorado high school, Shelley Donahue, one of WAIT/CRE's motivational speakers, . . . used a participatory activity outlined in the WAIT/CRE curriculum to show how sex prior to marriage negatively impacts a person's ability to bond to a mate in the future. Donahue had a boy join her at the front of the auditorium. She instructed him to bare his arm, then ripped a long piece of clear packing tape off a roll and held it up to the audience. Donahue applied the tape to the boy's arm and rubbed it briskly to ensure that it bonded, talking about how the tape would probably not become the boy's wife. She then ripped the tape from his arm--signifying their breakup . . . The tape was covered with bits of the boy's dried skin and hair. Donahue commented on how gross the tape was and repeated the operation over and over again. Each time the tape pulled up more debris and lost more of its ability to make a tight bond.

The implication is that the girl is now dirty, soiled for her future husband. She will go on to have problems trying to "bond" with another man. . . .

According to one Colorado blogger, an attendee of another Donahue WAIT/ CRE lecture reported that Donahue told the group that the HPV vaccine "will leave them sterile." This is a familiar lie used by the right wing based on their belief that for young women, a potentially life saving vaccine's most dangerous side effect is immorality and promiscuity. . . .[8]

Kopsa goes on to report that the Title V program recommends that grant recipients be inclusive of LGBT students and non-stigmatizing. WAIT/CRE applied for funding saying they had been vetted for inclusiveness by the American Psychological Association Gay and Lesbian Issues Team. However the APA denied having ever approved of the WAIT/CRE program.

Kopsa says that the programs he investigated are representative, and unfortunately he's right. Abstinence-only sex education programs are one of the most lucrative sources of government pork barrel funding, as Marty Klein demonstrates in *America's War on Sex: The Attack on Law, Lust and Liberty*. Here is Klein's breakdown of how extensively government subsidizes religion-based abstinence-only sex education programs.

Most of the $200,000,000 that goes to promote abstinence-only-before-marriage each year is awarded to agencies over which there is no oversight whatsoever. A huge amount of this taxpayer money goes to frankly religious organizations. Here are a few examples:

Pennsylvania:
Catholic Social Services	$46,000.00
Lutheran Social Services	$231,000.00
St. Luke's Health Network	$92,000.00
Shepherd's Maternity House	$50,000.00
Silver Ring Thing	$400,000.00

California:
Catholic Charities of California	$361,605.00

New York:
Catholic Charities of New York	$2,500,000.00

Illinois:
Roseland Christian Ministries	$800,000.00
Lawndale Christian Health Center	$461,278.00

To see which agencies are getting abstinence funding in your state and how much they are receiving, go to http://www.siecus.org/policy/states/. Almost one billion dollars has been spent on abstinence-only-until-marriage programs . . .[9]

This religion-based promotion of abstinence-only sex education is ludicrous to anyone old enough to remember the "good old days" when contraception was unreliable and no one ever admitted to having sex outside of marriage. Eight-pound babies born suspiciously soon after a marriage were charitably acknowledged by saying, "The first one can come any time. After that it takes nine months." Truthfully, and from experience, I can say that we didn't need abstinence-only sex education in those days. We girls were absolutely terrified at the prospect of getting pregnant and did our best to avoid it. Not always successfully. Nature's imperative could defeat the best intentions, resulting often enough in either a quick wedding or a secretive stay in a home for unwed mothers, or a visit to a "back alley" abortionist where, sometimes, the girls died. No, we did not need abstinence-only sex education. The daily-life realities of unwed pregnancy were far more terrifying than preachers' threats of hellfire. If such traumatic inducements to chastity didn't work well then, why would this silly abstinence-only stuff work now? At least the taxpayers weren't billed for the reality-based terror inflicted on us by nature's mindless sex drive.

According to a CDC poster I have, teen birth rates are highest in the South, where abstinence-only sex education is still playing teens and taxpayers for suckers in its cruel and costly con game. Here are the teen birth rate figures for 2006: U.S. average teen birthrate for 15- to 19-year-olds: 41.9 births per thousand females. For South Dakota, Minnesota and Nebraska: 18–30 per thousand, with New Hampshire lowest at 18.7. For the northern tier of states and the west coast: 31–40 per thousand. For the middle tier of states, including the District of Columbia, Delaware and Arkansas: 41–50 per thousand. And for the southern tier of states: 51–68.4 per thousand, with Mississippi highest at 68.4. (Mississippi also leads the nation in rates of STD transmission.)

On the bright side, the latest news from the CDC is better—there has been a significant decline is teen birthrates. In the U.S. as of 2010, the birthrate has dropped 44% from what it was in 1991. The drop is credited to an increased use of contraceptives, comprehensive (*not* abstinence-only) sex education, and Planned Parenthood's peer education programs.[10] It's all about self-respect, responsibility, and knowledge. It's about knowing how to control nature's mindless imperative so we are benefited by it, not victimized.

Teaching About Religion in the Public Schools

Some states include elective courses in comparative religion in their curriculums. The idea is to help students appreciate diversity. Well and good, but it is difficult to see how anyone could teach such a course in an unbiased way. Could a teacher discuss the Christian, Islamic and Hindu scriptures objectively, given the morally inconsistent teachings and factual and doctrinal contradictions in all of them? Could a teacher dissect the factual errors and contradictions in Christian scripture with as little fear of repercussion as he or she could when dissecting, for example, Hindu scripture?

Discussing noteworthy religious leaders and the rationale for various rituals and practices may be interesting, but it's not useful in understanding the breadth and depth of the social and political impact of religion. Will comparative-religion classes discuss Pope Pius IX's 1864 Syllabus of Errors, an "infallible" document listing 80 "errors" of the secular world, in which he condemned almost every progressive idea about democracy, state-church separation, human rights, civil liberties, and freedom of conscience? Will they discuss the inquisitions, persecutions, massacres, and wars waged over doctrinal differences? Of course not. That would bring on a firestorm of rage from religious zealots bent on trivializing such events or blaming individuals rather than the institutions whose orders they followed.

Religious beliefs—whether one accepts them or not—are a massive, controlling force in our society. Constitutionally we are a secular nation, yet we have been politically polarized and paralyzed for years by a religious war (euphemistically called a culture war) instigated and maintained by authoritarian fundamentalists, Catholics, and Mormons. For that reason alone, religion should be taught in public schools. But taught how? A superficial skimming of beliefs may be helpful in understanding the ritualistic worldviews of believers, but what about, "By their fruits ye shall know them"?[11] Throughout history, religion has borne many more thistles than figs. That's why our First Amendment separated religion from government: to keep forever from these shores the religious strife that for centuries had soaked the soil of Europe in blood. What is there about religion that causes so much strife? Why have religions supported slavery, the subjugation of women, persecution of gays, torture, murder, massacres, wars, and terror-ism? (Christian terrorists bomb abortion clinics and murder their doctors and staff, but are almost never labeled as what they are: Christian terror-ists.)

At a Religion in Public Life symposium in Minneapolis, Minnesota, on April 28, 1998, the Lutheran theologian Martin Marty said, in his keynote speech, "It is the role of unbelievers to force religions to be benign." That's it. There is no point in an atheist movement if religion is no more of a prob-lem than belief in astrology. Comparative religion classes should examine that; they should examine why religions are so often malignant.

Ideological certainty is the problem. That mindset must be explored, and it has been, with the rise of democracy and the freedom to speak one's mind publicly. The practice of examining religion's effects should be en-couraged, as this would contribute to the common good far more than superficial knowledge of different religions' sacred books and rituals. Such examination has led to the growth of liberal religions whose beliefs come as close to an atheistic worldview as one can get without completely aban-doning the god idea. William Sierichs Jr., a journalist and historian from Baton Rouge, Louisiana, who writes about the history of Christianity cit-ing original sources, says, "Liberal religionists had to abandon traditional Christianity so they could be moral." One has only to read about the inhu-mane religious beliefs of only two hundred years ago (beliefs that only the authoritarian/fundamentalist religions still accept) to recognize the truth of that statement.

Censorship: Who Says What Can Be Said?

Some have said that the strongest drive is not love or hate, but the drive to censor another's opinions. There's a lot of truth there. All societies have allowed prostitution in one way or another, but few if any have allowed people to speak critically of their rulers or their culture's religious beliefs. Such criticism has generally been a criminal act—and in many places, it still is. To get the full flavor of how bad things used to be—and to under-stand where the current remnants of censorship originated—consider the pronouncements of the Catholic Church in the wake of the Enlightenment. (Protestants were just as extreme, but not as extravagantly verbose.) The encyclical *Christianae Reipublicae*, issued on November 25, 1766 is typical:

The well-being of the Christian community which has been entrusted to Us by the Prince of shepherds and the Guardian of souls requires Us to see to it that the unaccustomed and offensive licentiousness of books which has emerged from hiding to cause ruin and desolation does not become more destructive as it triumphantly spreads abroad. . . . unless We lay the scythe to the root and bind up the bad plants in bundles to burn, it will not be long before the growing thorns of evil attempt to choke the seedlings of the Lord Sabaoth.

[Through bad books] They have not restrained their impious minds from anything divine, holy, and consecrated by the oldest religion of all time; rather in their attack they have sharpened their tongues like a sword. They have run first of all against God to their pride. . . . They do not respect His providence nor do they fear His justice. They preach with a detestable and insane freedom of thought . . .

Finally, who can avoid deep sadness when he sees the bitter enemy exceed the bounds of modesty and due respect and attack with the publication of outrageous books now in open battle, now in dissimulated combat the very See of Peter which the strong redeemer of Jacob has placed as an iron column and as a bronze wall against the leaders of darkness. . . .

Therefore since the Holy Spirit has made you bishops to govern the Church of God and has taught you concerning the unique sacrament of human salvation, We cannot neglect our duty in the face of these evil books. . . . It is necessary to fight bitterly, as the situation requires, and to eradicate with all our strength the deadly destruction caused by such books. The substance of the error will never be removed unless the criminal element of wickedness burn in the fire and perish. Since you have been constituted stewards of the mysteries of God and armed with His strength to destroy their defenses, exert yourselves to keep the sheep entrusted to you and redeemed by the blood of Christ at a safe distance from these poisoned pastures. For if it is necessary to avoid the company of evildoers because their words encourage impiety and their speech acts like a cancer, what desolation the plague of their books can cause. . . ."

Catholic advocates of censorship go on and on and on like this, pronouncement after pronouncement, one pope after another—and the effort to impose censorship continues today.

Outright censorship in the United States (not just dumbing down or hiding information) has historically focused on sex, and still does. In 1873, Congress passed the infamous Comstock Act; twenty-four states followed suit with similar laws (collectively known as the Comstock laws).

The Comstock Act targeted sexually explicit paintings and literary works as well as publications and advertisements for contraception and abortion. The Comstock Act remained in force (if not always *en*forced) until the *Bolger v. Youngs Drug Products Corp.* Supreme Court decision in 1973, which held that the provisions of the law relating to advertisements were unconstitutional under the First Amendment. Another 1973 ruling, *Miller v. California*, rendered the Comstock Act (and all similar censorship statutes) moot as regards the arts: a work of art could not be banned as long as it had "redeeming social value" (whatever that is).

But censorial zealots still ban books, though not as aggressively as they once did. The targets are mainly books that say anything straightforward about sex, sexuality, homosexuality, and the four-letter words we all hear every day. Today, book banning is mainly an issue in public schools, when school libraries stock a book religious fundamentalists dislike. The National Coalition Against Censorship regularly publishes reports on what the censors are up to. As the Coalition says:

> While rarely in the national news, book censorship is an everyday event in the U.S. It takes only one person to launch a challenge: because a book contains "sex" or "violence" or a character is a "bad role model" or because it "denigrates religion" or "undermines parental authority" (and on and on ...). The goal, invariably, is to remove the offending material and keep all students (in a class, grade, school or district) from reading it.[13]

Pope Paul VI officially abandoned the Catholic Church's infamous Index of Prohibited Books in 1966, but Catholic authoritarians still do their best to censor the more publicly visible arts. In October 2010, Catholic political pressure forced the Smithsonian Institution to remove a video from an exhibition in the National Portrait Gallery titled, "Hide/Seek: Difference and Desire in American Portraiture." The video was "Fire in My Belly," by David Wojnarowicz, who had died of AIDS. It contained 11 seconds showing ants crawling across a crucifix, and The Catholic League objected to the Smithsonian's showing it. The Catholic League contacted Republican politicians, including House Speaker John Boehner and House Majority Leader Eric Cantor. Government funding for the Smithsonian was suddenly in jeopardy, and it pulled the video.[14]

A more insidious form of censorship is the hiding of information in libraries through misleading cataloging. Retired Hennepin County, Minnesota librarian Sanford Berman regularly takes the Library of Congress to task for not cataloging material under headings the user might actually look up. It does no good to use technical or clinical terminology for sexual topics, he says, when users are familiar only with street -language terms. Crude as they may be, those are the terms that should be cataloged (with cross references to other terms), if the goal is to help the user find the information he or she wants. Berman also objects to cataloging historical topics in a way that smacks of whitewashing unpleasant facts about wars, invasions, massacres, and the like. He gives the example of a long out-of-print book, *1492: What it Means to Be Discovered*, about the conquest of America. The book has reproductions of woodcuts depicting the horrific tortures and brutal murders inflicted on native people by the Spaniards. The book was cataloged under "Fine Arts." That's just where someone might look who was seeking information about the European treatment of native peoples in America, wouldn't you say?

What are the reasons for such miscategorization? Berman thinks there are several reasons librarians do this: bureaucratic lethargy, individual bias, political expediency, or failure to recognize the significance of a topic. Regardless, he says, libraries have a responsibility to the public to do better than that.

Censoring Critics of Politically Predatory Religion

Religious apologists almost invariably describe *any* criticism of religious beliefs or institutions as "religion bashing." If you criticize religious beliefs (and the attempt to impose them on others via the law), and if by chance your criticism ever sees the light of day, editorials, columnists, right-wing hate radio, and letters to the editor will jump all over you, no matter how accurate your criticism. Why don't we ever hear about "ensoulment" in a discussion of "personhood," abortion, or stem cell research? Because the ludicrousness of the belief underlying the laws restricting abortion and stem cell research would be exposed. The defensive reactions to criticism of religious beliefs are driven by the Catholic Church's canon law #1369:

> A person is to be punished with a just penalty, who, at a public event or assembly, or in a published writing, or by otherwise using the means of social communication, utters blasphemy, or gravely harms public morals, or rails at or excites hatred of or contempt for religion or the Church.[15]

That includes everyone outraged enough by dogmatic religion's misanthropy and misogyny to speak out, including public officials who put their duty to support the Constitution above dogma. It also includes those who incite laughter by quoting Church beliefs about the Eucharist—the "sacred host"—an unleavened flour-and-water wafer elevated to transcendent dignity in Canon Law #1367:

> One who throws away the consecrated species or, for a sacrilegious purpose, takes them away or keeps them, incurs a *latae sententiae* excommunication reserved to the Apostolic See; a cleric, moreover, may be punished with some other penalty, not excluding dismissal from the clerical state.[16]

What's this about it being a "species"? It's nothing but a tasteless cracker! The communion cracker's "species" is a wheat plant. It does not become a living flesh-and-blood God "species"—to put it more bluntly, sacred meat—by having magical incantations uttered over it. If it did, how could a vegetarian ingest it in good conscience? If it did, why is communion still allowed on the Catholic Church's ritualistic meatless days? (The church still commands its followers not to eat meat on Ash Wednesday, all Fridays during Lent, and on Good Friday.)

The bigger question is why on Earth must we respect such utter nonsense? Incantations have no power just because they are uttered by a priest who was ordained by a bishop who claims (with no credible evidence whatsoever) to be a successor of the apostles. We're not supposed to laugh at this? No wonder the Church tries to silence critics with meaningless excommunications. (Sadly, all too many liberal Catholics bow to this illusory threat.) Reread chapters 2, 3 and 4 and ask yourself why the bizarre beliefs described in them, which so clearly form the framework for our restrictive laws on sex, cannot be discussed.

Censoring Sexual Expression

Even a brief glance at current television and movies shows that the censors seem to have lost this battle But only on film and TV. You still can't watch live sex, see thong bikinis at Daytona Beach, or drink liquor in a club with nude dancers.

Yes, there are regulations, such as they are. Prostitution—defined as paying someone for sex or offering sex for payment—is against the law, but paying porn stars to have sex in front of a camera is legal. So prostitution is not OK, but paying actors to have sex in a porn film is just fine. Such is the status of sexual censorship laws in this country.

Sex clubs are another target for regulation. Admittedly, places such as swing clubs and S/M clubs do not appeal to everyone (including this author, who is happy to be culturally deprived in this area), but if they are not causing trouble, why not leave them alone? But that's not what moral busybodies do.[17] Whatever else goes on in such clubs, it doesn't involve harmful criminal behavior or abuse of children (unlike the goings-on in some Catholic rectories and sacristies). Yet many on the religious right continue to advocate prohibition of consensual sex in private venues that hurts no one.

No Secular Justification

Would society be better off if dogmatic religious doctrines had no influence on our laws and public policies regarding education and science? Of course it would. Restrictive laws that do nothing but validate and enforce sectarian religious beliefs undermine the common good. It's true that opinions about morality evolve over time, so that what was once viewed with distaste, if not outright horror, is now accepted as normal. This does not mean that past and present views are equally valid. As Supreme Court Justice Anthony Kennedy put it in his opinion supporting the *Lawrence v. Texas* decision that overturned laws criminalizing sodomy:

> Had those who drew and ratified the Due Process Clauses . . . known the components of liberty in its manifold possibilities, they might have been more specific. [But] [t]hey did not presume to have this insight. They knew times can blind us to certain truths, and later generations can see that laws once thought necessary and proper in fact serve only to oppress. As the Constitution endures, persons in every generation can invoke its principles in their own search for greater freedom.[18]

Justice Antonin Scalia strongly dissented from Kennedy's view, apparently believing that what was true for some people at one time should be true for all people forever after:

> State laws [that are only based on moral choices include laws] against . . . bigamy, same-sex marriage, adult incest, prostitution, masturbation, . . . fornication, bestiality, and obscenity. . . . Every single one of these laws is called into question by today's decision. . . . This [decision] effectively decrees the end of all morals legislation.[19]

And so it should. The only secular reason for laws prohibiting sexual behaviors is to ensure that there is no coercion or exploitation of innocents, especially children (and animals).

Do as you will, but harm no one. And try not to be publicly disgusting. Maybe someday everyone will think copulating with your dog at high noon in the parking lot at Wal-Mart is perfectly acceptable performance art, but most of us aren't there yet—and never will be. Until then, those who can't resist challenging cultural hangups in public shouldn't be surprised if someone turns a water hose on them. That's life. Deal with it. Thank you.

---

1. Rob Boston, "Creationism Crusade," *Church & State*, July/August 2011, p. 9.

2. Miller et al, "Science," *Science* 313 765–766, as published, with ranking chart, in *The Secular Humanist Press*, Spring 2011, p. 23.

3. Wilson, Bruce, "The Loch Ness Monster is Real; The KKK is Good: The Shocking Content of Publicly Paid for Christian School Textbooks," www.Alternet.org, June 18, 2012.

4. "New Challenges for Evolution Education," National Center for Science Education newsletter, March 2011, p. 6.

5. "Applications flood stem cell bank," BBC News, http://news.bbc.co.uk/go/pr/fr/2/hi/science/nature/4396156/stm, published Nov. 1, 2005.

6. Neal St. Anthony, "Biotech executives call 'anti-cloning' bills anti-business," *Minneapolis Star Tribune*, May 2, 2011, p. B1.

7. Rob Stein, "1st stem cell recipient: 'It was meant to be,'" published in the *Washington Post*, as reprinted in the *Minneapolis Star Tribune*, April 17, 2012, p. A8.

8. Andy Kopsa, "As Attacks on Planned Parenthood Aim for Sex-Ed Funding, Let's Remember How Bad Religious-Backed Abstinence Only Programs Are," http://www.alternet.org/story/152755/as_attacks_on_planned_parenthood_aim_for_sex-ed_funding%2C_let%27s_remember_how_bad_religious_backed_abstinence_only_programs_are, posted Oct. 16, 2011.

9. Marty Klein, Ph.D., *America's War on Sex: The Attack on Law, Lust and Liberty*. Praeger Publishers, Westport, Connecticut, 2006, pp. 15-16.

10. Gail Rosenblum, "Surprisingly sharp decline in teen birthrates worth cheering," *Minneapolis Star Tribune*, April 19, 2012, p. B1.

11. Matthew 7:15-20, King James Version. "Beware of false prophets, which come to you in sheep's clothing, but inwardly they are ravening wolves. Ye shall know them by their fruits. Do men gather grapes of thorns, or figs of thistles? Even so every good tree bringeth forth good fruit; but a corrupt tree bringeth forth evil fruit. A good tree cannot bring forth evil fruit, neither can a corrupt tree bring forth good fruit. Every tree that bringeth not forth good fruit is hewn down, and cast into the fire. Wherefore by their fruits ye shall know them."

12. Courtesy of researcher William Sierichs Jr.

13. *Censorship News*, "Keeping Kids in the Dark," Fall 2011.

14. National Coalition Against Censorship letter to members, March 5, 2011.

15. Canon Law, Book VI: Sanctions in the Church; Part II: Penalties for Particular Offenses; Title I: Offenses against Religion and the Unity of the Church.

16. Ibid.

17. Klein, op. cit., pp. 133-134.

18. Ibid., p. xiv.

19. Ibid.

7

RELIGION AND TAXES:
FREELOADING AT ITS FINEST

*"When a religion is good, I conceive it will support itself; and when it does
not support itself, and God does not care to support it—so that its
professors are obliged to call for help of a civil power—it is
a sign, I apprehend, of its being a bad one."*

—Benjamin Franklin

Public frustration has, once again in a recurring political scenario, reached the "throw the bums out" level over government deficits and an economy in free fall. There is much agonizing, blaming, and demonizing over the need to cut spending and/or increase taxes, with little agreement on where and how to do it. Yet, one potential major source of revenue—tax exempt organizations—is seldom mentioned, much less acted upon. Over the years, as a political activist, I have had discussions about religious tax exemptions with many politicians. All understood the problem, even expressing eagerness to tax religious institutions and musing about ways to do it, but all concluded that (as one former U.S. senator admitted to me), "Anyone who told the truth about taxes could never get re-elected." There certainly are many nonreligious aspects of our tax system that are questionable, but given our First Amendment's religion clauses, we should not be paying higher taxes so religions benefit by paying nothing.

We need to hear the truth, and this is it. Death and taxes are not certain, only death is certain. Those who are classified as tax exempt and escape taxes are primarily religious, educational, and charitable nonprofits. For religious organizations, there is not only escape from taxation, but complete lack of financial accountability. Secular nonprofits have to file a financial report annually with the IRS; religious organizations do not. Generally (there are state-specific variations), religious organizations pay no state or federal income taxes, no sales, gas, car, or excise taxes, no user fees, no inheritance taxes, no taxes on investments, stocks, mutual funds and bonds, no capital gains taxes on the sale of property, and no property taxes to cover the cost of fire and police protection, libraries, and schools. Religious organizations don't even have to verify to the IRS the donations taxpayers claim on their income tax forms. Related businesses, such as religious bookstores, biblical and creationist theme parks, schools, hospitals, fitness centers, recreational facilities, and campgrounds are tax exempt. (About the only things religious institutions have to pay taxes on are any completely unrelated commercial businesses they might own, such as shopping centers and hotels.) They receive these exemptions simply because they're religious. There is no secular justification for these exemptions, and they compromise the economic wellbeing of everyone else.

No Good Deed Goes Unpunished

The law of unintended consequences never applied so well as it does to the decision to exempt religious institutions from taxation. These exemptions lead one to think that the cynical quip, "No good deed goes unpunished" has some truth in it. As our nation grew and state constitutions began to allow tax exemptions, churches received them, more or less as a charitable gesture, since in the early years of this country most churches were too small and poor to easily pay taxes.

As churches grew, exemptions were considered justified because churches dispensed charity, augmenting that of community poor houses and county poor farms. (The social safety net—Social Security, unemployment insurance, and later food stamps, Medicare and Medicaid—didn't exist until the New Deal in the 1930s; so, the charitable work of churches was much more important in the 19th century than it is today.) But then, through bequests, business investments and gifts from wealthy donors, religious institutions began prospering immensely. With wealth came power and influence, and so, through political pressure, the exemptions grew and grew. Today almost nothing churches do can be taxed, even when they generate millions of dollars of income and return little or nothing of value to the community. What began with some justification now borders on being criminal.

How Did This Happen?

Efforts to bring this unfair situation under control are as old as the initial tax exemptions, which began in the 1830s. Numerous pieces of state and federal legislation have been introduced since then to end the preferential treatment of churches, but to no avail. In 1874, the issue had become such a matter of public concern that James Garfield (later President Garfield) addressed Congress on the matter. He said:

> The divorce between Church and State ought to be absolute. It ought to be so absolute that no church property anywhere, in any state, or in the nation, should be exempt from equal taxation; for if you exempt the property of any church organization, to that extent you impose a tax upon the whole community.[1]

In 1875, President Ulysses S. Grant also addressed Congress. He came bearing a 900-foot-long petition with 35,000 signatures of people opposed to tax exemptions for religious institutions. He said:

> I would also call your attention to the importance of correcting an evil that, if permitted to continue, will probably lead to great trouble in our land . . . it is the accumulation of vast amounts of untaxed church property. . . . In 1850, the church properties in the U.S., which paid no taxes, municipal or state, amounted to about $83 million. In 1860, the amount had doubled; in 1875, it is about $1 billion. By 1900, without check, it is safe to say this property will reach a sum exceeding $3 billion . . . so vast a sum, receiving all the protection and benefits of government without bearing its portion of the burdens and expenses of the same, will not be looked upon acquiescently by those who have to pay the taxes. . . . I would suggest the taxation of all property equally, whether church or corporation.[2]

There have been a number of such efforts in my state, Minnesota, to end religious tax exemptions; none of them have been successful. The situation here is fairly typical, so it's worth considering.

In the 1970s, an amendment to Article X of the Minnesota Constitution passed by over 70 percent to allow taxing the business operations of churches. The amendment was supported by a coalition of business associations and labor unions. Despite the overwhelming popularity of this amendment, it has never been implemented.

In 1987, Minnesota Governor Rudy Perpich proposed eliminating the sales tax exemption of nonprofits and got nowhere. In 1988, Rep. Tom Osthoff sponsored a bill in the Minnesota legislature that, as reported in the *Minneapolis Star Tribune*, would have:

> [R]emove(d) $4 billion in property tax exemptions, which would have raised $180 million and cut homestead taxes by an average of 7.3 percent statewide, according to a study by Minnesota House researchers. The bill would have taxed hospitals, nursing homes, nonprofit organizations other than churches and schools, civic centers, arenas, auditoriums, leased airport property, college property not used for education, and residential property owned by churches, educational institutions and governments. Church property was included in everything except possibly the civic centers, arenas, auditoriums and airport property. To no one's surprise, the bill failed.[3]

And in 1989 I was involved in getting Article X implementation language into the tax bill. The bill was pulled at the last minute (according to my legislative contact) due to political pressure by religious institutions. Nothing of note has happened on the state level since then.

On the federal level, in 2011, U.S. Senator Charles Grassley, a Republican representing Iowa, opened a Senate Finance Committee investigation of the financial irregularities of several mega-ministries run by "prosperity gospel" televangelists. These preachers occasionally make the news by living over-the-top lavish lifestyles, with mansions, private jets, yachts, air-conditioned dog houses, and other luxuries. Grassley, although a religious-right supporter who shares the religious beliefs of his targets, has tried to stop these tax exemption abuses, but has succeeded only in publicizing their excesses, which is certainly a good thing in itself.

However, for reasons best known to himself—he retired in 2012 and was thus under no re-election pressure—he dropped financial inquiries into mega-churches in favor of supporting legislation that allows them to engage in political activity while retaining their tax exemptions.[4] At the same time, he started going after nonprofit hospitals, whose tax exempt status is based on providing a certain amount of charity care. An October 15, 2011, news report by Tony Leys in the *Des Moines Register* detailed Grassley's efforts and the effect on taxpayers when "nonprofits" profit from unjustified tax exemptions. Leys writes:

> [M]ore than $1.9 billion worth of hospital property in Iowa is tax-exempt, state records show. If those hospitals were normal businesses they would pay more than $58 million in annual property taxes, which would help fix roads, hire teachers and keep police on the beat. The result: Everyone else pays higher taxes because of such exemptions.[5]

As for the free care, Leys adds:

> [Iowa's 46 nonprofit] hospitals made nearly $295 million after expenses, about three times the amount of free care provided to patients too poor to pay. Fifteen of the hospitals provided less than 1 percent of their overall expenses in free care to the poor. Only 11 hospitals provided free care equal to 2 percent or more of their expenses. . . . nonprofit foundations are required to spend 5 percent of their assets on charitable activities per year.

Churches, of course, are not required to spend anything on charity, despite the huge incomes of the larger churches. Any significant charity they provide is normally funded by the government under contract, and by other public entities such as the United Way.

The most serious obstacle to eliminating church and secular nonprofit tax exemptions has been the 1970 Supreme Court decision in *Walz v. Tax Commission of the City of New York*. The justices ruled 8 to 1 that exempting churches from taxation was a benevolently neutral accommodation—although neutrality by definition can be neither benevolent nor malevolent.

Part of the *Walz* decision was based on the assumption that churches do charitable work and contribute to American culture. But many do little or no charitable work, and of those that do, anything significant is often paid for by government grants and/or private foundations and civic organizations. Many businesses do more good (as anyone who has faced a car breakdown or plumbing disaster knows), but they are not tax exempt.

As for culture, the most notable contribution from religious organizations in recent decades has been a divisive culture war. While some churches may do some good, many of them do far more harm than good. Every chapter in this book exposes a body of theology-based laws that victimize all of us in some way, while causing damage that requires tax dollars to remedy. (To cite but one example, consider the costs of unwanted children resulting from restriction of both abortion and contraceptive availability.)

What is often overlooked about the *Walz* ruling is that it did not say (as many suppose) that churches must be tax exempt, only that they could not be denied tax exemption if secular nonprofits were exempt. States were free to tax or exempt all or none. The states chose to exempt all.

Because secular nonprofits want to keep their tax exemptions, religious organizations are no longer the sole beneficiaries of this unfair system, but they play a major part in keeping it going. They are, in fact, the primary movers in keeping the system in place. Although *Walz v. Tax Commission* did not say churches cannot be taxed, the ruling is often understood to mean that taxing churches violates the religious freedom clause of the First Amendment. If it did, we'd have a schizophrenic First Amendment that, on the one hand, prohibits an establishment of religion (so that no one is forced to carry these freeloaders) while, on the other hand, guaranteeing freedom of religion (so that everyone is forced to carry them). Such are the political contortions this nation struggles with to keep religious institutions fat and happy, regardless of the burden this places on everyone else, religious or not.

Property Taxes: We Pay More Because They Pay Nothing

Tax inequities show up most clearly and affect most people directly in real estate taxes. In every community, government provides certain services: fire and police protection, road and bridge repair and maintenance, street cleaning, emergency response, education and recreational facilitie— all these and more if we are to have what we call civilization.

Local governments assess property taxes to cover these expenses, but only on some property. Those with a property tax exemption get all the benefits of a city's services but pay nothing. That revenue shortfall is made up by the rest of us, who pay more. Of this group, owners of business and commercial real estate can pass their tax costs on to customers and clients. Homeowners and renters cannot. For them there is no way out. They must cover the shortfall created by the tax exempt while also paying higher prices to cover the taxes on business property. This can be especially hard on senior citizens, whose retirement income is usually far below their former income.

Given the difficulty of taxing churches, some proponents of tax fairness have suggested charging churches a service fee for the many city services they enjoy at taxpayer expense. Some cities have tried this, but the churches put up such a fight that the efforts have not succeeded. To their credit, there are religious organizations that, at least occasionally, voluntarily pay a fee to cover their use of public services. For example, in 1967, the minister of the First Universalist Church of Minneapolis wrote a lengthy editorial for the (then-named) *Minneapolis Star* pleading for his fellow religionists to reject church tax exemptions as a threat to their integrity and religious freedom. He detailed instances of church wealth that he considered unconscionable. Almost nothing came of his efforts.[6]

However, his views have received some support. The 1988 *Star Tribune* report on tax exemptions referred to earlier noted that Augsburg Publishing House (owned by the Lutheran church) donated about $325,000 between 1975 and 1988 to the City of Minneapolis for the services it received.[7] Also, St. Olaf College and Carleton College in Northfield, Minnesota, donated about $20,000 a year for services, in addition to donating larger amounts for special projects, such as a hospital and an ice arena. I have heard of Unitarian-Universalist churches doing the same thing. These donations, of course, indicate the huge amount of money available to fund city services and lower everyone's property taxes if all property was taxed.

How much lost revenue must homeowners and renters make up to cover the tax exemption shortfall? In Minnesota, for example, tax exempt property statewide is valued at $84 billion.[8] In Minneapolis, one-fourth of the property is tax exempt; in St. Paul one-third is. (The difference is due to St. Paul being the state capital, and thus having many government buildings). This is probably typical among all the states.

Preacher Perks

The clergy even get tax exemptions just for being clergy. This goes back to 1954, when Cold War hysteria caused our elected officials to put religious bigotry in many forms into law as a barrier against "godless communism" (details in Chapter 9). The legislator who proposed the clergy exemption, Rep. Peter Mack Jr., a Democrat from Illinois, explained it this way:

> Certainly, in these times when we are being threatened by a godless and antireligious world movement, we should correct this discrimination against certain ministers of the gospel who are carrying on such a courageous fight against this foe. Certainly this is not too much to do for these people who are caring for our spiritual welfare.[9]

There's no discernable secular purpose in this rationale, since tax-exempt clergy could hardly affect the Soviet Union. This added tax exemption did, however, affect U.S. taxpayers, who had to make up for the lost revenue.

A former Episcopal priest, Dick Hewetson, reported on the clergy exemption in *Freethought Today*, the newspaper of the Freedom From Religion Foundation (FFRF):

> I have an income tax break that most members of FFRF do not share. Because I receive a pension from the 11 years that I served as a clergyman, a portion of that income is not taxed. It is called my "housing and utility allowance." It goes back to a tax law that allows clergy pay to be divided into two separate categories: salary plus housing and utility allowance. The latter

amount is excluded from federal tax. It is not included on Form W-2 as taxable income (although it can show up, with an explanation, in Box 14 of the W-2). Wouldn't you like it if your employer could divide your pay like this? Well, god is not on your side.

The tax code has been amended at least twice. In 1971 the Internal Revenue Services limited [tax exempt income of clergy to cover housing] to the "fair market rental value" of the furnished home, utilities included. Evidently, some god-fearing clergy were accepting housing and utility allowances above the amount they actually paid! . . . To add insult to injury, if clergy own homes, they can still deduct their real estate taxes and interest on their mortgage payments . . . Remember that the money they are paid for their home expenses is not part of th[eir] taxable income.

In the Oct. 11, 2006, *New York Times*, reporter Diana B. Henriques wrote: "The tax break is not available to the staff at secular nonprofit organizations whose scale and charitable aims [are comparable] . . . or to poorly paid inner-city teachers and day care workers who also serve their communities. The housing deduction is one of several tax breaks that leave extra money in the pockets of clergy members and their religious employers. Ministers of every faith are also exempt from income tax withholding and can opt out of Social Security. And every state but one exempts religious employers from paying state unemployment taxes--reducing the employers' payroll expenses but also leaving their workers without unemployment benefits if they are laid off."

A Vermont clergyman, Jay Sprout, wrote in the May 8, 2002, *Christian Century*: "The question this issue always raises for me is, what principle? The principle that ministers are entitled to a tax break available to no other taxpayers except, I believe, certain military personnel? I am not eager to pay more tax than the law requires and have received thousands of dollars of benefits, thanks to the housing tax break for clergy. But I have never understood why I should enjoy such a privilege or why church institutions should be so vigilant in their efforts to protect this tax advantage. Jesus was particularly critical of religious authorities and others who claimed special status in society. Can you imagine 'the son of Man [who had] nowhere to lay his head' living in a house worth $80,000 a year?"

. . . I am sure that you agree with me that this is a totally unfair situation. I have always said that I do not object to paying taxes. I do object to paying taxes in an unfair way. And this tax code is definitely unfair.

Now, getting back to the fact that I still get the break. Because I receive a pension from the church, any amount up to what I pay for rent and utilities is not considered taxable income. Don't you wish you were in my shoes? Hey, it's legal.[10]

What Hewetson didn't mention was that this benefit allows clergy to buy several homes tax free. For example, a millionaire minister who bought a $408,638 second home at a lake in Tennessee got the clergy exemption on that in addition to his first home, courtesy of a favorable ruling by the U.S. Tax Court. Then there were the clergy housing allowances granted eight members (including five from the Robert Schuller family) of Robert Schuller's Crystal Cathedral Ministries in California that amounted to an annual total benefit of $832,000. Congressional budget records show that the total cost to taxpayers for this largesse is about $500 million a year.

What It's Like to Fight Property Tax Exemptions

Broadening tax exempt property to include all nonprofits has led to a proliferation of secular nonprofits, which join with the churches in pressuring legislators to retain exemptions. An example of this occurred in 1996 in Colorado, when there was a business community-backed attempt to pass a referendum to tax the property of all nonprofits. The benefits to homeowners and businesses would have been substantial, and the measure provided generous exemptions for smaller nonprofits. Despite this, the nonprofits joined with the churches in opposing the measure. Billboards urging "NO on 11" depicted a little broken heart and the plaintive cry, "Don't Hurt the Helpers." The referendum lost 4 to 1. A report by a pro-referendum activist, Jackie Marquis, included this analysis:

Since 80% of the privately owned nonprofit properties in Colorado are owned by churches and religious organizations, . . . I would venture to say this was the real target. There were exemptions in the other 20% of nonprofit properties, so in reality only a few of these would [have been] affected. Why did [the proposition] fail? There were many reasons. Let me start with the opposition's strength and power. Most nonprofits are big business and operate as big business. The opposition took in over $700,000 to fight this. Now you know where the money is. Nonprofits also have tremendous political power, just as corporations do. . . . They had many voluntary speakers everywhere. With their financial power, they were able to pay two full-time campaign organizers and purchase hundreds of thousands of dollars worth of television, radio and newspaper advertising.

Their television ads were very compelling, implying that every kind of service they render and little churches were going to close down. Little old grandma and grandpa were going to be out on the streets. The homeless would not be able to be fed. Kids would lose their daycare. The zoo, the

Humane Society, the blood banks, everything was going to have to close. . . . Politicians spoke out for them everywhere. They even have billboards now that say "Thank you from the helpers" with their little broken heart and a red circle with 11 on the inside with a red stripe through it.

. . . We spent $7,000, a drop in the bucket compared to our opposition. We did not get the funds we thought we would. We did not get the statewide media coverage we expected. . . . We had a letter of endorsement from the Business Coalition For Fair Competition, which is an alliance of 19 national trade associations. We could not get this letter of endorsement out to the public. What amazed me was how we could not get the press to cover the misinformation on the opposition's flyers and TV ads. . . . There was blatant, huge figure-switching going on. The rearranging of figures all over the state was evident, like showing nonprofit school properties where there are no schools, and showing that El Paso County had more nonprofit properties in the 1980s than it does now in the 1990s. This of course is impossible, but would the media pick it up? No! . . . The opposition kept saying homeowners' property [taxes] would go up. This was totally false. We couldn't even fight that, even when we had a letter from the El Paso County tax assessor saying the taxes could not be raised . . .

In Denver, Mayor Webb said [Proposition] 11 would drive churches into extinction. Well, all I know is that the "American Dream" has become extinct for many Americans. Many can no longer even think of owning a car, much less a house. Many can barely pay their rent. No politician, no government entity, no corporation, whether profit or nonprofit, seems to care to help the taxpayer-they just keep adding taxes on our backs constantly. The greed is unbelievable.

. . . None of [the liberal] organizations would back us. They stated that, while they think it is unconstitutional that churches don't pay taxes, they would not make a public stand . . . The cowards! Let's face it. They all protect their own pockets, even if it means they will be fighting the religious right for a lifetime. I for one am not donating to any of these, ACLU, AU, People for the American Way, etc., any longer, because if they had taken a stand behind our small group against the religious right, it would have made our fight a lot shorter. Even Planned Parenthood . . . lie in bed with their enemies only to avoid a little property tax.

Many said [Proposition 11] went too far. In my opinion, it didn't go far enough, in that I think all these entities are businesses and should pay taxes as any other business or individual pays, with no special privileges for anyone.[11]

Who Prospers from the Prosperity Gospel?

Churches fight to keep their tax exemptions and charitable perks—and to get more. The national Citizens for Tax Justice (www.ctj.org), founded in 1979, lobbies legislatures to ensure taxes are adequate to maintain social programs. Its coalition members and directors include religious organizations. In Minnesota, it works with the Joint Religious Legislative Coalition (www.jrlc.org) whose four sponsoring members are the Minnesota Catholic Conference, the Minnesota Council of Churches, the Jewish Community Relations Council of Minnesota and the Dakotas, and the Islamic Center of Minnesota. (JRLC, founded in 1971, was the first interfaith public-interest lobby group in the United States. Since then, groups in other states have formed.)

While JRLC cites the need for fairness and bemoans the plight of the poor, its members never offer to pay any taxes themselves. Yet in 1992 the Joint Religious Legislative Coalition made specific proposals for raising taxes by $649 million on businesses and on higher incomes to fund social programs, with no suggestion that their own tax-free havens be tapped to help achieve what they call a "need for fairness."[12] The JRLC, of course, sings the same tune whenever budget crises arise.[13]

Many social welfare programs are administered through churches, which contract with the government to provide services or are paid from government sources such as Medicaid and Medicare. In either case, taxpayers, not the churches, pay for these services.

The comfortable financial status of many religious institutions is fairly well known. Despite the Vatican's well over a billion dollars in losses in court judgments and in out-of-court settlements for shielding pedophile priests, it remains extremely wealthy, not just in its financial investments and property holdings, but in its collection of priceless works of art—a major tourist attraction in Rome. (As of this writing, five U.S. Catholic dioceses—including the dioceses of Tucson and Portland—have declared bankruptcy to avoid paying pedophilia victims in full, and eight other dioceses have filed for bankruptcy for the same reason.) As for Protestants, the media regularly report on the lavish lifestyles of televangelists, as documented by Senator Charles Grassley in his now-aborted campaign to make lavish-spending churches accountable for abusing their tax-exempt status.

In 1977, the *Minneapolis Star Tribune* ran a multi-part investigative piece that revealed that Billy Graham had millions of tax-exempt dollars deposited in foreign bank accounts, while paying most of his employees minimum wage or less.[14] In 1987, the paper reported that Graham's tax-free profits for 1986 amounted to $3.8 million.[15] There is no reason to think the Graham operation, which has ministries in several countries, is any less profitable today. Certainly his organization—now run by his son, Franklin Graham—can afford to pay taxes.

In 2011, Americans United for Separation of Church and State, a First Amendment watchdog group, reported the following multi-million-dollar annual budgets for several prominent religious right organizations:

Pat Robertson empire	$412,581,050
Jerry Falwell empire	$400,479,039
Focus on the Family	$130,258,480
Alliance Defense Fund	$30,127,514
American Family Association	$21,408,342
Family Research Council/FRC Action/	
FRC Action PAC	$14,569,081
Coral Ridge Ministries	$17,263,536
Traditional Values Coalition	$9,888,233
Ethics and Religious Liberty Commission	
of the Southern Baptist Convention	$3,236,000

Then there are the "prosperity gospel" evangelical megachurches—a huge national network inspired by Kenneth Copeland, "The Godfather of the Prosperity Gospel"—all of which have palatial facilities, acres of property, and thousands of members. Most of these churches seem to be prospering nicely. Several were featured prominently in the *Minneapolis Star Tribune* in September, 2011. One was the Substance Church, with an income that grew from $150,000 in 2004 to $2.5 million in 2010. The church has accomplished this by preaching Bible verses such as Proverbs 11:24-25: "One gives freely, yet grows all the richer; another withholds what he should give, and only suffers want. Whoever brings blessing will be enriched, and one who waters will himself be watered." The "evidence" that such giving is rewarded came from occasional reports by churchgoers who gave when it was difficult, then unexpectedly recovered financially, always certain their god was rewarding them, never realizing that it is a mathematical certainty that some of those thousands of donors will prosper financially, getting something they can interpret as a reward.[16]

One might argue that, even though a religious organization's financial activities are questionable, donors are free to support the institution regardless. Maybe so, but what if those activities cause considerable harm? We seldom see reports from those who gave and gave and gave, and whose finances worsened as a result. But some of them do surface to shed light on this particular aspect of religious tax-exempt activities.

In 2008, CBS Evening News investigated Kenneth Copeland Ministries (KCM). Highlights of the CBS report included:

> "It's a business, it's a bottom-line business," said a former ministry employee-who feared being identified. The employee answered hundreds of prayer requests a day, most sent in with donations, before quitting, feeling 'betrayed' by Copeland's gospel of prosperity.

> Michael Hoover, who worked for Kenneth Copeland Ministries for five years, quit in 2005 over disagreements with the church. He says he witnessed other employees doing work on behalf of for-profit businesses tied to the Copeland family. "In my viewpoint, I believe that they were using a lot of the ministry's assets for personal businesses," he said.

> "The nonprofit activity and the for-profit activity are so intertwined that you can't, you can't separate them," said Ole Anthony of the Trinity foundation.[17]

Chuck Gallagher, a "business ethics and fraud prevention expert," recently commented negatively on the Kenneth Copeland Ministries (KCM) on his web site.[18] Gallagher's site includes comments from visitors. Most said they supported the Copelands, noting that "rappers and thuggish figures" and other high living celebrities make millions and fly corporate jets and nobody investigates them. The fact that those celebrities paid taxes while FCM was tax-exempt and abusing that privilege did not seem to occur to them.

But there were other comments. This one says it all. It's from a woman who tried to get an accounting of all the money her mother gave to KCM:

> Being only human, our quest for health and wealth regrettably does lead some in the wrong direction. Promises and guarantees, made by the Prosperity Gospel ministers give people that have not obtained these blessings on their own a second chance at achieving their goals in life. An important discovery I made while reviewing testimonies revealed that numerous victims had very little knowledge of the Prosperity Gospel's dark side. These unfortunate victims appear to be [acquainted] with only a small portion of the web of deceit these ministers weave.

Picture yourself being raised in a small country town, with a population of only a few hundred, the closest city [having] only a population of a few thousand. Computers, Internet, cable, satellite TV, and other high tech gadgets are not needed or desired. You are living a simple, solemn life you wouldn't trade for any amount of cash. After your working day is done, you gladly remove your shoes, kick back in your easy chair, and relax without a care in the world for a while. After flipping on the TV to view the local evening news, you are reminded to give thanks that you don't have the worries that accompany life outside the safe haven of your home and your community. Religion is your safeguard, your faith is strong, and you have no doubts about the truth behind your sacred beliefs.

This was my life, before KCM. Prosperity Gospel ministers enter the homes of many victims through a 30-minute Sunday morning worship service on a local broadcast station. Growing up in Jigger, Louisiana, truly located in the middle of nowhere, I can testify that we only received on a clear day about three or four channels at most. Warnings of dangers associated with Prosperity Gospel ministries made by critics, ministers, and victims go unheard; therefore, tragically for many, when the realization of this scam is discovered it is already too late. Families have lost their homes, life savings and some even their lives due to the Prosperity Gospel's misleading doctrines.

Unfortunately, my mother was not one of the lucky ones. Her confidence and faith in this false Gospel ultimately cost her her life. After more than a decade of programming her mind to believe and think the Prosperity Gospel way of life she lost her battle with cancer. By refusing medical attention, she sealed her fate, but the programming she had acquired from Kenneth and Gloria Copeland proved strong all the way to her last breath. A diary she left behind revealed the horrific tale of her life from 1992–2002, the top of each page titled with Kenneth Copeland, Gloria Copeland or BVOV [Believers Voice of Victory—Copeland's Internet TV "station"]. . . . The use of miraculous healing confessions and newly found wealth testimonies are their sales pitch. Sadly, my mom among many others are proof that their sales pitch works.

When all is said and done, perhaps [it] will be tagged not as the Prosperity Gospel, but the false Gospel.[18]

Preaching a Prosperity Gospel is not the only way to take advantage of trusting people. For months, in 2011, doomsday was yet again prophesied—this time to occur on May 21st, 2011. It never happened, of course. The "prophet" this time was the Reverend Harold Camping, from Alameda, California.

If such foolishness were treated as just that, we could dismiss it with a few jokes and end-of-the-world parties. But it's not. Many people take doomsday predictions seriously. Camping's national promotion through billboards and other media resulted in people inflicting great harm on themselves and others. Some liquidated their assets to donate money to publicize the event, or incurred heavy debt to finance purchases and vacations in the expectation that they would be gone to Glory on May 22nd, or they quit their jobs; some even killed themselves and/or their loved ones to avoid the post-Rapture Tribulation.

Camping's tax-exempt organization, Family Stations, a multi-million-dollar radio enterprise, promoted Camping's doomsday prophesies, and it in turn was supported by donations. But Camping made no personal preparations for being Raptured. And he certainly wasn't among those who liquidated their assets. This sort of thing happens every time someone promotes a doomsday scenario.[19]

At the very least, it is difficult to see what justifies preferential tax treatment for Camping.

No Secular Justification

How equitable are religious tax exemptions? Many claim they are justified because of religion's supposed beneficent moral influence—but families are not tax exempt, and they are the basic source of moral guidance. One of the original reasons for the religious tax exemption was that churches offered a support system for dealing with economic hardships. But it was overwhelmingly a system in which churches helped only their own members—and sparingly at that. For those who did not get their help, the dreaded alternative was "over the hill to the poor farm." Now we have government programs such as Social Security, Medicare, Medicaid, unemployment compensation, and welfare assistance that are far more effective than religious charities in alleviating—however inadequately—the suffering of the poor.

Today, churches do little more than administer some of the smaller government assistance programs, for which they get paid—and get the credit, as they're beneficiaries of the perception that the churches fund the programs. Their non-government-funded charitable activities are paid for mainly by secular sources, such as foundation grants and the United Way. Very little comes from church funds.

Would paying property taxes—or any taxes—be a significant hardship for churches? Very likely not, since many nonprofits lease their facilities, and so they do pay property taxes indirectly as part of the rental price, with no apparent financial distress because of this. Why would paying taxes be any worse for churches than for homeowners? Homeowners pay property taxes, and ordinary people pay income taxes, sales taxes, and taxes on interest, dividends, and capital gains, while churches pay no such taxes. Most corporations pay taxes on money or property bequeathed to them, while churches don't. Businesses pay income and property taxes on nursing homes, publishing houses, and other enterprises, while churches that have similar income-generating assets are tax exempt, giving them an unfair competitive advantage. In bankruptcy proceedings in Minnesota, money tithed to churches is exempt from being allocated to satisfy creditors—one more way churches benefit unfairly at the ordinary citizen's expense.

The tax exemptions that encourage all this have no secular justification. As well as being a burden on taxpayers, they have encouraged the proliferation of religious, charitable, and educational nonprofits, some worthy, many questionable. We have churches that seem focused almost entirely on providing private jets and mansions for their preachers—often in communities where the public schools are deteriorating for lack of sufficient funding. We have nonprofit charities that seem interested primarily in socializing. (Fraternal organizations with membership bars and dance halls come to mind.) We have educational nonprofits whose purpose appears to be to convince the public to think as they do, and to use their financial resources to affect election outcomes. Why exempt any of them, even those that provide worthwhile services? If they can buy and maintain property, pay their utility bills, and hire high-salaried CEOs, they can pay taxes like any other business.

What would be the result if all nonprofit organizations, both religious and secular, were treated like any other business for income tax purposes? Taxes would be based on ability to pay, so small organizations would not suffer major financial hardship, while large ones would easily afford the extra expense. As with any business, a nonprofit would succeed or fail based on its ability to attract supporters. And those supporters would be in a better position to contribute to the religious or secular nonprofit of their choice, because their property tax burden would be eased by virtue of it being shared equitably.

It could be argued that there should be exceptions for nonprofits whose primary purpose is to provide a full-time social service under contract with the government. However, many for-profit companies also provide goods or services to the government under contract, often as their primary activity. Such a contractual arrangement does not exempt them from taxes; neither should it exempt nonprofit contractors.

Would taxing religious institutions violate the religious freedom clause of the First Amendment by involving government in church affairs? No more than making newspapers pay income and property taxes violates freedom of the press, and no more than making a privately owned meeting hall pay property tax violates freedom of assembly.

One of the tradeoffs for being tax exempt is that religious and secular nonprofits are (in theory) not allowed to take political positions or endorse candidates, although they can discuss issues. Would that change if the tax exemptions were removed? Of course. But would that be significantly different from what is already going on? Does anyone who pays any attention to politics not know where the liberal and conservative churches, and the liberal and conservative secular nonprofits, stand on hot-button "moral values" issues such as abortion rights, gay rights, stem cell research, and teaching evolution in public schools? When nonprofits "discuss issues," don't they always make it quite clear how they want their supporters to vote?

At election time, don't activities such as the Catholic Church in Minneapolis and St. Paul sending out thousands of pre-election DVDs opposing same-sex marriage tell voters something? Don't the Protestant fundamentalists' voters' guides distributed to "moral values" voters tell the recipients something (and make it clear which candidates support the religious right social agenda)? Don't pro-choice rallies organized by Planned Parenthood also tell voters something? It would be better to treat all nonprofits like businesses, tax them accordingly, and let them engage in politics openly rather than carrying on this "non-political" charade.

If religion-based laws were declared unconstitutional as Establishment Clause violations—which they clearly are—and churches were forced to pay their fair share of taxes, there would be no more point in pre-election voters' guides, candidate "litmus tests," and "single issue" voting than there would be in campaigns to reinstate slavery or deny women the right to vote. Until that happens, there will be no end to our culture war.

---

1. Stated as a congressman in 1874; Congressional Record, vol. 2, part 6, p. 5384.
2. Message to Congress, Dec. 7, 1875; Congressional Record, Vol. 4, part 7, p. 175.

3. "Taxing question of who's exempt again faces state," by Robert Franklin, *Minneapolis Star Tribune*, March 14, 1988.

4. "Grassley Withers Under Religious Heat" by Joseph L. Conn, *Church & State*, February 2011.

5. Tony Leys, "Hospitals avoid taxes despite little free care," *Des Moines Register*, October 15, 2011.

6. "Taxes and Church Duty" by Rev. John Cummins, *Minneapolis Star*, March 6, 1967.

7. "Taxing question of who's exempt again faces state," by Robert Franklin, *Minneapolis Star Tribune*, March 14, 1988.

8. "Billions in value, zero in taxes," by Chris Havens, *Minneapolis Star Tribune*, Feb. 6, 2011, p B1.

9. Quoted in *Freethought Today*, June–July 2011. p. 24.

10. "Ex-Priest Still Gets Special Dispensation from IRS" by Dick Hewetson (reprinted with permission), *Freethought Today*, April 2010, p.3.

11. "Colorado's Amendment #11: A Report from the Trenches," by Jackie Marquis (with permission), *Secular Nation* magazine insert in *The Freethought Observer*, November–December 1996.

12. "Deficit: Religious coalition says state should raise taxes and increase spending," by Dennis J. McGrath, *Minneapolis Star Tribune*, March 3, 1992.

13. "Legislators, there is no magic number," (op-ed piece) by Brian Rusche, *Minneapolis Star Tribune*, June 7, 2011.

14. "Immigration: Faith leaders call for compassion," (op-ed piece) *Minneapolis Star Tribune*, April 16, 2011.

15. *Minneapolis Star Tribune*: "Graham Association won't reveal finances to avoid rich image," 6-25-77; "Graham admits Association has secret $22.9 million fund," 6-27-77; "North Carolina paper says Graham Association worth $23 million," 6-27-77.

16. "A recession-proof gospel of giving," by Rose French, *Minneapolis Star-Tribune*, Sept. 24, 2011, p.A1.

17. See http://trinityfi.org/2008/01/29/cbs-evening-news-w-katie-couric-looking-at-kenneth-copeland/]

18. "Kenneth Copeland-Godfather of 'Prosperity Gospel'? Why Not Comply with Grassley?" at http://www.chuckgallagher.com.

19. "FFRF calls for fraud probe into Rapture campaign," news release distributed by Freedom From Religion Foundation, June 1, 2011. See http://ffrf.org/news/releases/ffrf-calls-for-fraud-probe-into-rapture-campaign/

8

THE NATION'S MOST FAVORED WELFARE RECIPIENT

"Giving to a humanitarian organization like the Red Cross is tax deductible; and giving to a church is also tax deductible. But a church is not a humanitarian organization. Being tax exempt doesn't make it a force for good. If I send $100 to the Westboro Baptist Church to march around with signs saying GOD HATES FAGS, it's tax deductible, but it's not charitable."

—Roy Sablosky

The aura of credibility and respect that envelops religious organizations is largely due to the perception of them as charitable institutions. They are seen as fulfilling a Gospel mission to feed the hungry and shelter the homeless. To some extent this is true, and to that extent they are admirable. Unfortunately, that part of their mission has seldom if ever reached very far. Religious charity has always been a day late and a dollar short.

Historically, those in need have never received much from religious institutions, although vast amounts of money seem to have always been available for building and maintaining extravagant cathedrals, acquiring priceless works of art and, more recently, buying mansions, private jets, and thousand-dollar suits for televangelists. Until well into the 20th century, feeding the hungry and sheltering the homeless was left primarily to local government-run poor houses and poor farms. What changed this was large-scale federal government social safety net programs, beginning in the 1930s, when Social Security and many housing, employment, medical and welfare programs began lifting people out of destitution.

Who Feeds the Hungry and Shelters the Homeless?

Several years ago I was doing public relations for a religious nonprofit that provided health-related services. It was an excellent organization and its services were of the highest quality. Although it was run by a church, it operated in an entirely secular manner. When I was hired, the nonprofit's attorney emphasized how strictly they adhered to state-church separation principles. I was not even to refer to "our mission" in describing their work, because of the religious connotation. I was to refer to "our programs" instead. I wrote newsletters, press releases and heartwarming booklets promoting the organization—all that I wrote was entirely true. My normally required skill at writing public relations b.s. was not needed there. It was a joy to write honestly. My boss and I were both atheists and the management (ordained ministers) didn't care. We did a good job and they appreciated it.

When an anniversary celebration approached, I researched and wrote about the organization's history, going back well into the 19th century. What I found was more informative than I had expected. The church had always tried to provide charitable services, but (as with churches generally) gave help only to a small number of its own members. Then the federal social welfare programs began. The funding these programs provided allowed the church's social services to expand and grow . . . and grow . . . and grow. By the time I was hired, the operation had become very large, occupying several buildings, and serving hundreds of people from the general population in varying states of need. And it was almost all publicly funded in one way or another. While I was there, I saw how the organization even got a fully funded government grant to buy and maintain vehicles to transport clients.

To the church's credit, their nonprofit was doing an excellent job—efficient, honest, professional, caring, and respectful—with no religious proselytizing at all. However, the highest paid employee was the person who went around to the families of the clients, primed with the booklets I'd written, full of heartwarming stories about the wonderful work the church was doing. (The stories, as I said, were absolutely true.) That staffer encouraged the families to remember the church in their estate planning. And why wouldn't they? All of the nonprofit's buildings and vehicles carried the church's name—everyone could see what the church was doing. So families remembered the church in wills, and the church prospered. But taxpayers funded it all, while the church, by default, got the credit. My pleasant job ended when the church closed down our little PR department. The non-profit was getting too big, they said, and we were attracting more public attention than they wanted. So no more public relations.

The job did teach me a lot about how religious charities provide the social services that generate such widespread public respect. If their good works don't come about because of funds available through social safety net programs, they come via direct contracts with government agencies to provide services on the government's behalf (Catholic Charities, Lutheran Social Services, etc.) and from secular public or private grant-making foundations. To take an example from Illinois (reported in the liberal Catholic magazine, *Conscience*), from 60% to 92% of the revenue Catholic Charities received in five of its six Illinois dioceses came from the state. However, the Illinois bishops were closing most of their Catholic Charities affiliates rather than conform to state requirements that they not discriminate against same-sex couples as potential adoptive or foster care parents. Although the bishops offered to refer such couples elsewhere as a compromise, the state's Department of Children and Family Services declined, saying, "Separate but equal was not a sufficient solution to other civil rights issues in the past either."[1]

Of course, to be fair, there are churches that do provide charity using their own money, collected from members and fundraising activities. Although this is laudable, church funds are almost never enough to develop a significant and effective charitable project of any size. If they were, government-funded programs would not be necessary.

There is nothing wrong in principle with what these religious organizations—if operated on secular standards—are doing. It is probably cost effective for government to farm out some of its social service responsibilities to churches, since the infrastructure, administrative skills, and volunteer resources are already in place. However, it is wrong to mislead the public (whether intentionally or not) into assuming churches provide social services with their own money and therefore deserve preferential tax exemptions. They may be feeding the hungry and sheltering the homeless, but the taxpayers, private foundations, and publicly supported organizations such as the United Way are footing the bill. The work would not be done otherwise.

Even more wrong—and shamefully dishonest—is the arrogance of religious social service agencies that agree to provide necessary secular services under government funding programs, then refuse to provide those services that conflict with their belief system (as the U.S. Catholic bish-ops have been doing under the cover of "religious liberty"). To demand the right to deny their clients and patients—even their employees—those services, while continuing to demand government funding for them, is to demand to be paid for work they refuse to do. It is dishonest.

So, significant church-related charities are funded largely by govern-ment agencies. And who are the recipients? Most visibly, poor people in dire need of help. They get Social Security, welfare, housing, medical assis-tance, and more. Not so visibly, religious institutions in no need whatsoev-er are, arguably, benefiting more. They get lavish tax exemptions, subsidies, grants, service contracts, and giveaways of all kinds that keep their revenue stream flowing. It's a business, but one with little or no financial account-ability. Religion is this nation's most favored welfare recipient.

Charitable Giving / Money Laundering

Roy Sablosky is a science researcher who evaluates the accuracy of so-ciological studies. He is writing a paper on his findings regarding religion-motivated generosity. Although it is still going through the peer-review process, he has given me permission to use some of his material for this book.[2] One of his conclusions is that studies on religious generosity tend to be unreliable. Many of them consist of self-reports, and there is no in-dependent standard against which claims of religiosity can be measured. Social desirability also skews studies, because people tend to say what they think is expected of them. And then there's the problem of terminology. "Charitable" does not always mean "generous," "kind," or "helpful." Sab-losky cites several behavioral and economic experiments on generosity that avoid a connection to religiosity (however that is defined). In all cases, the results showed that religious beliefs or the absence thereof had little or no observable effect on the subjects' responses to tests of generosity.

So how much charitable giving, when defined as generous (i.e., helpful to others, especially those in need), is going on out there? Sablosky notes that estimates of donations to churches run to about $100 billion per year. However, only 2% of that goes to humanitarian projects. The rest pays for buildings, maintenance, staff salaries, clergy housing, and so on. Donating money to a church is like paying a membership fee to a country club. And it's all tax-deductible as a "charitable donation."

Ryan T. Cragun, Stephanie Yeager, and Desmond Vega conducted a carefully researched investigation of charitable giving over several months that appeared as "Research Report: How Secular Humanists (and Everyone

Else) Subsidize Religion in the United States" in the June/July 2012 issue of *Free Inquiry* magazine.[3] The extensively documented report contains a comparison of religious and corporate charitable giving. The Mormon church, while touting its generosity, actually donates only about 0.7% of its annual income to humanitarian projects. Other churches generally do better, but still come in far lower than, for example, Wal-Mart, which donates "about $1.75 billion in food aid to charities each year, or twenty-eight times all of the money allotted for charity by the United Methodist Church and almost double what the LDS [Mormon] Church has given in the last twenty-five years."

And what about organizations such as the Red Cross? Direct help to people in distress accounts for 92.1% of their budget, leaving 7.9% for operating expenses. Assuming a generous 50-50 split between charitable donations and operating expenses in assessing whether an organization's function is primarily charitable, how many religious organizations would even come close to qualifying as charitable? Probably none. One of the authors' sources calculated the operating expenses of 271 churches and found that they averaged 71% of total revenue, mostly for clergy salaries.

One of the problems with defining religious charitability is that religious activities, such as providing worship services, administering sacraments, and attending to various other ritualistic tasks, are considered "spiritual charities," supposedly making them charitable activities. But they are not. As Cragun et al. point out, when you provide charity, you give something, you don't exchange something. "Spiritual charities" are activities that clergy are hired to do. That is not charity, it is paid labor. To be charitable for tax purposes implies that, if the charity were discontinued, the government might have to take over and provide services in place of the charity. The authors point out:

> There is one other argument religions could use to claim they are "spiritual charities." When religions pray for rain for the local community or when they baptize the dead to assure them salvation—as is done by the Mormon Church—isn't this a form of spiritual charity in the sense that even people not donating to the religion benefit? These acts certainly seem closer to charity, but they don't meet the criteria of what it means to be a charitable organization for tax purposes: If the function or service the charity provides were discontinued, would it result in a legal requirement for public funds to continue the function? Religious soup kitchens would probably meet this criteria, but would praying for rain or baptizing dead people? Although Texas Governor Rick Perry may have prayed for rain and Mitt Romney may

want past presidents baptized, but we think most people would agree that government has no interest in addressing such "spiritual concerns."

In summary, religions spend a relatively small portion of their revenue on physical charity, and while they spend a larger portion of their revenue addressing spiritual concerns, most of that qualifies as labor, not charity. What little qualifies as "spiritual charity" would not be replaced by government if discontinued. In short, religions are, by and large, not engaged in charitable work. . . . [R]eligions are more like for-profit corporations providing entertainment (such as movie theaters or amusement parks) rather than charities.

Underlying the imprecision and unaccountability that go with religious tax exemptions and subsidies is a deeper problem. Since the IRS cannot require a religious institution to disclose the identity of its donors or the amount received from them, the opportunity for fraud must be irresistible for some people. The IRS isn't even allowed to determine what is or is not a church. It pretty much has to take the organizer's word for it—and grant claimed religious tax exemptions and subsidies. So donations come in, with no way to account for where they came from or where they went. The "church" could be a front for all manner of illegal operations. For example, here is an item from the May 2012 issue of *Freethought Today*, the newspaper of the Freedom from Religion Foundation, with the headline "Church scams total $35 billion":

The *Wall Street Journal* reported May 7, 2012 that of the $569 billion that churchgoers and others are expected to donate to Christian causes worldwide in 2012, about $35 billion or 6% of the total will end up in the hands of "money launderers, embezzlers, tax evaders or unscrupulous ministers living too high on the hog." The article cites a study by the Center for The Study of Global Christianity at Gordon-Conwell Theological Seminary in South Hamilton, Mass. The article notes that churches aren't required to file IRS Form 990 that other 501(c)(3) nonprofits must file. (p. 14)

Given the ease with which "church" frauds can be pulled off, surely there have been, and are, illegal businesses that have set themselves up as churches. They are not taxed, not investigated, not required to report anything they do. What group of schemers would not take advantage of this to launder profits from drug-running, prostitution, or gambling enterprises—or just to live high off the tax-deductible "charitable donation" hog by exploiting the gullible? And it's not just criminals who might take advantage of this open door. Any corporation that wants to fund some political activity anonymously could arrange to make charitable donations to a like-minded church (genuine or set up for the purpose) that would take it from there. We all pay higher taxes to make up for the revenue lost to "charitable donation" tax deductions.

Subsidies, Grants and Giveaways

Both direct and indirect government subsidies of religion is widespread. The *Free Inquiry* article cited above includes a detailed account of the many ways that taxpayers are subsidizing religion for no reason other than that it is religion. Much of this is covered in Chapter 7 on taxes, but Cragun, Yeager, and Vega provide a table (reproduced here in part) that summarizes the nature of the subsidies to religion, then puts them in perspective.

Estimated annual government subsidies to religion in the U.S.

Federal income tax subsidy	$35.3 billion
State income tax subsidy	$6.1 billion
Property tax subsidy	$26.2 billion
Investment tax subsidy	$41.0 million
Parsonage subsidy	$1.2 billion
Faith-Based Initiative subsidy	$2.2 billion
TOTAL	$71.0 billion

Subsidies not estimated

Local income tax subsidy
Sales tax subsidy
Donor tax-exemption subsidy
Related-business income tax subsidy
SECA (Social Security tax)

TOTAL	probably billions more

Given our inability to estimate some of the subsidies, we are fairly confident that our estimates are on the conservative end of the spectrum. To put this into perspective, the combined total of government subsidies to agriculture in the United States in 2009 was approximately $180.8 billion. Compare this with the itemized $71 billion in subsidies to religion and then add in all of the unitemized subsidies.

Another way to illustrate the size of the religion subsidy may be to illustrate how much tax revenue would increase at the state level if religious institutions had to pay property taxes. In Florida, where the state government's budget was $69.1 billion in 2011, the amount of tax revenue lost from subsidizing religious property was $2.2 billion or 3% of the state budget. The additional revenue would have mostly prevented the $1.1 billion cut to fire-fighter and police retirement plans and the $1.1 billion cut to public schools. If that 3% ratio holds nationwide, the total property tax subsidy to religious institutions runs well up into the tens of billions of dollars annually.

Subsidies also extend to government-funded religious work done over-seas. In 2001, Catholic Relief Services got a 57% subsidy of their budget. The National Association of Evangelicals' World Relief agency got 47% of their budget. Seven religious charities received government grants totaling $409 million. 4 Religion affected some of the aid provided. Catholic Relief Services refused to provide condoms to prevent AIDS, and World Vision (a Protestant agency that got a 19%-of-budget subsidy) hired workers based on the applicant's religion. Interestingly, Oxfam America, a well-regarded secular international development agency, does its work without taking any government money. The report did not explain why they could do that suc-cessfully while religious groups apparently couldn't.

Despite the constitutional violations inherent in government funding of religion, the situation seems only to get worse. President Obama's cam-paign rhetoric was strongly supportive of a wall of separation between church and state, yet his administration continued its ongoing destruc-tion. That "wall" has been undermined, leapt over, and punched through so often and so badly that it is more of a sieve than a wall. There is hardly a religion-favoring proposal that doesn't get through it. For example, the February 2012 issue of *Mother Jones* reported:

> When it comes to religious organizations and their treatment by the federal government, the Obama administration has been extremely generous. Re-ligious groups have benefited handsomely from Obama's stimulus package, budgets, and other policies. Under Obama, Catholic religious charities alone have received more than $650 million, according to a spokeswoman from the U.S. Department of Health and Human Services, where much of the funding comes from. The USCCB [U.S. Conference of Catholic Bishops], which has been such a vocal critic of the Obama administration, has seen its share of federal grants from HHS jump from $71.8 million in the last three years of the Bush administration to $81.2 million during the first three years of Obama. In fiscal 2011 alone, the group received a record $31.4 million from the administration it believes is virulently anti-Catholic, according to HHS data.[5]

Reinforcing that assessment, the liberal Catholic magazine *Conscience* devoted much of its First Quarter 2011 issue to examining the extent to which President Obama not only ignored his campaign promise to reverse the Bush administration's violations of the Establishment Clause, but main-tained and even expanded them.[6] Administrative decisions that looked good, such as new requirements to address constitutional concerns about faith-based initiative funding under the Office of Faith-Based and Neigh-borhood Partnerships (OFBNP), were simply not implemented. Religious organizations continue to receive funding that goes directly to churches, even for church building repairs, instead of to their supposedly secular and separate social programs, with no serious attempt at oversight. The Obama Administration did not mandate non-discriminatory hiring poli-cies, but they were not even on the agenda of the advisory body charged with making the OFBNP function within constitutional guidelines. There are, of course, strict rules against using OFBNP funds to proselytize, but no one has been minding that store, especially in small towns and rural areas where social service recipients would be fearful of complaining.

Government involvement with religion at the local level is pervasive. In 2000, Congress passed the Religious Land Use and Institutionalized Per-sons Act (RLUIPA), which seriously restricts local governments ability to control how, when, and where religious institutions can locate and expand. So the institutions expand into residential neighborhoods, creating traffic congestion and parking problems as well as sometimes putting up huge buildings totally out of scale with the surrounding neighborhoods—this seems to be a special problem with Mormon temples, the temples in Oak-land and north Phoenix being prime examples—or they expand into in-dustrial areas, removing prime land for industrial development from the tax rolls. For cities to object would be to impose a "substantial" burden on the practice of religion. If local governments sue and lose, they must pay the plaintiff's attorney fees. Since the prospect of winning against a reli-gious institution is seldom good and the costs of losing high, local govern-ments tend to let religious institutions have their way.[7]

Publications that advocate state-church separation are often filled with reports of total lack of separation. Recently, the government has started to fund historic preservation projects for churches.[8] For at least a hundred years, such work was privately financed. But no longer. For example, in 2011 repairs to the National Cathedral in Washington D.C. cost $700,000 and were paid with a government grant. Two other churches also got grants for repair work, one for $178,615 and the other for $700,000.

That is how church preservation is financed these days, under the Na-tional Historic Preservation Act. At first, the government provided funds to preserve churches of clear historic interest, but it soon began funding repairs of almost any church building. Church-state separation finally hit bottom in 2007 when the Supreme Court decided, in *Hein v. Freedom from Religion Foundation*, that citizens, as such, had standing to challenge government funding of religion only if the funding was authorized by a legislative body. Therefore, money from a government agency's discretionary funds could be used to fund any religious activity.

The Establishment Clause never seems to be a hindrance to government support of religion. For example, in 1989 I attempted to dissuade the Minneapolis city council from giving away prime, downtown tax-producing land to a Catholic institution. They went ahead and did it. They gave land worth between $5 million and $10 million to the College of St. Thomas for a school of business administration, because the college said it could not afford to buy it.

The council tried to find a way to get around the constitutional problem of publicly funding a religious institution, and finally succeeded with a convoluted scheme that can only be called money laundering. Our mayor at the time, Don Fraser, was strongly opposed to the funding and gave me information to use in my efforts to stop the giveaway. However, Minneapolis has what is called a "weak mayor" system that prevents mayors from acting without substantial support from the city council. That left Fraser extremely frustrated. The Minnesota chapter of the American Civil Liberties Union and other state-church separation supporters wrote letters to the editor, but they had no effect. A Wisconsin colleague, Paul Keller, wrote to State Attorney General Skip Humphrey (son of the late Vice President Hubert Humphrey) urging opposition to the giveaway. Humphrey advised Keller to take the matter up with the city council. They gave the land to St. Thomas. This multi-million dollar property now generates no taxes because it is owned by a religious institution.

One of the arguments in favor of the giveaway was that St. Thomas would give several scholarships to low-income inner city students. It has done so, but those scholarships come with religious strings attached: No student can graduate from St. Thomas without completing at least three courses in religion. This is enforced indoctrination, courtesy of the taxpayers. In 1990, the business section of the *Star Tribune* had an article praising St. Thomas for its business success, but that success came courtesy of the City Council's prime downtown land giveaway underwritten by the city's property taxpayers.[9]

The College of St. Thomas always touted its school of business as operating in a secular manner. Yet one friend of mine who was taking a course in accounting told me that the first day she came to class, when the instructor walked in, he asked the class to rise. Then he began to lead the class in prayer. My friend says she abruptly sat down and of course did not pray. She wondered if that would have an effect on her grade. It apparently did not, but this type of thing is inherently coercive—with taxpayer support.

The hubris of religious institutions can be astonishing. They seem to feel entitled to government support for anything they want to do; they seem to lack any concept of fairness. For example, in June, 2012, three churches in downtown St. Paul, Minnesota, decided they were being charged unfairly for street maintenance.[10] The city's fee for cleaning and maintaining the downtown streets was $16.62 per linear foot for every building, regardless of its length, height, depth, purpose, or amount of use. After all, street cleaning is street cleaning. Outside the downtown area, the fee was lower because much less cleaning and maintenance were necessary. The three churches said they were being treated unfairly because churches outside the downtown area paid less, so they wanted to pay less too, just because they were churches. They wanted the city to place them in their own special category that ignored the "street cleaning is street cleaning" concept. After some legal wrangling, the attorney for the churches, Scott Nordstrand, came up with what he insisted was a fair solution. Here it is, as reported by the *Star Tribune*:

> Nordstrand said a logical alternative might be to once again fund routine street maintenance through the general fund, which would eliminate street assessments but raise property taxes overall. Nordstrand crunched the numbers and believes he has a good handle on how much the overall burden would go up or down for various properties."

And no doubt Nordstrand's number crunching revealed that his "fair alternative" would leave the churches paying absolutely nothing, because they pay no taxes into the general fund (or anything else) and no property taxes either. But overall property taxes would be raised, with everyone else paying more so the churches could pay nothing. And they really do think that is fair—or, probably more accurately, they *present* it as being fair, while knowing it's anything but.

Some government preferential funding for religious activities is so ludicrous as to be embarrassing. Kentucky, for example, which already touts a Creation Museum devoted to presenting the Genesis account as actual history (and, yes, featuring a kids' ride with a dinosaur wearing a *saddle*), is going for a Noah's Ark theme park next. Taxpayers will provide financial incentives covering 25% of the costs for the nonprofit (tax-exempt, of course) group Answers in Genesis to develop the (profitable, of course) multi-million-dollar tourist attraction, scheduled to open in 2014. The Ark will be 500 feet long and wooden (just like the Bible says, so of course it's authentic). And it will be educational, having among its passengers replicas of dinosaurs (but maybe just babies due to space limitations) and live animals including baby giraffes. The Tower of Babel will be there too.

Such noble intellectual efforts! And some people never seem to appreciate them! The National Center for Science Education objected that "students who accept this material as scientifically valid are unlikely to succeed in science courses at the college level." (What makes the NCSE think such students will even qualify for a high school diploma, much less college?)[11] Then there's P.Z. Myers, the notoriously outspoken biologist and evolution's one-man S.W.A.T. team, who tried to be supportive. Here is his take:

> I'm going to be a contrarian here. I think the Kentucky legislature has made a perfectly sensible budget decision. Here's the deal: in the current budget, a couple of interesting decisions have been made.

> Funding for K-12 education, reduced by $50 million. Tax breaks for the Ark Park, $43 million provided. Highway improvements for the Ark Park, $11 million provided.

> Almost perfectly balanced: all the money handed over to creationists is taken away from education. And it makes perfect sense too. It's not as if the next generation might need a high school diploma to take advantage of the employment opportunities provided by Answers in Genesis. In fact, it's probably a selling point to the creationists to have an especially ignorant work force already in place. Good work, Governor Beshear![12]

Taxpayer Subsidies to Religious Education

The battle to get taxpayers to fund religious education has been going on since the advent of public schools in this country. Religions have always seen public schools as missionary territory, and they have fought for control over them.[13] In the early years of European colonization, America was made up predominantly of white, Anglo-Saxon Protestants, so of course school activities and curricula reflected their cultural and religious views (as did the nation's laws, too many of which we still live under). In effect, the public schools were Protestant schools. Increasing immigration brought religious diversity, particularly Catholicism, into the schools, and it didn't go well. Catholics objected to Protestant prayers and Protestant

Bible reading in the schools. At one point, in 1844 in Philadelphia, hostilities got so out of hand that there were three days of bloody rioting. Thir-
teen people were killed, homes and stores set afire, and a Catholic Church
burned down.[14]

The Catholics finally decided they would have to build their own schools
and, from 1850 on, have wanted government funding for them. At the
time, it seemed reasonable, given the publicly funded *de facto* Protestant
nature of the public schools. But anti-Catholic sentiment ran high, and
state-church separation became popular—at least where public funding of
Catholic schools was concerned. President Ulysses S. Grant made stirring
speeches in favor of strict state-church separation and taxing churches.
This inspired a proposed constitutional amendment in 1876 when U.S.
Congressman James G. Blaine (R-Maine) offered the Blaine Amendment.
It prohibited any tax money from going to any religion for any purpose.
Although it failed at the federal level, almost all states added it to their
constitutions, with language noting religious schools especially as being
ineligible for public funding.[15] As far as putting these amendments into
practice, some states did but others didn't, and continued to allow prayers
and Bible readings. The text of the state Blaine Amendments closely follows the proposed federal amendment, which said:

> No State shall make any law respecting an establishment of religion, or pro-
> hibiting the free exercise thereof; and no money raised by taxation in any
> State for the support of public schools, or derived from any public fund
> therefor, nor any public lands devoted thereto, shall ever be under the con-
> trol of any religious sect; nor shall any money so raised or lands so devoted
> be divided between religious sects or denominations.

With many states banning prayers and Bible readings in public schools,
the U.S. Supreme Court began doing the same in 1947 in response to challenges, thus making such religious observances unconstitutional nationwide. First came *Everson v. Board of Education* (1947), then *McCollum
v. Board of Education* (1948), then *Engel v. Vitale* (1962), then *Abington
Township School District v. Schempp* (1963). Although these cases should
have ended the efforts to keep religion in the public schools, the battle
continues. It's waged primarily by Protestant fundamentalists, because the
Catholic Church still wants its own taxpayer-funded schools. (When the
Schempp ruling was announced, I—still a devout Catholic at the time—
cheered, even though the case included and supported a companion lawsuit filed by Madalyn Murray O'Hair, an atheist. I was happy that those

Protestant prayers were out of the public schools.) School prayer amendments in one form or another have been introduced in Congress every year since 1963, but have gone nowhere. Their purpose appears mainly to be bluster, a bullying tactic letting it be known publicly that this is a Christian nation, nonbelievers should just suck it up, and that to oppose religious intrusion is a mean-spirited attack on religious liberty.

While they have lost (at least for now) the school-prayer battle, fundamentalists have had success in many states in obtaining government funding for their schools. To avoid the restrictions of the Blaine Amendments in state constitutions, most raids on the public treasury have been in the form of state-provided tuition to be used at schools of the parents' choice. Such programs are currently operating in ten states (including Arizona, New Mexico, and Maine) plus the District of Columbia, but most have failed because voters have tended to favor their public schools, especially in suburban and rural areas.

Meanwhile, religious schools have obtained indirect funding rather easily by lobbying legislators to provide such things as bus transportation, nonreligious textbooks, classes for special needs children, various other services, and tax credits for parents for educational expenses. Religious schools and their allies claim this financing benefits the parents or the children, not the schools. And the courts have agreed, deeming these expenditures constitutional—even though the bottom line is a reduction in religious schools' operating expenses, while increasing the cost of public school education. Ironically, these increased costs sometimes incite taxpayer complaints that public schools do not operate in financially efficient ways and suggestions that more taxpayer support should go to the more "frugal" religious schools.[16] The campaign for public funding of religious schools is nationwide and never ends. Denigration of public schools, public school teachers, and teachers' unions is the norm in this campaign.

Publicly funded secular charter schools have proliferated to fill perceived gaps in traditional public school educational curricula or approaches, but this has provided cover for infiltration of education by religious groups. The mandated secularity of a charter school is often compromised when a curriculum that started out legitimately enough slides into blatant promotion of a religious viewpoint. For example, the June 2012, issue of *Church & State* reports that Life Force Arts and Technology Academy in Tampa, Florida, is under investigation for teaching Scientology, meanwhile collecting $800,000 a year in taxpayer support.[17] Likewise, the Ben Gamla charter schools in south Florida are apparently deep into the religious aspects of Judaism. In Pennsylvania, the Pocono Mountain Charter School is in trouble for allegedly funneling taxpayer-supplied school money to a local church. In Texas, a charter school organization called Cosmos is accused of financially favoring Turkish Muslim teachers and contractors. And all over the country, Catholic schools that are no longer financially sustainable become charter schools. But with the same teachers and administrators, what are the chances that they've abandoned their religious views?

Worse yet is that the Center for Research on Education Outcomes at Stanford University, after studying 2,403 charter schools, found that, "37 percent deliver [overall] learning results that are significantly worse than their students would have realized had they remained in traditional public schools." On math scores, the study also showed that 47% of charter school students did about the same as students at regular schools, and 37% did worse.[18]

But now the U.S. Supreme Court has stepped in, possibly settling the controversy over taxpayer funding of religious education the worst way possible, with a decision that allows funding religious schools through tax credits. It's a money laundering scheme (there is no other term for it) that is impressive in its legalistic subterfuge and far reaching implications. On April 4, 2011, in a 5–4 ruling in the case of *Arizona Christian School Tuition Organization v. Winn*, the Court upheld an Arizona law that allowed tuition-support organizations to collect money from parents, then send it to the school of the parents' choice as a tuition payment. The parents could then take this amount off their taxes as a credit. The private or parochial school gets the money, the parents get reimbursed by the government, the public schools get weakened by underfunding, and the taxpayers get the shaft, since somewhere down the line the state will raise taxes to make up for the tuition-reimbursement shortfall. (An NEA-backed proposition to permanently raise the sales tax—the most regressive type of tax—by 1% in Arizona, with the money earmarked for education, went down by a 2–1 margin in the 2012 election.)

So far the amount of laundered money in Arizona is limited to $500 per individual and $1,000 per couple. Will it go higher? Will the sun rise tomorrow? Worse yet, taxpayers cannot sue to stop this. Why? Because Supreme Court Justice Anthony Kennedy said it's not taxpayer money, it's the parents' money, and they can donate it to a tuition-support organization if they choose. And of course the tuition-support organization can donate it to whatever school it chooses. As expected the Justices divided ideologically: Chief Justice John Roberts, Justices Antonin Scalia, Clarence Thomas, Anthony Kennedy and Samuel Alito formed the majority. Justices

Stephen Breyer, Sonia Sotomayor, Ruth Bader Ginsburg and Elena Kagan were in the minority. Kagan (along with Breyer, Sotomayor and Ginsburg) wrote a strong dissent blasting the ruling, saying in effect that it means that states seeking to aid religion no longer need to develop constitutional workarounds to give cash grants—they can just give tax credits:

> Today's decision devastates taxpayer standing in the Establishment Clause cases. . . . The Court's opinion thus offers a roadmap-more truly, just a one-step instruction-to any government that wishes to insulate its financing of religious activity from legal challenge. Structure the funding as a tax expenditure, and Flast [the 1968 *Flast v. Cohen* ruling that allowed some taxpayer challenges to expenditures under the Establishment Clause] will not stand in the way. No taxpayer will have standing to object. However blatantly the government may violate the Establishment Clause, taxpayers cannot gain access to the federal courts.[19]

Religious Occupation of Public Schools

After the Supreme Court ruled that prayers and other religious observances in public schools were unconstitutional, Protestant fundamentalists tried another tactic—using public school property after hours to express their beliefs and recruit new members. Katherine Stewart has written a detailed report on this strategy in *The Good News Club*. The strategy originated with the formation of the American Center for Law and Justice (ACLJ), guided by attorney Jay Sekulow, as a counterpoint to the American Civil Liberties Union (ACLU).[20] Sekulow picked up on a 1981 Supreme Court ruling, in *Widmar v. Vincent*, that a state university had violated the free speech rights of a religious group when it denied the group permission to meet on campus. There was only one dissent, by Justice Byron White. With a clear perception of what the Court's ruling might mean for the future, he wrote:

> I believe the proposition is plainly wrong. . . . Were it right, the Religion Clauses would be emptied of any independent meaning in circumstances in which religious practice took the form of speech.[21]

And that is exactly what happened when the ACLJ and Sekulow began mounting challenges to claims of Establishment Clause violations by saying religious speech is free speech. Using the Widmar ruling as a precedent, Sekulow's first legal success was securing the right of "Jews for Jesus" to hand out pamphlets in airports. In a speech to supporters of ACLJ in 1990, Sekulow said:

> Our purpose must be to spread the gospel on the new mission field that the Lord has opened—public high schools. Yes, the so-called "wall of separation" between church and state has begun to crumble.[22]

As Justice White predicted, the Establishment Clause of the First Amendment has become almost meaningless where religious proselytizing by public school students is concerned. One of the more notable, but typical, examples of this has been the "See You at the Pole" movement. As Stewart describes it:

> Like many of the religious initiatives now taking place in America's public schools, "See You at the Pole" represents itself as a student-led program. It began when a group of students gathered around a flagpole in 1990 in Burleson, Texas, a small town just south of Fort Worth, and now claims to reach two million students at 50,000 schools. The events take place annually, usually at 7 a.m. on the fourth Wednesday of September at schools across the nation, and students often bring sophisticated sound systems, rock bands, and other accessories of the mega-church movement onto their public school campuses. The ceremony[ies] involve[ed] nailing pieces of paper [with the name of a non-Christian classmate] to a cross . . .

> In the technical terms of the public school missionary movement, "See You at the Pole" is an example of "peer-to-peer evangelism." The important thing about peer-to-peer evangelism is that, from a legal perspective, it is "private speech" by students, of the sort protected by the Free Speech Clause of the First Amendment. So, as the national leaders of the movement are fond of repeating, it's perfectly legal.[23]

Such events are supposedly student sponsored and led, but Stewart points out the heavy involvement of "pastors, teachers, administrators and parents" in organizing and setting them up. And it's not harmless. Sometimes students who refuse to participate are humiliated and bullied.

Fundamentalist groups such as the Fellowship of Christian Athletes (FCA) have gone further than "See You at the Pole," with pre-game prayers and public praise of Jesus at games. The Supreme Court has allowed such activities by assuming they are all arranged by students, and not recognizing the coercion of nonparticipating students that is bound to occur, as anyone who has ever been to high school knows.[24]

Nicole Smalkowski, a 15-year-old Jewish student and gifted athlete, who attended Hardesty High School in Hardesty, Oklahoma, was one victim of such coercion. The persecution was relentless, with efforts to get Nicole and her family to leave town; one teacher told her, "This is a Christian country, and if you don't like it, get out." The family refused to leave town, but Nicole doesn't participate in sports anymore. Such religious pressure in public schools occurs all over the country (including homophobic bullying as an expression of fundamentalist "free speech"), but only the few who are courageous enough to object publicly make the news.[25]

The Good News Clubs are a growing feature of this evangelical move into public schools. They are a product of the Child Evangelism Fellowship (CEF), a proselytizing movement that is well organized nationally and well funded. It aims at the "4–14 window," which refers to the ages of the large group of children they consider prime targets for religious proselytizing.[26] Again, a Supreme Court decision opened the public school doors to this campaign, with the June 11, 2001 ruling *Good News Club, et al. v. Milford Central School.* The case involved Milford (New York) Central School's denial of meeting space to a Good News Club because its purpose was purely religious. The Good News Club prevailed by arguing that the school violated its free speech rights. The ruling's summary stated:

> Restrictions on speech that takes place in a limited public forum must not discriminate on the basis of the speaker's viewpoint and be reasonable in the light of the forum's purpose. Because the school's exclusion of the Good News Club violates this principle, the school violated the Club's free speech rights guaranteed by the First Amendment. Furthermore, the school's claim that allowing the club to meet on its property would violate the Establishment Clause lacked merit and thus was no defense to the club's First Amendment's claim.[27]

So what do the 3,500 Good News Clubs in public elementary schools do? They claim to be nondenominational, yet promote only the fundamentalist biblical world view. They claim to hold Bible study classes focusing on history and a broadly religious perspective, but they actually conduct sectarian indoctrination. They insist that their program does not involve the school in any way, yet their mere presence gives children the impression of school sponsorship. They claim to reinforce the beliefs of the parents who send their children to these clubs, yet work to undermine those beliefs in favor of their fundamentalist beliefs. They claim to focus only on the children who join the clubs, yet use those children to recruit others.

They ultimately create a divisive student environment. Their goal, as Jerry Falwell (one of the movement's leaders) said, is this: "I hope to see the day when, as in the early days of our country, we don't have public schools. The churches will have taken them over again and Christians will be running them." Another movement leader, Robert Thoburn, said, "I would imagine every Christian would agree that we need to remove the humanism from the public schools." He also encouraged Christians to run for school boards, saying, "Your goal must be to sink the ship."[28]

And sinking it is. In August 2012, the U.S. Court of Appeals for the 8th District not only ruled in favor of CEF's incursion into Minneapolis public schools, but required the Minneapolis school district (aka the taxpayers) to pay CEF's legal fees, amounting to $100,000. The school district had created after-school community partnerships with local organizations to augment a school's efforts to boost student achievement with programs that (as stated in the Court of Appeals ruling) "encourage social, mental, physical and creative abilities, promote leadership development and improve academic performance." The district had accepted CEF as a community partner because it assumed CEF engaged in secular activities similar to those of the Boy Scouts, Girl Scouts, Big Brothers/Big Sisters, and Boys and Girls Clubs of the Twin Cities, which were also community partners. It removed CEF from the after-school program and filed an injunction against CEF when prayer and proselytizing surfaced. The school district allowed CEF to continue to hold meetings at the school, but only at the end of the 3 p.m. to 6 p.m. period. This meant CEF no longer had access to the school's bus and food services. Attendance dropped to five students, down from 47, so CEF appealed the injunction, charging viewpoint discrimination based on the religious content of its speech. The appeals court agreed, citing previous federal court rulings that religious speech is private speech when not school sponsored. So now, as reported in the *Minneapolis Star Tribune*:

> Dave Tunell, the Child Evangelism Fellowship's state director, said he hopes three or four more after-school clubs could emerge from summer events conducted by churches in city parks.[29]

Religion in public schools is on a roll in Minneapolis. Child Evangelism Fellowship regained its status as a community partner with the school, complete with taxpayer-funded literature distribution to recruit attendees, and free bus and food service (not free to the taxpayers, of course). But wouldn't that make it school sponsored, even though the school says it does not sponsor it? Even when the school's teachers are allowed to also teach the CEF classes? If this is not sponsorship, it would be interesting to see what is. As for the Minneapolis school district, it is not going to appeal for fear of getting hit with more and larger fees from religion-friendly rulings. If it wants to avoid a complete religious takeover of its schools, it has no choice but to discontinue all of its otherwise-valuable, after-school, education-enhancing activities, thanks to a judiciary that increasingly sees anything other that full support for religion as hostility toward religion.

It's also pertinent that these child evangelism groups do not have churches. They don't need to. They can meet and hold their services and proselytize for minimal costs out of public school classrooms. No mortgage, no maintenance costs, no utility bills, no liability insurance, and free parking besides. All thanks to a Supreme Court whose motives and/or judicial reasoning capacities are certainly questionable, and "watchdog" media entities that seem to have lost all interest in doing their job.

Boy Scouts and the Worst Type of Citizenship

The Boy Scouts of America (BSA) rank right up there with motherhood and apple pie in the American view of all that is noble and good. Yes, Boy Scouts are certainly that. They can help me cross the street any day. It's the dirty underside of this squeaky clean image that should bother any decent person; but it's not the kids' fault, it's the national Boy Scouts of America's right-wing, mean-spirited, Bible- and Mormonism-besotted, hypocritical, discriminatory leadership that is a disgrace to everything the Scouts are supposed to stand for.

By now, almost everyone knows the BSA leadership insists on discriminating against gays. (It also discriminates against girls, but girls have the Girl Scouts, with their higher ethical standards, so who cares?) What is not generally known is that the Scouts also discriminate against nonreligious boys as a matter of an official national policy they established in 1970:

> The recognition of god as the ruling and leading power in the universe and the grateful acknowledgment of His favors and blessings are necessary to the best type of citizenship. . . .

The Boy Scouts' adult application form says:

> The Boy Scouts of America maintain that no member can grow into the best kind of citizen without recognizing his obligation to God.

As usual, it would be useful to have some examples of the poor citizenship of the nonreligious (in contrast to the fine citizenship of David Koresh, Jim Jones, Fred Phelps, and thousands of pedophile priests). In the current culture war, the nonreligious are the group most solidly opposed to the religious right's mean-spirited authoritarian agenda, and the least likely to cause trouble to others. If there's a worst type of citizen, the BSA leaders are good candidates. Margaret Downey, president of the Anti-Discrimination Support Network, which documents instances of anti-atheist bigotry, has done extensive research showing the preferential treatment the government lavishes on scouting, despite the BSA's continuing violation of federal anti-discrimination laws.[30] Following court rulings against the BSA's discriminatory policies, the BSA settled for identifying itself as a religious organization instead of a secular civic organization. This allows it to discriminate in who it accepts as members. However, all the government perks that went with its civic status still apply. These include:

- A Congressional Charter as a "patriotic organization"
- The President of the United States as its nominal "Commander in Chief.
- A higher pay grade for military recruits who have been Eagle Scouts
- Direct federal funding through the Combined Federal Campaign
- Member recruitment through public schools
- Sponsorship by public schools and school boards
- Free meeting space in public schools
- Free or token rent of government property for Scout Jamborees

None of these should be available to a religious organization. Some local Scout troops have ignored the discriminatory policies; some schools have not allowed recruitment; some funding agencies have canceled their grants; but all resistance to the Scouts' discriminatory practices has been due to activism by the gay community. Anti-atheist discrimination remains, and the BSA ignores complaints by atheists. Frankly, this is of little consequence, because there are other and better organizations for boys to join. But since the BSA has declared itself a religious organization in order to allow it to continue to discriminate, it should not retain its civic organization perks.

In 1995 I helped Margaret Downey lobby the BSA leadership to stop its discrimination. I faxed letters to over 100 national BSA leaders. Responses were indifferent, intolerant, and hostile. For example:

You don't believe in God and that is your problem. . . . We are not the ones hurting the child. You are the ones that are teaching your children to be Atheists. This is the consequence of your choice. . . . I only hope that some-day, someone will open your eyes to God and an afterlife.

Fine, but don't promote this kind of ignorance with government sup-port. It's not the best type of citizenship.

No Secular Justification

Is there any secular value in giving away so much to religious institu-tions? What is the return on our tax investment? We lose revenue overall in subsidizing them through near-total tax exemptions, then compound that loss by allowing tax-deductible donations. We lose when churches get all the credit for doing good works, the most significant of which are funded by the taxpayers. Secular charities do as much or more (and they do it full time, undistracted by their "spiritual charities") without presenting us with problems about state-church separation, use of government funding for proselytizing, setting up programs and projects that undermine scientific knowledge and education, and setting off culture wars.

I know one politician who, at a not-open-to-the-public political meeting said that, when social services are needed, the government should provide them openly and transparently, and not give funds to churches to provide them. He was right, but of course he never says this publicly because he would very quickly be out of office.

Government support for the Boy Scouts also serves no rational purpose. BSA has clearly defined itself as a religious organization and should be treated as such. Even if the Scouts were entirely secular, the problem would be the difficulty of keeping Scout troops out of churches. They need spon-sors with meeting facilities and volunteer personnel to organize activities, so churches become the venue of choice. It would be better for troops to be sponsored by public schools or parks and recreation departments, but by and large they aren't. Meanwhile, the gay rights movement has made progress in denying BSA access to public schools for recruitment and to military bases for camping and other activities.

And what is the value of having government help fund religious theme parks? A few low-level jobs might result, but other businesses create jobs too, and with less damage to the intellectual development of children—

and other businesses pay taxes. There is no good reason to fund religious education in the many ways we do through constitutional end runs. Why should any religious or private K-12 school be funded by the taxpayers, directly or indirectly? Public schools have a long and laudable history of educating children. Where they fall short, the cause is in part external, in the child's environment—poverty, emotional deprivation, physical abuse, poor parenting, health problems, and so on. We must address those problems; transferring education funds from public schools to private and religious schools will not help and cannot help. It can only make matters worse by encouraging divisiveness and starving public schools of funds.

Some of their advocates claim that private/religious schools do a better job of educating students than public schools, and therefore all students regardless of income status should have the choice of attending a religious/private school rather than a public school. But there's no evidence that religious/private schools do a better overall job than public schools. If a private school does do a better job, it's at least in part because it can be selective about the students it accepts, whereas public schools are not allowed to discriminate.

But there is one possible non-educational advantage to attending a private school, as I learned from a politician I once campaigned for. Although he supported public schools, he sent his children to private schools. Why? Because it enabled them to meet and become friends with children from wealthy families—something that could be a great advantage to them later on in establishing a career. But these were a politician's kids, already with advantageous social connections and with parents able to afford an expensive private school. How many career-building friends would the vouchered-in children of a welfare mother find?

The argument that tax support for religious schools can be justified because they relieve the government of the cost of educating some students does not hold up when one considers the loss to the state from religious tax exemptions. Also, educating students at a religious school is a choice, just as installing a home swimming pool is a choice, yet this is no argument for taxpayer support for private swimming pools, even though private pools partially relieve the state of some of the burden of providing public swimming pools. But schools and swimming pools are in different categories of need. So what is the need for religious schools? Here is the Catholic perspective, probably shared in essence by all religions that seek public support for their schools. Religious belief may be sincere, but it is hardly something the taxpayers should be funding. It certainly has no secular value:

I would say to Catholics who send their children to public schools when there is a Catholic school within reach, that they are violating a grave law of their religion, and that no supposed temporal advantages can be sufficient compensation for that. Secondly, I would challenge their statement that their children will get a better education at state schools. Is it a "better" education to fit a child for this life by reading, writing and arithmetic than to fit it for both this life and the next by a solid formation in religion, reading, writing, and arithmetic? What is the use of bringing forth children to temporal life, if they are brought forth to eternal death? If a parent gives life, let him give life indeed, not only in this world, but in heaven also. Education, to be complete, must embody the formation of the whole being, intellectual and moral, body, mind and soul. The spiritual atmosphere is entirely absent from the state school. My own education as a Protestant was entirely in state schools, and I know by experience the irreligious atmosphere that prevails. They are no place for Catholic children. Conversing with me recently, an Anglican clergyman deplored the fact that only about 10 percent of Anglicans practiced their religion. He blamed state school secular education. "We Anglicans," he said, "played the part of Judas when we handed our children over to the tender mercies of the state, and accepted the policy of free, compulsory, and secular education." And a Catholic parent who sends his children to a state school without absolute necessity is also playing the part of Judas.[31]

Is there any secular value in allowing religious Good News Clubs and similar operations to use our public schools in ways that create division and controversy? If we are stuck with the Supreme Court decision that allows these clubs, we should charge rent sufficient to cover all maintenance costs and apply this policy equally to all groups that want to use public school facilities in off hours.

Given all these indefensible handouts, and the lack of social responsibility in how religious organizations use them, one could easily argue that religion is this nation's ultimate welfare cheat.

---

1. "Ignoring Views of Catholics, Illinois Bishops Close Doors on Same-Sex Adoptions," *Conscience*,Vol. xxxiii-No. 2, 2012, p. 9.

2. Sablosky, Roy, "Does Religion Foster Generosity?" Research paper not yet peer-reviewed in its entirety.

3. Cragun, Ryan T.; Yeager, Stephanie; Vega, Desmond, "Research Report: How Secular Humanists (and Everyone Else) Subsidize Religion in the United States." *Free Inquiry*, June–July 2012.

4. Associated Press, "Government has long funded faith groups," *Minneapolis Star Tribune*, July 21, 2001, p. A11.

5. See http://motherjones.com/politics/2012/02/what-war-religion-obama-catholic-charities.

6. Sarah Posner, "President Obama's Religion Problem," *Conscience*, Vol. XXXII, No. 1, 2011.

7. Mary Jane Smetanka, "Bloomington, others find restricting religious groups is dicey," *Minneapolis Star Tribune*, Sept. 1, 2012. p. A1.

8. Rob Boston, "Historic Shift," *Church & State*, April 2011.

9. Sources: *Minneapolis Star Tribune* articles: 1) "Minneapolis council questions giving land for St. Thomas campus," April 11, 1989; 2) "Minneapolis looks at St. Thomas options," April 15, 1989. 3) Letters to Editor, *Minneapolis Star Tribune*, May 13 & June 16, 1989; 4) Susan E. Peterson, "College of St. Thomas Inc.," *Minneapolis Star Tribune* Monday Marketplace, Feb. 12, 1990.

10. Frederick Melo, "3 downtown churches say city bills them unfairly," *St. Paul Pioneer Press*, June 10, 2012.

11. Joe Romm, Climate Progress. See http://thinkprogress.org/politics/2011/08/10/292379/kentucky-gives-creationist-theme-park-75-percent-tax-discount-for-the-next-30-years.

12. P.Z. Myers, "Kentucky has nothing to complain about," http://www.freethoughtblogs.com/pharyngula.

13. Lynn, Rev. Barry W., *Piety and Politics: The Right-Wing Assault on Religious Freedom*, Harmony Books, New York 2006, p. 51.

14. Ibid, p. 52.

15. Lader, Lawrence, *Politics, Power & the Church: The Catholic Crisis and its Challenge to American Pluralism*, Chapter 3, "Catholic Schools: The Church's 'Essential Instrument,'" Macmillan Publishing Company, New York, 1987.

16. Jean O'Connell, "Educating St. Paul Public School students: the actual cost," *St. Paul Pioneer Press*, Sept. 2, 2012, p. 10B.

17. Simon Brown, "Charter for Controversy" and "Showdown at Shekinah," *Church & State*, June 2012.

18. Ibid.

19. "Supreme Court OKs Arizona Tax Credits," *Voice of Reason*, No. 2, 2011.

20 Stewart, Katherine, *The Good News Club: The Christian Right's Stealth Assault on America's Children*. Perseus Books Group, New York, 2012.

21. Ibid. p. pp. 88-89.

22. Ibid, p. 90.

23. Ibid, Chapter 10, "The Peer-to-Peer Evangelical Loophole," p. 216.

24. Ibid. pp. 220-221,

25. Ibid, pp. 216-218.

26. Ibid, Chapter 6, "The Neighbor's Children: The 4/14 Window."

27. See http://www.law.cornell.edu/supct/html/99-2036.ZS.html.

28. Stewart, op cit. pp 3-7.

29. Steve Brandt, "Bible-club ruling to cost school district $100,000," *Minneapolis Star Tribune*, Oct. 11, 2013. See also the ruling of the 8th Circuit Court of Appeals, No. 11-3225, Child Evangelism Fellowship of Minnesota v. Minneapolis Special School District No. 1, filed August 29, 2012.

30. For detailed information on BSA discrimination, to go http://www.ftsociety.org/menu/anti-discrimination-support-network/

31. Rumble, Rev. Leslie & Carty, Rev. Charles Mortimer, *Radio Replies*, Vol. 3, Chapter 13, "The Church and Social Welfare," #1335, Radio Replies Press, St. Paul, Minnesota, circa 1940. Imprimatur: Joannes Gregory Murray, Archbishop of Saint Paul.

9

Public Religion: Insults and Injuries

Sticks and stones will break my bones, but names will never hurt me.

—Children's taunt

This book deals primarily with the abusive "sticks and stones" of theology-based laws. But there is also name calling disguised as "civic religion" or "ceremonial deism." This is the ritualistic religion practiced by government at all levels (sometimes court approved) and imposed on everyone, even though, if the First Amendment means anything, government shouldn't do this. It does hurt and it is socially divisive—as it's meant to be.

Governmental religion consists of using supposedly benign religious sentiments to, ostensibly, set a morally unifying or patriotic tone to an occasion or event. As well, it's the maintenance of religious symbols on public property by various subterfuges such as contrived "historical" or "memorial" designations or "land sales" shell games. Not so benignly, governmental religion has an insidious, proselytizing purpose that supports and validates majority beliefs, while marginalizing citizens who don't share those beliefs.

Although religion is constitutionally a private sector activity (since there is no need for it in the public sector), there are constant instances of government agents and entities using the power of the state to impose religious ritual on secular functions. Among public officials, from school teachers to mayors to prison wardens to military commanders, the urge to impose religious beliefs on others is ubiquitous:

• Presidents and governors declare an evangelical Christian National Day of Prayer every year on the first Thursday in May.

• Government meetings open with prayerful invocations.

- Public school events (graduation, football games, holiday celebrations, etc.) are infused with religion, especially with effusive thanks to god.

- The Ten Commandments and Christian crosses mark public buildings and parkland as Christian territory.

- Prison wardens make prisoners participate in religious activity.

- Military commanders encourage proselytizing on base, and some even require participation in religious activity.

This book provides only a few examples. The newsletters of church-state separationist organizations are replete with reports of First Amendment violations and the legal efforts to bring the situation under control. (To know more about what is going on around the country, contact the organizations listed in the appendix and ask for sample newsletters. One issue may be all you need to see the scope of the problem,)

A letter or phone call will occasionally spur officials to put an end to violations; other violations require serious legal action. It's a never-ending "Whack-a-Mole" game. In all cases, a citizen faced with government-imposed religion objects to it. But not many citizens do, because it does take courage. Typically, those who object and cannot remain anonymous are vilified, forced to leave town, or terrorized with death threats and vandalism. The landmark 1948 *McCollum v. Board of Education* case (see Preface) made Vashti McCollum and her family the targets of three years of community persecution and vandalism. The same goes for just about everyone who has challenged a religious institution's assumed right to use government to support its beliefs.

In August 2011, the Pew Research Center published the results of a major survey it conducted in 2005 and 2006—the Pew Forum on Religion & Public Life. This statement from the summary is particularly relevant:

> Americans remain conflicted about what the right mix should be between religion and politics. The public, however, is more critical of what it sees as efforts by the political left to diminish the influence of religion in government and the schools than with attempts by conservative Christians to impose their religious values on the country.[1]

This doesn't sound encouraging, but what it means in real-life terms is anyone's guess. The questions were hardly the kind to generate informative answers. They were: "Have liberals gone too far in trying to keep religion out of schools and government?" (69% said yes; 26% said no; 5% didn't know) and "Have conservatives gone too far in trying to impose their religious values on the country?" (49% said yes; 43% said no; 8% didn't know). These were the 2006 results, which were not significantly different from 2005.

Public reactions often reflect perceptions more than substance. Who knows what church-state situations the survey respondents were envisioning or if they conformed at all to reality? The Pew survey results may only be illuminating confusion and ignorance.

The corporate media, which usually focus on who did what, and only rarely on "why" in any useful depth, tend to mold public perceptions. Coverage of church-state separation lawsuits (such as challenges to government-sponsored graduation prayers and Christmas celebrations, religious statements on money and in the pledge of allegiance, and religious graven images on public property) is normally superficial, often dismissive, and sometimes sarcastic. This reinforces the view of such lawsuits, and the issues underlying them, as nitpicky by the marginally religious majority, and it does nothing to challenge the delusional view of such lawsuits as life-and-death matters by the deeply religious. The end result is that a large segment of the public is hostile toward groups that challenge long-standing, seemingly harmless social practices.

Understanding Civic Religion

The 1954 insertion by Congress of "under God" in the Pledge of Allegiance, which then became our nation's official loyalty oath, is perhaps the definitive example of imposition of name-calling laws. The pledge was uncontroversial and religion free for 62 years prior to 1954. It first appeared in 1892 when Francis Bellamy wrote it to give the Boy Scouts something to do with the flags his company was providing them as part of a marketing project. It soon became a common patriotic ritual.

The "under God" addition was finally challenged in 2004 and went to the U.S. Supreme Court as *Elk Grove United School District vs. Newdow.* Michael Newdow, a resident of California, had filed the lawsuit, saying the insertion of "under God" in the pledge was an unconstitutional imposition by government of religious beliefs.[2]

The public school Newdow's daughter attended required teachers to lead their classes in recitation of the pledge. Children who objected to reciting the pledge (either entirely, as do Jehovah's Witnesses, or just the added words "under God") could be excused, but being singled out as different is often traumatic for children. It may not be "sticks and stones" violent, but it hurts children just as much—possibly more—psychologically. Anyone who knows children knows this, so one would think that educators especially wouldn't inflict such abuse. But they do.

On June 14, 2004, the Supreme Court ruled against Newdow, reversing a Ninth Circuit Court of Appeals ruling in his favor. The Court did not base its decision on the First Amendment, but simply dismissed the case for lack of standing. The Court ruled that Newdow, because he was not his daughter's primary custodial parent (he and the child's mother were not married), had no legal right to challenge the school's action.

Was the Court's ruling a cop out? Newdow's case was so strong that the only decision consistent with reason, history, and evidence would have been in his favor. Yet the Court allowed the case to go through the system for months, taking up hundreds of hours and the production of numerous briefs, pro and con, only to throw it out in the end. One strongly suspects that the reason for this evasion was fear of the inevitable social and political explosion that would have been set off with a ruling on First Amendment grounds. So much for the power of the Constitution and the courts to protect the minority from the tyranny of the majority.

What was at stake here? The original phrase, "one nation indivisible," contains nothing controversial, and is in fact unifying. The addition of "under God" offers nothing of value, only mean-spirited divisiveness. Even capitalizing "God" makes it a proper noun that refers specifically to the Christian god. (See the Oxford English Dictionary 639–642, 2d ed. 1989.) Believers in Allah or Jehovah or Krishna may ignore this so as to avoid controversy, but the militant Christians who put the word there and will fight to the death to keep it there know who this "God" is—and it's theirs alone. Adding injury to this insult, the phrase itself implies a denial of the equal patriotic citizenship of nonbelievers. The advocates for putting "under God" in the pledge and keeping it there know this. That's almost certainly a big part of why they want it there.

My organization, Atheists For Human Rights, submitted an *amicus curiae* brief in support of Newdow.[3] We argued from credible sources such as the Congressional Record and case law that the sole purpose of placing "under God" in the pledge in 1954 was to attack the patriotism and citizenship of atheists. Here is an excerpt from our brief:

On February 12, 1954, upon introducing the bill to insert "under God" (H.J. Res. 243), Rep. Louis C. Rabout, stressed the need for the nation to affirm a belief in God: ". . . You may argue from dawn to dusk about differing political, economic, and social systems, but the fundamental issue which is the unbridgeable gap between America and Communist Russia is a belief in Almighty God. From the root of atheism stems the evil weed of communism and its branches of materialism and political dictatorship. Unless we are willing to affirm our belief in the existence of God and His creator-creature relation to man, we drop man himself to the significance of a grain of sand and open the floodgates to tyranny and oppression. . . . An atheistic American, . . . is a contradiction in terms.

"This country was founded on theistic beliefs, on belief in the worthwhileness of the individual human being which in turn depends solely and completely on the identity of man as the creature and son of God. The fraudulent claims of the Communists to the role of champions of social, economic, and political reform is given the lie by their very own atheist materialist concept of life and their denunciation of religion, the bond between God and man, as the 'opium of the people.' . . .

"It is therefore, most proper that in our salute to the flag, the patriotic standard around which we rally as Americans, we state the real meaning of the flag. From their earliest childhood our children must know the real meaning of America. Children and Americans of all ages must know that this is one Nation, which 'under God' means 'liberty and justice for all.'"

On signing the 1954 Act into law, President Dwight D. Eisenhower said (again quoting our *amicus*):

From this day forward, the millions of our school children will daily proclaim in every city and town, every village and rural schoolhouse, the dedication of our Nation and our people to the Almighty.

Eisenhower's message told nonbelievers that they were social and political outsiders, morally suspect, and barely to be tolerated within the circle of community life. For Christians, this carried a message too: that they and they alone were correct in their religious beliefs, for their God would henceforth be daily recognized by school children throughout the nation.

On June 22, 1954, there was a ceremony celebrating the addition to the pledge. It was attended by Sen. Homer Ferguson (sponsor of the Senate version of the bill) and President Eisenhower. The Senate chaplain, Frederick Brown Harris, had this to say (from our *amicus*):

The results of blasphemous denials of God on a tremendous scale already are being shudderingly shown by the baneful social pattern of atheistic materialism. Suspicion begins to grow that it is not the believer who is irrational, but the cynical denier.

Following the addition to the pledge, Congress, in 1956, changed our nation's official motto (created by Benjamin Franklin) from "E Pluribus Unum" ("From Many, One") to "In God We Trust." (Michael Newdow has challenged this also, without success.) Congress replaced a motto designed to bring people from many nations together as one nation with a motto designed to divide and marginalize along religious lines.

It cannot be argued that putting "under God" in the pledge, and making "In God We Trust" our nation's motto, was based only on pious religious sentiments or to oppose communism. Both the legislative history and the social history of the time show such a virulent anti-atheism that the purpose can only have been a desire to harm a politically unpopular group. As for opposing communism, the Soviet Union could not have been affected by or cared less about our pledge and motto. If communism itself was the object of this legislative hostility, shouldn't the pledge and motto have reflected that with "under capitalism" and "In Capitalism We Trust"?

This marginalizing of unbelievers went so far that (quoting again from our amicus):

> Rep. John Ashcroft offered this amendment to the Civil Rights Act of 1963: "Notwithstanding any other provision of this title, it shall not be an unlawful employment practice for an employer to refuse to hire and employ any person because of said person's atheistic practices and beliefs." Debated on February 8, 1964, in the House, where it passed 137 to 98, but it failed in the Senate. . . .

One way or another, the hammer keeps falling. On March 22, 2011, the Republican-controlled House Judiciary Committee, despite the Republican Party's no-compromise opposition to government spending, voted to put the motto "In God We Trust" on all 9,000 of our nation's Federal Buildings. On November 1, 2011, the resolution (H. Con. Res. 13—Reaffirming "In God We Trust" as the official motto of the United States) passed the full House 396 to 9. The motivation for this was that President Obama had visited Jakarta, Indonesia, in 2010, where he made a speech in which he noted that our national motto was "E Pluribus Unum."[4] It made sense to cite our unifying, inclusive original motto in a nation of mostly Muslims instead of the divisive and vacuous "In God We Trust." That Obama chose our original motto points up its inherently positive meaning, while exposing the negative effects of the mean-spirited "In God We Trust" relic from the Cold War.

Religious Coercion in the Military

Of all the "patriotic" displays of religiosity forced on unwilling participants, the exploitation of men and women in military service has to be the most despicable. The victims are citizens who willingly left jobs and families to be part of the defense of this nation's freedom, yet they found the very freedoms they were willing to fight for denied them by proselytizing base commanders. Was there coercion? Not unless the choice of either attending worship services or being harassed, assigned onerous duties, being physically threatened, or denigrated as spiritually unfit for the military counts as coercion.

But some members of the armed forces have been challenging proselytizing in the military with some success. Mikey Weinstein, Founder of the Military Religious Freedom Foundation (MRFF), is one of them. Weinstein graduated from the Air Force Academy, served 10 years in the U.S. Air Force as a Judge Advocate, has been a federal prosecutor and a defense attorney, and served for several years with the Reagan Administration, including as Assistant General Counsel in the Executive Office of the President. Now, as a private attorney, he has filed lawsuits against the Department of Defense for failing to protect the right of military personnel to be free of religious coercion from Christian commanding officers set on proselytizing. Weinstein says these religious zealots have a national outreach and are formally organized as the Officers' Christian Fellowship and the Christian Military Fellowship. Their goal is to bring all non-Christian and nonreligious military personnel into the religious-right fundamentalist fold through pressure tactics.[5]

For Weinstein's efforts, he and his wife have received death threats that included the threat to murder their children, and anonymous criminals have vandalized their home and left dead animals on their property. The Weinsteins are now licensed to carry concealed weapons to protect themselves and their children. This, however, has not stopped them.[6] Weinstein's ongoing piecemeal fight, individual case by individual case, stemming from the zealotry of individual base commanders, became national news in December, 2012. According to media reports, an atheist West Point cadet, Blake Page, resigned just short of graduation to protest the egregious proselytizing he and other nonreligious military personnel were subjected to. Working with Weinstein, Page is writing a book and says he intends to become a public spokesperson to expose the bigotry in the military in order to draw attention to it nd to eliminate it. He has moved to Minnesota to begin the campaign.

Then there are the annual military base prayer breakfasts featuring fundamentalist preachers in conjunction with the National Prayer Breakfast in Washington, DC. These can be intimidating. For example, Weinstein says that an anonymous Air Force Academy cadet contacted him and claimed to be part of an underground group of about 100 cadets who came together because they could not rely on legitimate channels to address pressure from evangelicals in the academy. Weinstein's source said that some cadets pretended to be evangelical and attended services and Bible studies to maintain standing among their peers and superiors. One graduate of the U.S. Air Force Academy (USAFA) describes how the pressure affected him:

> I am married with kids, and my wife and I are Protestants but try to keep it on the down low because we know we'd be judged poorly for not being "energetic Christians" as my boss likes to say. Like the time my boss asked me if Jesus was in control of my life or if I felt that I was the one in control and then gave me some literature from Focus on the Family as a "gift." It has also been made very clear that we are expected to support USAFA by personally attending this "National Prayer Luncheon." I saw in the news that the Academy is trying to downplay this whole mess which the MRFF brought to the public by saying that it's "voluntary" to go to it and that this USMC Lt. is just a "motivational speaker" and that "nobody will be taking names." LIES! My USAFA boss and even his boss left it very clear that if we didn't go to this "patriotic Christian" event we'd be "letting him down." Seriously, "patriotic Christian" event? That says it all.[7]

One of the more insulting aspects of the proselytizing heavy handedness has been the Army's mandatory Soldier Fitness Tracker, a survey that includes "spiritual fitness" among a number of fitness categories. Soldiers who don't express a belief in the supernatural are deemed "unfit to serve." To ensure "spiritual fitness" there are spiritual fitness centers, programs, concerts, runs, and walks. This has been a fairly widespread project, but it will probably be dismantled due to the efforts of nonreligious army personnel who have been organized by Weinstein's MRFF and the Military Association of Atheists and Freethinkers (MAAF).[8]

Then there's the Army's sponsorship of the Billy Graham Evangelical Association's "Rock the Fort" concert at Fort Bragg in 2010, a clearly proselytizing event. Despite protests, the concert went off as scheduled. Science blogger Chris Rodda then worked with Weinstein to force the military to allow a counter event. MRFF, MAAF, and national atheist and secularist organizations then held a "Rock Beyond Belief" concert as big as the Billy Graham event in 2011.

The same type of religious coercion goes on in schools, sports programs—anywhere there is a captive audience, including prisons, where there really is no getting away from it. To cite one instance among many, in the Bay Minette, Alabama jail offenders can get out of serving time if they attend church services.[9]

And woe to public officials if they cross the religious right. Charles Nichols is a good representative of the courageous politicians whose commitment to the First Amendment has brought on the wrath of religious zealots. (This is another case in which I was personally involved.)[10]

In 1996, Charles was on the city council in Brooklyn Center, a Minneapolis suburb. Given his track record and base of support, he was a shoo-in for reelection. That was until the city council invited Reverend Steve Loopstra to give a meeting invocation. What he said offended everyone except his Christian-nation, racist-sexist-homophobic followers. The city council, upset by the divisiveness, voted to have only a moment of silence from then on. In the next election, Charles was the only incumbent running due to staggered terms. For supporting that moment of silence, he got the full religious-right treatment in the form of door-to-door flyers distributed by "The Minnesota Truth Tellers Association" accusing him of banning prayer invocations at city council meetings, ". . . a slap in the face to people of faith in our Brooklyn Center community" and urging "On November 5, just say NO to Councilman Charles Nichols."

Charles lost the election. Initially the strong front runner, he came in last among four candidates. Should we blame religious fanatics? No. It was a low-profile election. Most people stayed home, either not caring or assuming Charles would win and didn't need their vote.

This is how the religious right gains political power. It's handed to them by those who, like Charles' would-be supporters, don't bother to vote.

Graven Images on Public Property

Challenges to religious plaques, crosses, statues and monuments on public property have been frequent since the first state-church violation cases began to be litigated in the 1940s. Results have been mixed. Where courts have found a secular justification for such displays, the reasoning has been strange indeed. Christian crosses, plaques and monuments on public land and property are sometimes ruled to be "secular" symbols or deemed "historic" even if they have been there for far less than an average lifetime. The courts have even allowed a few feet of land under a cross on public parkland to be sold to a "private party" in an obvious maneuver to keep the cross in a highly visible location within, but not technically on, public parkland.

The increasingly conservative makeup of the Supreme Court offers scant hope for de-Christianizing much government property any time soon. The understanding of what state-church separation means is just not there, as shown by Justice Antonin Scalia's dissent on a ruling (in *McCreary County v. ACLU*) against placing the Ten Commandments on public property:

> [T]oday's opinion suggests that the posting of the Ten Commandments violates the principle that the government cannot favor one religion over another. That is indeed a valid principle where public aid or assistance to religion is concerned, or where the free exercise of religion is at issue, but it necessarily applies in a more limited sense to public acknowledgment of the Creator. If religion in the public square had to be entirely nondenominational, there could be no religion in the public forum at all. One cannot say the word "God" or "the Almighty," one cannot offer public supplication or thanksgiving, without contradicting the beliefs of some people that there are many gods or that God or the gods pay no attention to human affairs. With respect to public acknowledgment of religious belief, it is entirely clear from our Nation's historical practices that the Establishment Clause permits this disregard of polytheists and believers in unconcerned deities just as it permits the disregard of devout atheists. . . .

Scalia has no business being on the Supreme Court, since he seems completely ignorant of the constitutionally defined role religion should or should not play in the public square. ("Congress shall make no law . . ." means exactly that—no law!) He doesn't even understand the Ten Commandments—the worst possible document to put on public buildings to represent morality and the rule of law. (See Chapter 10 under "The Morally Compromised Ten Commandments.") As for the rest of his statement, "public acknowledgment of the Creator" certainly sounds like favoring one religious belief over another. It also sounds like an establishment of religion, that is, government establishing a particular religious view. Government does not have freedom of religion, only individuals do. And what is wrong with keeping government-endorsed religion out of the public square? Individuals could still speak about their religion in public if they spoke as individuals, not as representatives of government. Is there any reason why government officials cannot address the public on special occasions without insulting and marginalizing non-Christian citizens? As for historical practices, they don't mean much, since violations of the Constitution were rampant until the mid-20th century. Before that, until the ACLU was founded, woe to anyone who tried to challenge any of those "historical practices." (See Chapter 1.)

Attempts like Scalia's to Christianize the Constitution go on constantly. Entire books could be written about this. Here, I'll provide just two examples. They show the length to which religious organizations will go to maintain the symbols of their perceived entitlement to power and control of the culture.

The first example involves the ongoing legal battle over a cross that has been permanently installed and maintained at taxpayer expense on public parkland on Mt. Soledad in California, near San Diego.[11] (The endnote references document the astonishing lengths to which government entities will go to placate religious sentiments.) The cross was originally wooden and put up in 1913 by private citizens. Over time it was stolen, replaced, burned by the Ku Klux Klan, replaced again with a wood-and-stucco version, blown down, and finally replaced in 1954 with the concrete version that stands today—43 feet tall, overlooking Interstate 5, and visible for miles.

In 1989, two Vietnam veterans sued the city of San Diego in an attempt to have the cross removed as a violation of the First Amendment. Religious groups countered by claiming that the cross was only a "secular" symbol or a "patriotic memorial." Court rulings have gone back and forth in favor of removal or retention, each ruling followed by an appeal. Propositions passed to allow sale of a small piece of land under the cross to a nonprofit to maintain it as a veterans' memorial. There were attempts to sell the land with noncompetitive bids. The federal government got involved and allowed the city of San Diego to claim the land under the cross under eminent domain. Then, Congress designated it a veterans' memorial and took it out of San Diego's hands.

In 2011 a federal court again ruled the cross unconstitutional, but issued no order to remove it. The ruling said the cross "primarily conveys a message of government endorsement of religion that violates the Establishment Clause. This ruling implies that the memorial could be modified to pass constitutional muster, and that a cross could be part of this veterans' memorial." How this "memorial" could be secularized with that huge cross dominating the landscape for miles, the court did not say. Perhaps the cross could be "modified" (at least on holidays) to celebrate our cultural diversity by nailing a very large secular object to the cross as the occasion requires—Santa Claus at Christmas, the Easter Bunny at Easter, and the Bill of Rights on the Fourth of July.

The legal fight has continued, always centered on whether the cross is a Christian symbol or a veterans' memorial, so what are the facts? The actual history is that maps of the area from 1954 to 1989 identified the cross site as "Mt. Soledad Easter Cross." After 1989 (when the first legal challenge was made) the map notations suddenly changed to "Mt. Soledad Memorial." No markers or other signs at the park indicated a "memorial" significance to the cross until after 1989. From 1954 on, Christian worship services took place every Easter sunrise at the cross. No non-Christian religious group ever held religious services there. The 1954 event dedicated the Mt. Soledad Easter Cross to "Our Lord and Savior Jesus Christ." When the Mt. Soledad Memorial Association dedicated the site to the veterans of the Korean War, they did it on Easter Sunday.

Despite these facts, the Republican-controlled Congress in January 2012 voted in favor of two bills approving religious language and/or symbols as war memorials. Although they would affect all such memorials, one bill aimed specifically at preserving the Mt. Soledad cross and a cross in the Mojave National Preserve. The other mandated that the World War II Memorial in Washington D.C. include the D-Day prayer by President Franklin D. Roosevelt. (The Memorial had already been planned, designed and commissioned, making the addition of a prayer difficult.)

Americans United, the American Civil Liberties Union, the American Jewish Committee, the Interfaith Alliance, and the Religious Action Center of Reform Judaism challenged these bills in court. None of these groups think Christian crosses and Christian prayers properly represent and respect the diverse religious views of the deceased defenders of this country.[12]

Finally, however, after 21 years of litigation (at great cost to the taxpayers, of course) the Mt. Soledad case landed at the U.S. Supreme Court. On June 25, 2012, the Court let stand the federal district court's ruling that the cross is unconstitutional. The cross is now controlled by the Navy, which is expected to oversee its removal.[13]

The second example is a more typical religious-symbol controversy that starts with a letter of complaint, this one from Freedom From Religion Foundation. I will let FFRF tell the story as reported in the November 2011 issue of its newspaper, *Freethought Today*:

A letter from the Freedom From Religion Foundation to the U.S. Forest Service protesting an unconstitutional Jesus shrine in the middle of Big Mountain in Montana's Flathead National Forest has ignited a Religious Right firestorm.

On behalf of one of its Montana members, FFRF Staff Attorney Stephanie Schmitt sent a letter in May pointing out that religious symbols may not be posted on federal property. She filed a Freedom of Information Act request to review the leasing agreement with the Knights of Columbus Council #1328. The lease refers to the purpose "to provide a site for a religious shrine."

Documents reveal the government charged no money for the special lease permit for use of 625 square feet of land near Whitefish Mountain resort's Chair 2.

The Forest Service had quietly agreed this summer not to renew the lease to the conservative Roman Catholic men's club. The violation has been going on since the mid-1950s with "leases" renewed every 10 years. The permit was up for renewal this year.

Then U.S. Representative Denny Rehberg, R-Mont., got into the act. In October, he wrote Forest Service Chief Tom Tidwell: "Removal of this symbol of hope and faith is an insult to the sacrifices they so willingly gave our great country."

Forest Supervisor Chip Weber capitulated and announced Oct. 21 that Flathead National Forest was withdrawing its decision not to renew the permit and would "formally seek public comment." Also getting into the act is the Montana State Historical Preservation Office, which absurdly claims "the site in question is eligible for listing on the National Register of Historic Places."

FFRF immediately wrote Tidwell to protest the notion that public opinion can supersede the Constitution. The majority does not rule in matters of personal conscience. Just because a violation is of long-standing does not diminish the violation, FFRF further pointed out—quite the contrary. By that reasoning, the longer an abuse goes on, the less egregious it becomes.

FFRF also called it a "sham" that the shrine to Jesus is belatedly being called a World War II memorial. The shrine promotes one religion's deity and excludes all non-Christians, including "the many 'atheists in foxholes' who have served our country with distinction and valor," FFRF wrote Tidwell. Courts have rejected such ruses.

Since the Forest Service was seeking "public comment," FFRF also sent Tidwell representative samplings of its vicious hate mail on the issue . . . , showing how the statue has given believers a sense that they are political insiders, and that nonbelievers are outsiders worthy of deportation or even death.

The concrete statue is one of thousands manufactured by the Knights of Columbus to place on their lawns. "They overstep their rights when they appropriate federal property to broadcast their religious message," said FFRF co-president Annie Laurie Gaylor. . . .[14]

Unfortunately, rational arguments are ineffective against religious zealotry, as this followup report on the controversy shows.

A statue of Jesus on federal land in Montana may remain where it is for at least another ten years, thanks to a decision by the U.S. Forest Service. The Forest Service had sought to end a special lease for the statue on Big Mountain, but bowed to pressure from the Knights of Columbus, a Roman Catholic fraternal group that erected the monument. U.S. Rep. Denny Rehberg (R. Mont.) also made saving the statue a pet project. Forest Service supervisor Chip Weber said the reversed decision came about because the statue is historic.

"I understand the statue has been a long-standing object in the community since 1955, and I recognize that the statue is important to the community for its historic heritage based on its association with the early development of the ski area on Big Mountain," Weber said.[15]

FFRF has filed a lawsuit challenging this decision.

This controversy gives a good idea of the sense of entitlement some religious organizations have in regard to use of government resources, and their belief (like Supreme Court Justice Scalia's) that the religious majority (at least as long as it's Christian) can impose its will on the minority just because it's the majority.

Ironically, religious-right legislators have introduced bills in many states to prevent Islamic Sharia law from being considered by the courts. In Oklahoma (with an under 1% Muslim population), voters in 2010 passed a constitutional amendment to that effect. There's no chance of Sharia Law ever being imposed in the U.S.—among other things, the First Amendment already prohibits it—but does this reflect a fear that Muslims might one day become the majority religion? And fear that what "Christian nation" zealots are trying to do to non-Christians now might one day be done to them? And does this make the anti-Sharia advocates consider the value to everyone of the First Amendment's religion clauses? No. At least not yet.

Challenging Government Religion

I've already mention Vashti McCollum's experience. Damon Fowler[16] and Jessica Ahlquist[17] are representative of the many high school students who have objected to their schools being proselytizing arms of a local church. Their experiences are typical, but the happy outcomes are not.

Damon Fowler, an atheist, was a student in Bastrop, Louisiana, in 2011, when he got into trouble for trying to stop an unconstitutional prayer at his graduation. The community reacted with hostility and few people were brave enough to support him openly. His parents kicked him out of the house and threw his belongings on the porch. His brother Jerritt, in Dallas, took him in initially, and he has since been staying with his sister Heather, also in the Dallas area. Jerritt and Heather helped Damon register at Dallas Community College, where he plans to go until he can attend a four-year college. Meanwhile, thanks to the Internet (a huge help to victims of religious extremism, so they do not have to fight entirely alone) supporters around the country donated to help fund Damon's continuing education. Along with this, state-church separationist groups are working to eliminate the Bastrop high school's unconstitutional graduation practices. But the bottom line is that Damon's devout Christian parents turned their backs on him simply because he didn't share their religion and had the guts to follow his conscience.

Jessica Ahlquist objected to an eight-foot-tall Christian prayer banner permanently displayed at Cranston West High School in Cranston, Rhode Island. She contacted the Freedom From Religion Foundation to see about getting it removed. The reaction from her classmates and community included death threats (anonymous, of course) and obscene comments, plus public defamation by David Bradley (the man who wrote the prayer) and state Representative Peter Palumbo (D-Cranston). Both men went on WPRO Radio where Bradley called Jessica a "trained seal" and Palumbo called her an "evil little thing." On the other side, FFRF gave Jessica a $10,000 scholarship grant along with $2,000 in appreciation for her student activism. Jessica plans to graduate early so she can move on to a college out of state.

When Jessica's case went to court, the judged ruled in her favor. To congratulate her, FFRF ordered a bouquet of flowers for her. However, no florist in Cranston would fill the order, either out of agreement with the community's hatred or out of fear of inciting a boycott. FFRF finally found a florist, Glimpse of Gaia, in Putnam, Connecticut, to deliver the flowers.

Michael Bristor is representative of all the little kids who have been victimized by religious zealotry. It is unconscionable that young children are forced into the front lines of the culture war, but they are, and have been for decades. I was involved personally with the following case. It is fully documented.[18] The story is a bit long, but it's instructive. It shows how religious zealotry can prevail even in a socially liberal environment when abetted by bureaucratic rigidity.

In 1990, Mary Lou Bristor's son Michael (then six years old) started first grade at Wilder elementary public school in Minneapolis, in one of the most liberal areas in an overwhelmingly liberal city. His teacher had replaced the public school curriculum with one from the Catholic schools. She held regular prayer time and brought religion into class activities. Michael knew his family didn't pray, so he told his mother, who was a regular volunteer teacher's aide at the school. Mary Lou spoke to the teacher, who said she had been doing this for 12 years and no one had ever complained. She said she thought Michael "needed a little God in his life." Mary Lou told her what she was doing was unconstitutional and told Michael he didn't have to pray in school.

The teacher ignored Mary Lou's complaint and Michael refused to participate in the prayers, so the persecution began and, with the connivance of the school principal, escalated. Throughout the school year, Michael often came home crying. He was ridiculed by the teacher and punished with time-outs for not praying. Forced to make a religious book mark, he drew a crying face on it. Some parents refused to let their kids play with "that atheist kid." Some classmates would not go near or touch his desk for fear of something having to do with "satanic contamination." He was suspended for an "unprovoked attack" even though the "victim" denied vehemently that Michael had attacked him.

During a Boy Scouts recruitment meeting, the teacher announced that all the boys could join "except Michael, because he doesn't believe in God." The school denied him placement in a class for gifted students, and his teacher disdainfully remarked, "What makes you think you're so smart?", although Michael's grades were always very high. When he was nine years old, he tested at the 8th-grade level. The final blow came when the teacher refused Michael placement on the class math honor roll although his grades were far above the eligibility level. The teacher said it was because God knew what Michael was thinking and he was not thinking good thoughts, so he didn't deserve to be on the honor roll. That was the last straw for Mary Lou, so she took the case to the Minneapolis Civil Rights Department.

The Minneapolis School Board and the school district's legal firm began stonewalling. For three years, Mary Lou wrote letters, made phone calls and tried to get appointments with school officials to no avail. Everything she tried failed. At that point she called me, looking for help from a non-religious source. I put her in contact with the Minnesota chapter of the American Civil Liberties Union and they took care of business. The facts were not in dispute and the school board had no choice but to settle.

I wondered why the school board had been so resistant to settling the issue. Every member claimed to be dedicated to civil and constitutional rights. All opposed voucher systems. None was a fundamentalist Christian. However, it seems that liberal and moral principles become negotiable when they might create bureaucratic problems. I found this out when I called a school board member. After acknowledging that he knew about the Bristor case, he said, "Do you realize it costs over $140,000 to fire a tenured teacher?" In other words, they were more concerned about a lawsuit and their finances than protecting a small child from abuse. The only punishment the teacher got was five days suspension without pay; the principal received no punishment at all.

Mary Lou received a settlement of $10,000. The school board acknowledged the facts of the case (but was not required to admit guilt), and sent a notice to all teachers restating the school board's policy forbidding religious proselytizing. Had Mary Lou refused the school board's offer and taken the case to federal court, she may have gotten more money. However, she said she wanted Michael to learn right then, while still a child, the importance of standing up for one's rights. She said that dragging the case through federal court would take several years and by the time it was settled both the issue and Michael would have been too old for Michael to care any more.

Michael was finally awarded his honor roll certificate as furtively as possible. His classmates had received their honors in a public ceremony. Michael was handed his three years later by an assistant superintendent at

11:30 a.m. on Tuesday, February 1, 1994, in an empty room in the school administration building. The presentation was unapologetic and perfunctory. Michael was given his certificate, not because it was right, but only because it was legally required. To memorialize the event, Michael had his certificate printed on a T-shirt—in ever larger sizes year by year as he grew. The certificate is dated as earned in 1990 and presented in 1994.

Some time later, I was on a committee to screen school board candidates for endorsement. I asked about the Bristor case. One candidate knew exactly what I was talking about. All she would say was that the school board had fired that law firm. Apparently the firm had insisted on stonewalling. That advice cost the school board $30,000 in legal fees.

Such mean-spirited attacks should make any decent religious person ashamed. Religious zealots attempt to enforce conformity, abusing their positions of authority to threaten and hurt *children.*

What would happen if the religion brought into a public school was not Christian but Islamic? Would Christian proselytizers, who demonize those who object to having a public school "Christianized," suddenly see great value in taking the First Amendment seriously? These are not rhetorical questions.

In Minneapolis, where liberalism seems to be in the water, but where Michael Bristor learned how easily the First Amendment can be trampled, a public charter school opened in 2003. It received millions of dollars in state and federal funding every year, and its title was the Tarek ibn Ziyad Academy (TiZA); it served the Muslim population, but operated by secular standards. The school appeared to be doing a good job, so it was noticed by the media and liberal politicians eager to promote multiculturalism. It was noticed also by the *Minneapolis Star Tribune*'s religious-right columnist Katherine Kersten. She raised questions. Very good ones. The school, as it turned out, was promoting Islamic beliefs and had questionable business practices, besides. Thanks to Kersten's efforts, the Minnesota Chapter of the American Civil Liberties Union (ACLU-MN) became involved, and on October 3, 2011, after much publicity and a lengthy and expensive legal battle, TiZA closed.

Kersten's column on October 9 gave an excellent account of the chain of events.[19] But, interestingly, here's how she starts it, amazed at how successful her protests had been: "How did it come to this? In America today, we rush to fumigate our public schools at the slightest hint of religion." That's Kersten—always concerned about efforts to keep Christian prayers and observances out of public schools and public venues in general, to tout the

Christianity of the nation's founders, to promote the religious right version of moral values, and to criticize the ACLU for keeping religion out of government. Yet, here she is, defending and applauding them when the intrusive religion receiving government support is not Christianity, but Islam.

Kersten made the following accurate, but unconsciously ironic, statement:

> Thanks to ACLU-MN, those who tried to hold TiZA to the same constitutional standards as other public schools have been vindicated. But charges of anti-Muslim "bigotry" remain a powerful weapon in the hands of those willing to use them in an effort to play by their own rules.

Well said! But never so well said (or said at all) when unbelievers are routinely called bigots for opposing Christian religious intrusions into public school events and other public activities. It may take a few more non-Christian religious impositions on the "Christian nation," but multiculturalism should eventually spur everyone to appreciate the First Amendment.

Currently, such appreciation seems limited to the less religious and non-religious end of the belief spectrum. Consider this in the light of the TiZA case: In 2006, two award-winning psychologists, Bruce Hunsberger and Bob Altemeyer, published a statistical study of atheist worldviews and attitudes, and compared them to religious worldviews and attitudes. Their book, *Atheists: A Groundbreaking Study of America's Nonbelievers,*[20] focused on nonbelievers who join atheist organizations, so their ideological commitment could be safely assumed. In comparing these atheists with agnostics, inactive believers, modestly active believers, regular church attendees, and fundamentalists, a consistent pattern appeared across the board. In regard to zealotry, authoritarianism, and prejudice, atheists scored lowest and fundamentalists highest, with the other groups in between. But atheists ranked almost as high as fundamentalists in dogmatism regarding the certainty and strength of their own beliefs. However, when measuring the extent to which groups wanted to impose their beliefs on others, atheists were always at the bottom and fundamentalists always at the top. For example, in answering the question, "Would you favor a law requiring your beliefs to be taught in public schools?", atheists were rock bottom at 0%; agnostics 1%; inactive believers 37%; modestly active believers 42%; regular church attenders 51%; vehement fundamentalists 84%. As the authors say, "However ambiguous the causal direction of these relationships, the associations themselves could hardly be clearer. It is almost as if a law had been passed saying that as religiosity ranges from 0 to 100, so also will dogmatism, zealotry, authoritarianism, and prejudice increase." (p. 128)

No Secular Justification

Is any valid secular purpose served by government imposing religious observances on us? The 1954 insertion of "under God" in the Pledge of Allegiance was not politically necessary. It meant nothing to the Soviets and served only to marginalize law-abiding, non-religious U.S. citizens. Even the Pledge of Allegiance is not necessary. The only other nations with patriotic pledges are dictatorships. The 1954 act to change our nation's motto from "E Pluribus Unum" to "In God We Trust" was also unnecessary and regressive. It changed an inclusive motto to a divisive one. It is also meaningless. Which god? (Jesus? Yahweh? Allah? Krishna?) Trust how? For what? The only use I have seen for this motto is in taverns where a sign behind the bar says, "In God We Trust. All Others Pay Cash." Do other nations have religious mottoes? Well, yes, but let's not emulate the likes of these: Iraq has "God is the Greatest." Nicaragua is right there with us with "In God We Trust." Saudi Arabia uses the wordy motto, "There is No God other than God and Muhammad is His Prophet." So how have these "God" mottoes worked for the citizenry? And there's one more: The secessionist, slave-holding Confederate States of America had "Under God, Our Vindicator."

Some claim that government god-talk is just ceremonial deism, not meant to be religious, only to convey harmless but inspiring sentiments. This idea first appeared in 1984 when Justice William Brennan, dissenting from the Supreme Court's decision upholding, in *Lynch v. Donnelly*, the constitutionality of a government-sponsored nativity scene, wrote:

> Finally, we have noted that government cannot be completely prohibited from recognizing in its public actions the religious beliefs and practices of the American people as an aspect of our national history and culture. . . . While I remain uncertain about these questions, I would suggest that such practices as the designation of "In God We Trust" as our national motto, or the references to God contained in the Pledge of Allegiance to the flag can best be understood, in Dean Rostow's apt phrase, as a form of "ceremonial deism" protected from Establishment Clause scrutiny chiefly because they have lost through rote repetition any significant religious content. . . . Moreover, these references are uniquely suited to serve such wholly secular purposes as solemnizing public occasions, or inspiring commitment to meet

some national challenge in a manner that simply could not be fully served in our culture if government were limited to purely nonreligious phrases. . . . The practices by which the government has long acknowledged religion are therefore probably necessary to serve certain secular functions, and that necessity, coupled with their long history, gives those practices an essentially secular meaning . . .[21]

An opinion like this, coming from a Supreme Court Justice, makes one question whether reasoning ability, or plain common sense, is actually a qualifier for such a high position. How lacking in significance are god phrases to the persecutors of those who object to them? Why did the Supreme Court not dare to rule on the merits of Michael Newdow's case? The only religious phrases or terms that come to mind as lacking in significance due to long use and repetition are "goodbye" (God be with you) and "Halloween" (All hallows [saints] eve). And just because an unconstitutional practice has a long history does not thereby make it constitutional. Slavery has a long history, and subjugation of women has an even longer one. As for their necessity, I have personally been instrumental in getting religious sentiments, quietly and unobtrusively, removed from public events and replaced with secular observances—and no one noticed the difference. (Well, in one instance they did. Christian zealots asked the chair of an event, who favored state-church separation, to open a meeting with a prayer. He opened it with a group of Native Americans doing a drumming and chanting ritual. The Christians demanded to know where their promised prayer was. He said, "That was it.")

Have prayers at government meetings ever accomplished anything worthwhile? If only they did! It would be hard to find a group of people more in need of them. The only value, such as it is, is that politicians can look like they are doing something to help, while actually doing nothing. In the summer of 2011, Governor Rick Perry of Texas called the entire state to a prayer rally to ask God to end the historic drought and intense heat. God's "answer"? A huge area of the state the size of Lake Erie went up in flames from devastating wildfires.

What is accomplished by forcing prayer on school children, school events, military personnel, and prison populations? Nothing. As with the TiZA case, where the beneficiaries of government funding were Muslim, government support is bound to generate inter-religious rivalry, as believers begin competing for government preference and favoritism. The role of government is to stay on the sidelines and just ensure that religions are benign. After all, the reason the religion clauses were put in the First Amendment was to keep America free of the religious strife that had drenched the soil of Europe in blood for centuries. It was a valiant attempt to ensure that religion in this country would be benign. It hasn't worked nearly as well as it should have, but it could—if we work to make sure that it does.

1. See www.pewforum.org under "More Dissatisfaction with Left than Right," Aug. 18, 2011.

2. *Elk Grove Unified School District, et al, v. Michael A. Newdow, et al*, (02-1624) 542 U.S. 1 (2004).

3. *Amicus Curiae Brief of Atheists For Human Rights in Support of Respondent, Jerold M. Gorski, Esq., Counsel of Record. Amicus* is archived as a pdf at www. atheistsforhumanrights.org under "Articles."

4. Audrey Hudson, "House Votes to Reaffirm 'In God We Trust' as National Motto," www. HumanEvents.com, Nov. 2, 2011.

5. Ben Burrows, "An Interview with Michael Weinstein," *The Philadelphia Jewish Voice*, http://www.pjvoice.com. 2008.

6. William Rivers Pitt, Onward Christian Soldiers . . . to Hypocrisy"; http://archive. truthout.org/onward-christian-soldiers-to-hypocrisy67164

7. Mike Ludwig, "Air Force Academy Taps Member of 'Lord's Army' to Speak at National Prayer Luncheon," Truthout Report, Jan. 19, 2011. www.truth-out.org.

8. http://scienceblogs.com/dispatches/2010/12/mandatory_us_army_survey. SEE ALSO: http://richarddawkins.net/articles/574342-army-s-spiritual-fitness-test-comes-under-fire, The Richard Dawkins Foundation News, Jason Leopold, "Army's 'Spiritual Fitness' Test Comes under Fire," Truthout Investigative Report, Jan 6, 2011.

9. "FFRF objects to 'probation officers for God,'" *Freethought Today*, Nov. 2011, p. 5.

10. Documentation is in newsletters (MarieAlena Castle, ed.) recording the events in detail published by Minnesota Atheists, and in "Running in Place" (MarieAlena Castle, ed.) a history of the atheist movement in Minnesota, published by Atheists For Human Rights (AFHR). All documentation is archived by AFHR.

11. See the following web sites: http://en.wikipedia.org/wiki/Mount_Soledad_cross_ controversy; http://www.kpbs.org/news/2006/may/03/judge-orders-mt-soledad-cross-removed-in-90-days, KPBS Public Broadcasting; http://www.kpbs.org/news/2011/jan/04/ federal-court-rules-mount-soledad-cross-unconstitutional, Susan Murphy.

12 Rob Boston, "Misguided Military Maneuvers," *Church & State*, March 2012, p. 14.

13. See appeals decision at http://caselaw.findlaw.com/us-9th-circuit/1551143.html.

14. "FFRF Jesus shrine protest sets off firestorm," *Freethought Today*, op cit. p. 1.

15. "Forest Service Renews Lease For Jesus Statue," *Church & State*, March 2012, p. 22.

16. See web site by Hemant Mehta: http://www.patheos.com/blogs/ friendlyatheist/2011/05/21/what-happened-at-damon-fowlers-graduation/

17. "Rhode Islanders go ape over prayer; freethinkers show floral support," *Freethought Today*, Jan.–Feb. 2012, p. 1

18. Documentation is in newsletters (MarieAlena Castle, ed.) recording the events in detail published by Minnesota Atheists, and in "Running in Place" (MarieAlena Castle, ed.) a history of the atheist movement in Minnesota, published by Atheists For Human Rights (AFHR). All documentation is archived by AFHR.

19. Katherine Kersten, "TiZA is gone, but lawsuit and questions remain," *Minneapolis Star Tribune*, Opinion page 3, October 9, 2011.

20. Hunsberger, Bruce E. and Altemeyer, Bob, *Atheists: A Groundbreaking Study of America's Nonbelievers*, Prometheus Books, Amherst NY, 2006, pp73-130.

21. Brennan, J., Dissenting Opinion, Supreme Court of the United States. 465 U.S. 668, *Lynch v. Donnelly*, Certiorari to the United States Court of Appeals for the First Circuit. No 82-1256 Argued: October 4, 1983-Decided: March 5, 1984.

10

To The Barricades

"It is the role of unbelievers to force religions to be benign."

—Lutheran theologian Martin Marty, Religion in Public Life symposium,
Minneapolis Minnesota, April 28, 1998.

We live in a democracy. We the People have a right and a duty to act when religious fanaticism attempts to impose its dogma-driven morality on us by law and wages a destructive culture war to achieve its goals. We have been in that war for a long time and it may be a long time before it ends, but it will, and perhaps not well. But the barricades have gone up and they are ours to defend.

What we are facing should be clear, but it is not. Polls constantly assess public opinion on the issues raised in this book. The pollsters treat the issues as though they are in the same category as, say, farm policy, and respondents apparently think so too. There is no recognition of their essential dogma-driven nature. They are simply seen as moral issues, with no understanding or acknowledgment that the morality is the antiquated theocratic kind that only causes misery. As such, there is no valid secular reason for even discussing these issues other than to persuade legislators to take theocratic laws off the books.

This culture war is a struggle to keep the dogma-driven Catholic and Mormon churches, and Bible-obsessed Protestant fundamentalists, from destroying our freedoms. (If the pollsters asked people if that's what they want, they might get useful answers.) Their theologies differ, but the social-political legitimacy they seek is the same. For the Vatican, the culture war is about maintaining its historical role as a political power, arbiter of social morality, and beneficiary of governmental preference and funding. For the fundamentalists, it's about establishing this country as a Christian nation with laws based on biblical values, and with institutions that reflect fundamentalist ideology. For the Mormons, it seems to be about imposing their moral views on everyone, and acceptance as a mainstream religion. For all three factions this requires a return to the pre-1940s era when all sexist, racist, homophobic, anti-science and puritanical religious beliefs were supported by our laws, and preferential treatment for religion was automatic and unquestioned.

At most, perhaps a fourth of the voting public supports a moralistic rollback. Perhaps a similar number reject such a rollback. The rest of the voting public seems to have no idea what or whom they are voting for, if voter surveys are reasonably accurate. (Having done many of these surveys, I can attest that, sadly, they are.) Add to this the nearly 50% of eligible voters who don't vote at all. That well-known observation by Walt Kelly's comic strip character Pogo that "We have met the enemy and he is us" still applies. Regardless, there are many citizens who want to take action to end the divisiveness of politicized religion. The actions suggested below can be effective and don't take much effort. At the very least, everyone can find out where candidates stand on the issues and vote accordingly.

Supporting Secular Government

Because of the one-sided ferocity of the culture war, many legislators who want to defend secular government cannot do so safely. We need to publicly support them and work to ensure their election if we expect them to maintain the courage to support us.

As a long-time political activist involved in my party, I know how this works. A few years ago, our then-state representative was truly committed to public service; he was honest, responsible, and effective. Then one day he voted in favor a very regressive bill. We called a meeting. We asked him how he could have done such a thing. He said if he hadn't voted that way the fanatical element that favored the bill would have turned out against him en masse in the primary election. He would have been defeated, and that would have ended all the legislative good he was doing. He said too many people don't understand the importance of primary elections, and don't bother to vote. We had to agree. We all knew how hard it was to get out the vote for primary and low-visibility elections, and how often that leaves the gate to government wide open for the religious extremists.

Another time three of us progressive activists drove to a nearby town to help knock on doors for a very good candidate. It was a perfect sunny day for campaigning. Our candidate had a list of 70 volunteers who had promised to show up for his door-to-door outreach. Not one of them did. Our candidate lost the election by a wide margin to a zealous advocate for religion-based laws. I have seen this happen far too often. As they say, "All power lies with those who show up." We have to show up. The religious extremists always do.

The Morally Compromised Ten Commandments

In the United States, the Ten Commandments are commonly advanced as the ultimate guide to moral behavior, yet they embody the opposite of everything this nation is supposed to stand for. When this comes up for public discussion, it's good to know the truth about these Commandments to counter the "moral teachings" claim. When there are attempts to place them on public property, we should make every effort to discredit them, not assume they have some value.

Roy Moore, Chief Justice of the Alabama Supreme Court, became a hero of the religious right by insisting on placing a wooden plaque of the Ten Commandments in his court room, opening court sessions with prayer, and speaking at Christian rallies about how the United States is a Christian nation and Christians should take it back. His crowning achievement was having a massive granite "Ten Commandments" monument installed on the Capitol grounds. Challenged in court for violating the Establishment Clause of the First Amendment, he fought tenaciously and repeatedly to keep up his proselytizing, and lost every time. In *Glassroth v. Moore* (2002), a U.S. district court ordered him to remove the monument.[1] When he refused to comply—even after the court of appeals affirmed the ruling—Moore's fellow Alabama Supreme Court justices removed him from the Court. (He was re-elected to the Court in 2012.)

Eventually, the U.S. Supreme Court took up the issue. There were two rulings on the same day, June 27, 2005. In *Van Orden v. Perry*, the Court ruled in favor of allowing the Commandments to remain on Texas capitol grounds. In the other, *McCreary v. ACLU*, the Court ruled that a display of the Commandments in a county court house was unconstitutional. Basically, the Court said that such placement may or may not be constitutional, depending on when, how, and with what other objects the Commandments are displayed.

Although such placement does indeed suggest government sponsorship of a specific religious code, it's worse than that—it's sponsorship of a morality that is appalling in its barbarity, and this is what we should bring to the public's attention. Few people—including the Supreme Court justices—are aware of what the Ten Commandments actually say. If they were, they might not want to display them anywhere other than in a museum of primitive artifacts. They are far from being the basis for our laws, or the foundation of our government, or our moral standards, despite claims that they are. In the case of the Ten Commandments, we *should* try to get people to read the Bible.

Get one and read the relevant passages, primarily Exodus chapters 19–24 and 31–34, and all of Deuteronomy (written about 150 years later), especially 4:44 through 5. You will find many commandments in addition to the well-known ten, all mandated by the Hebrew tribal god Yahweh as equal in importance. It will be obvious to you that the writers are talking about a covenant between the Hebrew people and their god. This covenant is clearly part of a specific tribal identity and nation-building process. It has no relevance in today's world. The Christian fundamentalists' insistence on state validation of these relics by placing them on public property is based solely on a fanciful perception of them, not on their reality.

What is that reality? We can limit this discussion to the commandments in Exodus 20, since they are the only ones involved in legal challenges, and the only ones most people think exist—thanks, in part, to the Cecil B. DeMille movie, "The Ten Commandments." But they are an arbitrary selection from among dozens of commandments. They are also hopelessly flawed and outright barbaric. Only three of them have a bearing on our laws: don't kill, don't steal, don't commit perjury. That these commandments meant less under Yahweh than they do under our Constitution is evident from the massacres and land confiscation Yahweh ordered right after giving the commandments not to kill and steal. Despite the prohibition against telling lies (bearing false witness), the Bible is notorious for doing just that against believers in other gods and atheists. As Psalm 14:1 says: "The fool says in his heart, 'There is no God.' They are corrupt, their deeds are vile; there is not one who does good." (Frank Zindler of American Atheists replies to this slur, "Well, if even the fool can figure it out, what's your problem?")

The commandment to honor one's parents is not only dangerous to children of abusive parents, but contains an implied threat: "that thy days may be long on the earth." There was a definite possibility that your days might *not* be long on the earth if you disobeyed the commandment, as suggested in Deuteronomy 21:18–21: "If a man has a stubborn and unruly son who will not listen to his father or mother, and will not obey them even though they chastise him, his father and mother shall have him apprehended and brought out to the elders at the gate of his home city where . . . all his fellow citizens shall stone him to death."

The prohibition against adultery reflects the primitive level of family values in biblical times, in which adultery was entirely related to male ownership and control of women, and men could have several wives as well as any number of concubines.

An especially chilling aspect of those Iron Age values is apparent in Yahweh's instructions for carrying out the commandment to worship him by offering sacrifices. Exodus 22:28,29 gives this order from Yahweh: "You shall not delay the offering of your harvest and your press. You shall give me the first-born of your sons. You must do the same with your oxen and your sheep; for seven days the firstling may stay with its mother, but on the eighth day you must give it to me."

Some will argue that this does not refer to a bloody sacrifice of a first-born son (although lumping the son with animals that are to be sacrificed suggests otherwise), but simply the dedication of him to the service of Yahweh. However, in the rewritten version of the commandments, in Exodus 34:19,20, Yahweh modifies the order to allow substituting something of lesser value: "To me belongs every first-born male that opens the womb among all your livestock, whether in the herd or in the flock. The firstling of an ass you shall redeem with one of the flock; if you do not redeem it, you must break its neck. The first-born among your sons you shall redeem. No one shall appear before me empty-handed." "Redeeming" the son in this version supports the interpretation that the earlier commandment, Exodus 22:28,29, refers to human sacrifice.

Of the remaining commandments, the first three (Catholic numbering) or four (Protestant numbering) do not allow freedom of religion, one of this nation's most cherished values. We do not require citizens to express loyalty to a deity—except, of course, in the case of "under God" in the pledge of allegiance and "so help me God" at the end of various required oaths. Although lawsuits have eliminated legal coercion, social and political coercion remains, and apparently most people favor that coercion.

The Commandments support slavery (as does the Bible generally) via references to male and female slaves (the word translated in the Bible as "servants" means "slaves") and instructions for how they are to be treated—and mistreated. They also treat women as chattel, listing them among the animals and household belongings that are not to be coveted. As for coveting, that is what consumerism is all about in today's world. It keeps our economic engine running and tax revenue flowing into those same governmental hands that seek to enshrine the Commandments as a moral guide.

If the government is to promote the Commandments, shouldn't it also enforce the penalties for breaking them? In the Bible, disobeying the Commandments is mostly a capital crime, with stoning to death the usual penalty. One of the penalties is especially relevant to our Constitution. Failure to worship Yahweh (treason in those days of total state-temple unity) earns Yahweh's promise to punish the offender's children "down to the third and fourth generation." This is known as "corruption of the blood" and was part of English common law, upon which our legal system is modeled. This law required punishment (such as confiscation of property) of the children of those convicted of treason. Our Constitution's authors specifically prohibited this practice. In opposition to the Commandments, Article III of the Constitution forbids Congress to "work Corruption of the Blood, or Forfeiture" on anyone other than the person convicted.

So it is not true that, as is claimed by their advocates, the Commandments embody concepts we live by, such as democracy, freedom, justice— or even common decency. Contrary to the Commandments, we have freedom to worship any god or no god, spend Sabbaths as we please, use Yahweh's name frivolously, and make a graven image (Exodus Chapter 20) or molten image (Exodus Chapter 34). If we covet a neighbor's possessions, that might spur us to buy similar possessions, which would be good for the economy. As for coveting a neighbor's wife, our laws ignore that as none of the government's business; the Commandments forbid it only because she is the neighbor's property.

Contrary to the Commandments, our Constitution no longer allows us to have slaves or to treat women as property, and we can't punish a man's children for his misdeeds. Our laws against murder, stealing and perjury, while conforming to the Commandments, are common civic virtues necessary for social harmony, gods or no gods. A careful look at this issue shows that the Ten Commandments, taken as a whole, as presented in the Bible, are nothing more than an interesting but irrelevant relic of a primitive culture. They are as out of place and time today as slavery, Jim Crow laws, and laws denying women the right to vote. Given this, it is difficult to see how insisting that the state support and display these religious icons can be justified—or even makes sense. Unless, of course, their advocates yearn to return to a time when this country actually followed those barbaric mandates rather closely. The culture war does seem to point in that direction.

A Religious Test for Candidates

Article VI of our Constitution states, "no religious Test shall ever be required as a qualification to any Office or public Trust under the United States." Article II states: "Before he [the President-elect] enter on the execution of his Office, he shall take the following Oath or Affirmation:— 'I do solemnly swear (or affirm) that I will faithfully execute the Office of President of the United States, and will, to the best of my Ability, preserve, protect and defend the Constitution of the United States.'"

So—no religious tests and no religious oaths of office are required. Social coercion, of course, is another matter, and almost everyone elected to public office has added "so help me God" to the swearing-in oath, and given the voters assurances (whether heartfelt or pandering) of his or her religious beliefs. Because of Article VI, questioning a candidate's religious beliefs has historically been off-limits—as it should be—to tamp down any inclinations to start yet another battle over transubstantiation, infant baptism, antinomianism, and other theological snake pits (including, lately, whatever fine points of Islamic beliefs might rile competing sects).

 Candidates for public office should not have to run a gauntlet of questions about why they believe this or that religious doctrine. Such quesioning is tedious and irrelevant. Candidates should, however, be questioned about the impact of their beliefs on legislation. In other words, do they intend to keep their religious beliefs—whatever they are—to themselves or do they intend to impose them on the public? Voters have a right to know this, but candidates rarely spell this out in election campaigns. Usually, the only way voters can know a candidate's legislative intent is if the candidate's literature lists endorsements by easily identified, specifically issue-based, organizations.

Religion does matter in election campaigns, because of candidates' religious beliefs and their willingness (or unwillingness) to impose those beliefs on others. Some religion-supported values, such as feeding the hungry and sheltering the homeless, coincide with basic civic virtues that any civilized nation supports. Measures implementing such values have a valid, demonstrable, and entirely secular justification.

Religion-supported beliefs that are specifically sectarian are another matter. These support particular religious doctrines that cannot be justified in secular terms. These doctrines, when incorporated into law, are inevitably hurtful in a society that values human rights and individual freedom.

Yet Protestant fundamentalists and the Catholic and Mormon hierarchies are notorious for attempting to do just that—making their doctrines legally binding—with their insistence on their version of morality being *everyone's* morality.

The U.S. Catholic bishops regularly threaten to excommunicate Catholic politicians who support abortion rights. Along with their Protestant fundamentalist and Mormon allies, they organize in opposition to abortion and contraceptive rights, gay-lesbian rights, the right of the hopelessly ill to end their lives on their own terms, and medical research involving embryonic stem cells. The bishops also oppose any attempt to hold taxpayer-funded Catholic hospitals to the same standard of care as secular hospitals, and continually apply political pressure for tax support for parochial schools.

If a Catholic politician is challenged on First Amendment grounds for seeking to put Catholic beliefs about abortion and related issues into law, the wrath of the Church descends on the challenger. I was just such a challenger a few years back, and was publicly defamed in a newspaper op-ed opinion piece by the local apologist for the Catholic Church as a "slimy bigot."[2] No matter that I clearly limited my challenge to state-church issues and that I regularly supported Catholic and other religious politicians who understood the meaning and value of state-church separation. Given that the bishops threaten pro-choice Catholic politicians with excommunication if they don't toe the church line on abortion, it is legitimate to ask Catholic candidates how far their church loyalties go—especially if they say outright that they intend to be guided by church doctrine in their tax-supported public life. This is not anti-Catholic, it is pro-separation of state and church.

Questioning Candidates for Public Office

Jamie Raskin, Democratic state senator in Maryland, said this to a legislator who was proposing Bible-based legislation: "Senator, when you took your oath of office, you placed your hand on the Bible and swore to uphold the Constitution. You didn't place your hand on the Constitution and swear to uphold the Bible." Such is the state of the union now, that it's necessary to ask legislators if they intend to support the Constitution or the Bible—or increasingly, the demands of the U.S. Conference of Catholic Bishops.

The most prominent feature of the culture war has been the rise of Bible-based politics, yet this is rarely mentioned. Voter guides published by mainstream newspapers to encourage voting pay scant attention, if any, to the candidates' views on politicizing religion. It's therefore the civic duty of citizens who value freedom and civil liberties to ask candidates questions such as those listed below, to do it as publicly as possible, and then to make the results publicly available, through the Internet, letters to the editor, and news releases to the media. (One caveat: In areas where the religious right is influential, do not put candidates on the spot whom you know will favor secular government. They probably need to lie low to be elected.

Insist that candidates' position statements include the reasons—ethical and/or pragmatic—why they take specific positions. Do not settle for vague answers such as, "I'd have to see the specific legislation," or "I'd be guided by my ethical principles." Ask this basic question about every religion-based issue: "Do you see any reason for the government to be involved in these matters, and why?"

Ask questions about the following:

1. Scientific literacy. The United States has a low level of scientific literacy. Do your best not to allow candidates to pander to ignorance. The problem is especially acute regarding evolution. Ask candidates how their beliefs might affect their views on evolution, teaching it in public schools, and whether "alternative" views such as Intelligent Design should be allowed in the curriculum, and why.

2. Reproductive issues. Ask candidates how their beliefs would affect their position on legislation regarding comprehensive sex education, teenage access to affordable contraceptives, parental notification and other restrictions, family planning programs (local, national, global), abortion, and women's autonomy. Ask them why they think abortion should even be a topic for discussion or why there should be any restrictions at all, other than those that apply to any medical procedure. Ask why they think women need all this control and reproductive oversight.

3. Gay issues. Ask candidates how their beliefs would affect their position on legislation regarding the civil rights and liberties—including same-sex marriage—of sexual minorities (gays, lesbians, bisexuals, transgender people, etc.). Ask if they think sexual orientation is genetic or learned. Ask if they can identify any useful secular reasons for laws that limit the rights and liberties of sexual minorities where sexual activity is between consenting adults.

4. End-of-life decision-making. Some states now allow physician aid in dying. Ask candidates how their beliefs would affect how they vote on legislation to allow this in your state. Since government does have a role to play in protecting vulnerable sick people from coercion, ask what that role should be and to what extent it should interfere with individual autonomy. Ask who they think is a better judge of a mentally competent person's end-of-life decision—the person, their physicians, or a legislative body.

5. Other questions. There are many other questions you might ask, concerning children's health care (faith healing), tax policy, religious accommodations, faith-based initiatives, civic religion, etc. This book covers most of those that are of current (and probably ongoing) political interest. Refer to it for candidate-questioning material.

Preferential treatment of religion is ubiquitous at the local level. Question it closely, as this is where state-church separation troubles most often occur. You are likely to find many local problems well worth your concern, such as public schools that allow religion classes and services in their buildings, or dumb down the teaching of evolution, or allow books to be removed from their libraries to avoid offending religious or ideological believers. There may be government plans to donate publicly owned land to a religious organization, or place religious icons on government property, or enact zoning laws that restrict how close businesses involving liquor or adult entertainment can be to a church. The list goes on. It's almost endless.

The task of getting religion out of government may seem like trying to win a Whack-a-Mole game. But you can win sometimes. Join others. Work the Internet. Get to know your local politicians. (They value their supporters highly and are always as accommodating as possible short of doing or saying something that might jeopardize their electability.) The grip of religious fanaticism is loosening. Thanks to the Internet, curious people can research religion and secular alternatives anonymously, and find more information than they could have ever found in their library a few years ago.

The truth is out there. Challenge the religious fanatics on their inexcusable abuse of the victims of their religion-based laws. Emphasize that abuse and don't focus on justifying the victims' actions. They don't need to be justified. It's the religious busybodies who need to be put on the defensive. Their hearts have been hardened; it's time they were challenged on that and forced to come to terms with their own cruelty.

When it Comes to Healthcare, You're On Your Own

As long as the law supports conscience clauses for medical personnel, there is little you can do in terms of political and organizational activism. Religious beliefs can prevail in the most unexpected ways. You will have to be very careful and willing to ask questions and raise objections. There are problems you could face without even knowing they are there. I am indebted to Niles Ross, a retired medical professional, for offering this summary:

> Dogma-based health care can be hidden in the specific delivery person. A non-Catholic hospital can have a specific doctor or nurse who has a conscience objection. (They need not be Catholic, of course. Members of other religions, particularly the more orthodox ones, can also exercise objections.)

> Outsourcing agreements to provide the service of what are called "hospitalists" can trip you up. A non-Catholic hospital can purchase the services, often in bulk, from Catholic institutions. Although you are inside a non-Catholic hospital, you might be seen by physicians or other health care workers provided by a Catholic hospital—and those personnel are required by the terms of their employment to follow the Catholic Directives for health care. And they don't have to tell you this.

> The bottom line is that getting health care that accords with your values and needs could depend almost entirely on you.

Mitch Lipka, a journalist blogger and Reuters contributor makes the following suggestions: 1) Read what you are asked to sign very carefully; 2) Ask a lot of questions; 3) Be firm about what you want or don't want; and 4) Walk out if you don't like what you are getting into. [3]

Lipka makes it clear than none of this is easy. Once you sign something, you have lost control. It could help in potential litigation if you either write "Do not understand" next to paragraphs you are signing reluctantly or cross them out and write "Do not agree" next to them. However, you can do this only in a real medical emergency where federal law requires the hospital to treat you regardless of your objections. And so they will. But your objections could be useful later on if you decide to take legal action. In a non-emergency situation, if you object to signing something you will simply be sent home without treatment.

"They Stand with Us"

Not one of the theology-based laws described in this book serves any useful social purpose. On the contrary, every one causes harm to innocent people. Every one requires those who reject their foundational belief system to live by that system. Every one could be eliminated from our statutes and social policies with significant benefit to the common good. If these laws were eliminated, the culture war would become pointless and our political system would stabilize. Whatever social services religious institutions provide now—at government/public expense—would continue to be provided at government/public expense, but by non-divisive, non-doctrinaire, non-discriminatory providers.

Those who understand the value of a secular society and meaningful state-church separation need to do more. Unfortunately, freethought and secularist organizations tend not to mount legal challenges to the religious right's "moral values" agenda, when it is exactly those twisted "morals" that most need to be challenged. Instead of claiming the moral high ground and challenging religion-based laws that inflict real harm on real people, secularist legal challenges usually focus on symbolic affronts—religious wording in the Pledge of Allegiance, religious mottoes on currency, and religious icons on public land. All well and good, but challenges to the religion-based laws that really hurt—the sticks and stones of religious beliefs about women, gays, and the hopelessly ill—must be prioritized, not given lip service. Symbolic challenges haven't worked, and they won't work. The general public sees the symbolic lawsuits as nitpicking. Those of us who value state-church separation are not viewed as friends, but as irritants.

What would happen if we focused our legal challenges on protecting the victims of religious tyranny?

I'm reminded of one of the events members of our Atheists For Human Rights organization attended recently. We had given a scholarship grant to an LGBT funding organization. At the awards ceremony, our recipient accepted the grant, and the emcee called out our organization's name and shouted joyfully, to applause, "They stand with us!"

If our state-church separationist organizations showed through our lawsuits that we stand publicly and proudly with women, gays, the hopelessly ill, and other groups abused by religion-based laws—if all those groups could say, "They stand with us!"—what might happen when we then challenged the symbolic stuff? Instead of being viewed as nitpickers and irritants, we might get sympathy and support. Just as our society has learned that the expression "That's mighty white of you," once given mindlessly as a compliment, is a disgusting racist insult, society might come to see government god-talk as a mean-spirited insult to good and decent nonreligious fellow citizens.

---

1. Austin Cline, "Judge Roy Moore: Ten Commandments & the Law. Moore's Beliefs, Decisions, Reactions." http://www.about.com, The New York Times Company, 2011.

2. *The Progressive DFLer*. A Report from the DFL Feminist Caucus, "Progressive Agenda at Stake in November Elections," September 1993, Marie Castle, ed.

3. Mitch Lipka, "Make a stand with hospital paperwork," July 31, 2012, http://blogs.reuters.com/mitch-lipka.

Resources

American Atheists
225 Christiani Street
Cranford, NJ 07016
908-276-7300
www.atheists.org

American Civil Liberties Union
125 Broad Street, 18th Floor
New York NY 10004
www.aclu.org

American Humanist Association
1777 "T" Street NW
Washington, DC 20009
800-837-3792
www.americanhumanist.org

Americans for Religious Liberty
P.O. Box 6656
Silver Spring MD 20916
www.arlinc.org

Americans United for Separation of Church & State
1301 K Street NW, E. Tower, Suite 850
Washington D.C. 20005
202-466-3234
www.au.org

Anti-Discrimination Support Network
P.O. Box 242
Pocopson, PA 19366
610-793-2737
www.ftsociety.org/menu/anti-discrimination-support-network/

Atheists for Human Rights
5146 Newton Ave. No.
Minneapolis, MN 55430
612-529-1200
www.atheistsforhumanrights.org

Catholics for Choice
1436 U Street NW, Suite 301
Washington D.C. 20009-3997
202-986-6093
www.CatholicsForChoice.org

Children's Healthcare is a Legal Duty (CHILD)
136 Blue Heron Place
Lexington, KY 40511
405-684-3970
www.childrenshealthcare.org

Final Exit Network
P.O. Box 665
Pennington, NJ 08534
866-654-9156
www.finalexitnetwork.org

Freedom From Religion Foundation
P.O. Box 750
Madison WI 53701
608-256-8900
www.ffrf.org

Military Association of Atheists and Freethinkers
1380 Monroe St NW, PMB 505
Washington, DC 20010
202-656-6223
www.maaf.info

Military Religious Freedom Foundation
13170-B Central Avenue, SE #255
Albuquerque, NM 87123
800-736-5109
www.militaryreligiousfreedom.org

Secular Coalition for America
P.O. Box 53330
Washington, DC 20009
202-299-1091
www.secular.org

BIBLIOGRAPHY

Barnstone, Willis, ed. & trans. *The Other Bible*. San Francisco: HarperSanFrancisco (*a division of* HarperCollins *Publishers*), 1984.

Boston, Robert. *Why the Religious Right is Wrong about Separation of Church and State*. Amherst, NY: Prometheus Books, 2003.

Bothwell, Cecil. *The Prince of War: Billy Graham's Crusade for a Wholly Christian Empire*. Asheville, NC: Brave Ulysses Books, 2007.

Bothwell, Cecil. *Whale Tales: An Exploration of Belief and its Consequences*. Asheville, NC: Brave Ulysses Books, 2010.

Brief Amicus Curiae of Atheists For Human Rights in Support of Respondent in the Supreme Court of the United States No. 02-1024: Elk Grove Unified School District and David W. Gordon, Superintencent, Petitioners, v. Michael A. Newdow, Respondent, 2004.

Castle, Marie Alena. *Running in Place* (a history of atheism in Minnesota, 1982-2010). Minneapolis, MN: Atheists For Human Rights (privately published; available by request at www.atheistsforhumanrights.org), 2010.

Chase, Annie. *My Purpose Driven Death: How I Managed to Become One Luncky Stiff*. Minneapolis, MN: Atheists For Human Rights (privately published; available by request at www.atheistsforhumanrights.org), 2010.

Fraser, Arvonne. *She's No Lady: Politics, Family and International Feminism*. Minneapolis, MN: Nodin Press (*a division of* Micawber's Inc.), 2007.

Holy Bible, Catholic Family Edition. New York: John J. Crawley & Co., Inc., 1953.

Holy Bible, King James Version. New York: American Bible Society, 1998.

Hughes, Philip. *A Popular History of the Catholic Church*. Garden City, NY: Image Books (*a division of* Doubleday & Company, Inc.), 1954.

Lader, Lawrence. *Politics, Power & the Church*. New York, NY: Macmillan Publishing Company, 1987.

Lynn, Rev. Barry W. *Piety & Politics*. New York, NY: Harmony Books, 2006.

Mumford, Stephen D. *The life and Death of NSSM 200: How the Destruction of Political Will Doomed a U.S. Population Policy*. Research Triangle Park, NC: Center for Research on Population and Security, 1996.

O'Brien, Rev. John A., Ph.D. *The Faith of Millions*. Huntington, IN: Our Sunday Visitor, 1938.

Pinker, Steven. *The Better Angels of Our Nature*. New York, NY: Viking Penguin Group, 2011.

Pollitt, Katha. *Virginity or Death!* New York, NY: Random House Trade Paperbacks, 2006.

Ranke-Heinemann, Uta. *Eunuchs for the Kingdom of Heaven*. New York, NY: Doubleday, 1990.

Ranke-Heinemann, Uta. *Putting Away Childish Things*. San Francisco: HarperSanFrancisco, 1994.

Rumble, Rev. Dr. Leslie, and Carty, Rev. Charles Mortimer. *Radio Replies*, Second Volume. St. Paul, MN: Radio Replies Press, 1940.

Rumble, Rev. Dr. Leslie, and Carty, Rev. Charles Mortimer. *Radio Replies*, Third Volume. St. Paul, MN: Radio Replies Press, circa 1940s (binding destroyed; cover and publication pages missing).

Sloan, Richard P., Ph.D. *Blind Faith: The Unholy Alliance of Religion and Medicine*. New York, NY: St. Martin's Press, 2006.

Stewart, Katherine. *The Good News Club*. New York, NY: Public Affairs Books, 2012.

Swomley, John M. *Compulsory Pregnancy: The War Against American Women*. Amherst NY: Humanist Press, 1999.

Toobin, Jeffrey. *The Oath: The Obama White House and the Supreme Court*. New York, NY: Doubleday, 2012,

INDEX